The
Learning
Society

INTERNATIONAL

PERSPECTIVES

ON CORE SKILLS

IN HIGHER

EDUCATION

Elisabeth Dunne

KOGAN
PAGE

First published in 1999

Apart from any fair dealing for the purposes of research or private study, or criticism or review, as permitted under the Copyright, Designs and Patents Act 1988, this publication may only be reproduced, stored or transmitted, in any form or by any means, with the prior permission in writing of the publishers, or in the case of reprographic reproduction in accordance with the terms and licences issued by the CLA. Enquiries concerning reproduction outside these terms should be sent to the publishers at the undermentioned address:

Kogan Page Limited
120 Pentonville Road
London N1 9JN

© Elisabeth Dunne and contributors, 1999

The right of Elisabeth Dunne to be identified as the author of this work has been asserted by her in accordance with the Copyright, Designs and Patents Act 1988.

British Library Cataloguing in Publication Data

A CIP record for this book is available from the British Library.

ISBN 0 7494 2895 3

Typeset by Kogan Page
Printed and bound by Biddles Ltd, Guildford and King's Lynn

The
Learning
Society

Contents

PART 1: SKILLS FOR A LEARNING SOCIETY: WHO WANTS WHAT FROM HIGHER EDUCATION?

List of figures

List of tables

List of contributors

Peter Bacher is Director of the Danish Research and Development Centre for Adult Education where he has worked since 1985 as a counsellor and then as deputy director. He is also acting President of the European Research and Development Institutes – European network. For many years he was a teacher and study counsellor in adult education, as well as a researcher and evaluator of experimental and developmental work. He holds a Master's degree in Sociology.

Neville Bennett is Professor of Education at the University of Exeter and a Director of the Centre for Research on Teaching and Learning. He was Co-Director (with Elisabeth Dunne) of a study on the Acquisition and Development of Core Skills, funded by the Economic and Social Research Council within their 'Learning Society' programme. He is the author of 16 books and dozens of articles; the Editor of Teaching and Teacher Education and the President of the European Association for Research on Learning and Instruction.

Alan Brown is a Principal Research Fellow in Education, Training and Employment at The Institute for Employment Research, University of Warwick. He has worked in the area of skill formation, work-based learning and the comparative analysis of education and training for over 20 years. He was an evaluator of the national Core Skills Development Programme in the mid-1980s, and is currently a member of an expert group looking at the development of core skills/key qualifications in Europe.

Clive Carré was, until he took early retirement, Senior Lecturer in the School of Education at Exeter University. He has a particular interest in Science education and has worked extensively in this area in the UK and Australia. He was coordinator of a major research programme on learning to teach and, more recently, Research Fellow to the project on the Acquisition and Development of Core Skills. His research interests include the role of subject matter knowledge in teaching (*Learning to Teach*, with Neville Bennett, Routledge, 1993) and core skills in higher education and employment.

James L Cooper is Professor of Graduate Education at California State University Dominguez Hills, located in Los Angeles, CA. He holds an MA in experimental psychology and a PhD in educational psychology, statistics and measurement, both from the University of Iowa. He is editor of the *Cooperative Learning and College Teaching* newsletter and has published extensively in personalized instruction and applications of cooperative learning to college teaching. In 1991 he received the Lyle F Gibson Distinguished Teaching Award from Dominguez Hills.

Peter Danby works as a leadership and team development tutor. He is an Associate with the London Business School and the Institute of Directors. His work is mainly with the Chalybeate Partnership which he helped to found in 1992. This work has involved the design and delivery of leadership and team development programmes across Europe for organizations such as BP, Mars and Pepsico. He is a qualified football and cricket coach as well as a spiritual healer working with local community groups.

Elisabeth Dunne now works in the Staff Development Unit at the University of Exeter, having previously been a Senior Research Fellow in the School of Education and Co-Director (with Neville Bennett) of the study on Core Skills within the 'Learning Society' programme. She has over 20 years' experience in teaching and research at every level of education. The last few years have been devoted to research on core skills in higher education, the development and maintaining of initiatives to promote such skills, and the evaluation of innovative practices. Her many publications reflect a specific interest in the processes of learning.

Richard Dunne is a consultant in instructional design for all phases of education. In over 30 years of teaching in schools and higher education across the country, he has developed a model for planning teaching that focuses on the nature of representation, and emphasizes teaching as assisted performance. This model, influenced by the Soviet psychology of Galperin and Leont'ev, underpins his current work in the development of methods of teaching numeracy. His ideas are reflected in many publications, in particular those on mentoring in higher education and a new series of mathematics texts for teachers and pupils.

Terry Evans is Director of Research in the Faculty of Education at Deakin University, where he also teaches and supervises postgraduate students. His recent research is in the fields of open, flexible and distance education, including work on professional and vocational education and training, internationalization, new educational technologies and postgraduate pedagogy.

He is the author of *Understanding Learners in Open and Distance Education* (Kogan Page, 1994) and the co-editor of nine books including *Opening Education: Policies and practices from open and distance education* (with D Nation, Routledge, 1996) and *Shifting Borders: Globalisation, localisation and open and distance education* (with L Rowan and V Bartlett, Deakin University Press, 1997).

Robert Fox is a Senior Lecturer, Teaching Learning Group, Curtin University of Technology, Perth, Western Australia. He works mostly in distance and flexible learning environments, assisting staff develop courses and materials. He has an MA in Education and his doctorate studies are concerned with technological change and practice in higher education. He has conducted educational consultancies in Europe, the Middle East, South Asia and Australia.

June Harwood is a Senior Lecturer/Development Officer in Educational Development Services at the University of Plymouth. Her specific remit is employer links into the undergraduate curriculum. She has a background of education within the health service, teacher education and further education. Her current research interests are innovative approaches to the skills curriculum and integrating work-related experience.

David Harwood is a Senior Lecturer in Organic Chemistry and Environmental Science at the University of Plymouth. He is the Manager of the Extended Science Programme and has a particular interest in teaching and learning strategies in Science, particularly with regard to widening access. Prior to his university appointment in 1990, he worked as a research chemist in the public sector and in industry.

Dai Hounsell is Head of the Department of Higher and Further Education at The University of Edinburgh. His many publications include *The Experience of Learning* (Scottish Academic Press, 1997), *What Is Active Learning?* (CVCP/USDU, 1992) and *Reviewing Your Teaching* (UCSDA, 1998). He is a member of the Staff Development Advisory Group of the Scottish Higher Education Funding Council and the Joint Funding Councils' Teaching and Learning Support Network Advisory Service.

Zoran Jelenc is a Senior Research Fellow at the Slovene Adult Education Centre where he was previously director for five years. His prevailing research themes are: non-formal adult education; conceptualization and systemic regulation of adult education; lifelong learning strategies and the learning society. He is Associate Professor of adult education theory and comparative adult education at the Faculty of Arts at the University of Ljubljana.

Ligija Kaminskiene is Director of the Lithuanian Institute of Management. She has been an Associate Professor at Lithuania Christian Fund College and at Vilnius University. She has a PhD in Linguistics and has been a teacher for 24 years. Formerly she was Director of Soros International House, an English language school affiliated to International House, London. After independence (1990), she became Adviser to the Minister of Culture and Education, and Head of the International Relations Department. Her major commitment is to the implementation of educational reform in the independent, democratic Lithuania.

Kathryn Lamble has a background in environmental science and chemistry and is currently working as a researcher at the Royal Institute of Technology in Stockholm, Sweden. During her post at the University of Plymouth she investigated how the University's science degree programmes could be made more relevant to the needs of graduates in the workplace, especially through the development of appropriate skills.

Peter Levin taught Social Policy and Administration at the London School of Economics (LSE) for 25 years before taking early retirement in 1995. Since then he has worked as a consultant in teaching and learning methods in higher education. Projects include the use of information technology in teaching, and the BP Team Development in Universities programme. He earlier acquired a PhD in Solid State Physics and worked as a researcher in industry, at the Building Research Station, and at the LSE and Centre for Environmental Studies. His most recent publication is *Making Social Policy: The mechanisms of government and politics and how to investigate them* (Open University Press, 1997).

Heather MacLennan has lectured for 22 years in Art Theory for Fine Art Degree programmes and her present post is at Cheltenham and Gloucester College of Higher Education. An exhibiting artist, she also researches into the history and aesthetics of printmaking. Recent research interests are in Art Education, particularly investigating students' perceptions of their learning experiences in Fine Art and in relation to the world of work following graduation. Publications include papers on printmaking and connoisseurship and on Fine Art Education.

Mary McCulloch is a Project Officer at the Department of Higher and Further Education at The University of Edinburgh. She is currently pursuing research interests in student involvement in assessment and evaluating the use of computers in undergraduate teaching.

Yvette Miyazaki graduated from the University of Hawaii with a BA in psychology, earned an MA and credential in school psychology from California State University, Dominguez Hills. She is currently in an MA in Human Development program at St. Mary's University of Minnesota and working as a school psychologist in the Montebello Unified School District.

Alistair Morgan is a Senior Lecturer in Educational Technology and Head of the Student Research Centre in the Institute of Educational Technology at the Open University (OU) in the UK. He has an extensive experience of research and teaching in open and distance education both at the OU and internationally and has published widely in the field. His books include *Improving your Students' Learning* (Kogan Page, 1993).

Sue Prince is a Tutor of Law at the University of Exeter and is responsible for teaching core subjects and legal skills. She was previously a student in the same Law department. She has also worked in industry where she has experience of training and managing staff.

Alex Radloff is Senior Lecturer in Academic Staff Development, Teaching Learning Group, Curtin University of Technology, Perth, Western Australia. She has an MA in Psychology and a PhD in Education, and over 20 years' experience in university teaching. Her research interests include self-regulation of learning and the development of communication skills, especially academic writing. She has undertaken consultancy work for both the public and private sectors in Australia.

Mike Rawlins works in the Chalybeate Partnership, which he founded in 1992, as a leadership and team development tutor. These skills were developed with BP where, besides management responsibilities in Research and Development and Commercial areas, he was involved in team development and quality programmes. His facilitation and coaching skills are based on 16 years in a large multi-national business environment and he has worked in the UK, Europe and the Far East. He enjoys applying these skills in sport and is a qualified skiing coach for the disabled. The BP Team Development in Universities programme, based on his original concept and initiative, is now offered to 10 universities in the UK to support existing links with BP.

Pamela Robinson holds a BA in Psychology from California State University, Dominguez Hills and an MA in Experimental Psychology from the California State University, Fullerton. She is a Lecturer in the School of Education at California State University, Dominguez Hills where she teaches courses in motivation and learning, research methods and multicultural issues in education. She is Associate Editor of the *Cooperative Learning and College Teaching* newsletter. She currently serves as evaluation consultant for a five-year school-to-work project jointly funded by the US Department of Labor and the US Department of Education.

Kenneth E Sinclair is an Associate Professor in the Faculty of Education at Sydney University and a former Dean and Head of School. He is the author of books and articles on classroom motivation and learning, the integration of technology into teaching and learning, and the transition of graduates into the workforce. In recent years he has completed a number of commissioned projects for the Australian Business/Higher Education Round Table on graduate competencies for the workplace and on career progression and development.

Lee Sutherland is employed at the University of Zululand as an Academic Development Practitioner, with a specialist interest in assessment. She has taught in a number of secondary schools in South Africa, both State-run and independent, as well as in teacher training. She holds a Master of Education from the University of South Africa and is presently reading for a PhD, entitled 'Reflective assessment practice: a model for staff development', at the University of Witwatersrand.

Simon Unwin has taught architectural design and lectured on the history and theory of architecture since the late 1970s. For the majority of that time he has been based in the Welsh School of Architecture, which is part of the University of Wales, Cardiff, but he has also lived in Australia and taught for a while at the schools of architecture in the Technical University, Stockholm and Pennsylvania State University. His book, *Analysing Architecture* (Routledge, 1997), relates to a course of the same name offered as a module to architecture students in Cardiff.

Preface

The purpose of this book is to provide a series of perspectives on what underpins the vision of a democratic, educated and functional society, and how this is translated into expectations for learning and teaching in higher education. This includes conceptualization and interpretation of the notion of core skills and their relationship to a learning society. It provides a set of overviews and perspectives that interweave, support and extend each other, as well as providing a series of challenges premised on philosophical, psychological and pedagogical grounds. It is in no sense designed to be a comparison between nations, nor a complete overview of the international scene, but serves more to show how certain similarities in influence can be seen within a variety of contexts.

The chapters represent, first, the forefront of current thinking on both what *might* or *should* be; and second, what is being achieved in practice. They are premised on both theoretical and pragmatic stances rather than unattainable visions or goals. The book is firmly premised on what is already known, and how this can be adapted and worked at to promote realistic change. From different national, disciplinary and personal perspectives, academics and others discuss what is 'core' – or of central importance – in their own perceptions of what higher education is, and must be, about in a learning society. Linked to this are important questions about what it means, in practice, to learn, or to be a learner in a learning society. What kinds of learning? What content and which skills? How can appropriate contexts be provided for learning and how do we foster learning? How can we enable students to become 'better learners', now and for the future?

The key issues examined include:

- the role of core skills/generic skills/transferable skills/employment skills/skills for lifelong learning, or any similar term, and their relationship to an economic or personal future. Critical analysis of problems in the development of such skills, or of a learning society, in higher education: for example, conceptual issues, practical implementation, resistance to change, vision as opposed to reality, utilitarianism as opposed to academe;

- how to prepare students/adults for a productive economic future, a professional future, lifelong learning;
- how to ensure that students recognize themselves to be part of an active learning society – both now and for the future.

The book draws together wide themes and issues at the same time as ensuring that they remain embedded in the context of practice. Some papers are research-based and present important findings; others examine theoretical issues or personal practice. All have an underlying theme of 'core' skills, however this is interpreted. What is developed through the book is a critical awareness of the issues that surround practices and personal views, alongside alternative perspectives, discussion of 'where do we go from here?', what has been learnt and what this tells us about a learning society. It is the range of conceptions, the potential tensions and also the commonalities that provide the interest and enable a broad-based characterization of skills.

The book is divided into three parts:

Part 1: Skills for a learning society: who wants what from higher education?

The first seven chapters provide an introduction and a background context for the rest of the book. They highlight perspectives on the requirement for core skills, and allow consideration of what there is in common and what is markedly different in philosophy and development according to context and country. These chapters explore issues of core skills in countries emerging from difficult political situations as well as in those that have a history of democracy and affluence, and how the particular issues or problems associated with each have led to a determination for reassessment and change – through a national strategy or through developing specific kinds of skill.

Part 2: Strategies for teaching and learning – issues and theory

The next seven chapters fit firmly within the issues already raised, providing a critique of present provision in higher education and suggesting strategies for analysis and improvement. In so doing, they illuminate a set of views on what constitute core skills, and on how these contribute to a learning society. The major focus is on learning, and on the barriers to learning – whether societal, institutional or personal. Discussions focus on the necessary conditions and contexts for promoting learners who are well-equipped to cope with a complex future, both personal and in the world of work. The role of teaching and of teachers is also considered in relation to achieving desired ends.

Part 3: Strategies for teaching and learning – in practice

The final nine chapters focus on the actual provision of the kinds of condition for skill development outlined above. The first few chapters deal with practical ideas for promoting change, both at the level of academics as teachers and at the level of tried and tested activities for students, and initiatives for assessment. The remaining chapters have been selected as examples of worthwhile practice in the context of core skill development, and as an illustration of many of the issues raised throughout the book. The selection of a range of disciplines is important in discussion of different approaches and motivations, but each chapter also holds an interest for any reader interested in practice. The issues contained within them are not essentially discipline-based but are, rather, generic in nature. Each provides a personal story of the teaching or provision of core skills, not always without difficulties, and demonstrates a commitment to enriching the lives of students, both within higher education and for the future.

A concluding chapter pulls together the threads running through the book. The emphasis is on the provision of frameworks which can be used to analyse the rhetoric and practice of the present, as well as to enhance decision-making and planning for the future.

The contributors

Many of those who have agreed to contribute are leaders in their field or discipline, or at the forefront of good practice in higher education. Some work both within and outside higher education, and make critical observers. Several authors are from countries that usually receive little international attention – at least in terms of education. Some papers have been selected from presentations at international events; many have been invited from those who have demonstrated themselves to have an important voice in the issues under consideration, and who have been prepared to write specifically for this book.

PART 1

SKILLS FOR A LEARNING SOCIETY: WHO WANTS WHAT FROM HIGHER EDUCATION?

Chapter 1

Introduction

The first seven chapters provide the background to the rest of the book, highlighting requirements for core skills in a variety of contexts.

Chapter 2 provides an introductory overview of the area of core skills and the concept of a learning society. It is mainly set in the context of the UK, but shows that the issues and practice are of international concern. It is suggested that, alongside radical structural changes, there has been a powerful movement towards a reconceptualization of higher education. The purposes and practices of the past have been challenged and undermined in an agenda that requires higher education to serve as a preparation for employment.

Chapter 3, 'Perceptions of the importance of skills for employment', by June Harwood, David Harwood and Kate Lamble, provides evidence of the kinds of perspective outlined in Chapter 2. It serves as an example of the relationship of general government and employer demands for skills to the reality of one specific community. The chapter outlines the findings from three large-scale surveys centred on the University of Plymouth, its present students, its past students and employers of its graduates. These surveys explored how much importance students attach to the skills and abilities increasingly seen by employers as necessary for employment, and how well they perceived these skills to have been encouraged and developed within their higher education programmes. The enquiry was continued within the context of the Faculty of Science. It allowed the examination of graduate and employer views on ways of enhancing the relevance of the chemistry, environmental science and geological science programmes to meet the needs of the workplace.

Chapter 4 reinforces that, as outlined in Chapter 2, there have been similar considerations and pressures impacting on higher education in Australia. Ken

Sinclair, in 'The transition of graduates from universities to the workplace', describes how there have been a number of influential reports addressing the question of competencies needed for effective workplace participation (Finn Report, 1991, Mayer Report, 1992). The skills under consideration have many similarities with the British approaches. In the Mayer Report, seven key competencies were identified, collecting, analysing and organizing information; communicating ideas and information; planning and organizing activities; working with others and in teams; using mathematical ideas and techniques; solving problems and using technology. The reports have fuelled a lively debate, but have also been influential in finding application at the school and post-school levels of education. The results of a series of surveys are described, the findings of which have very similar outcomes to those outlined in Chapter 3.

The prior chapters have focused on countries where traditional cultural characterizations and a clear national identity have become somewhat submerged within a multicultural society. However, similar moves towards the conceptualization of core skills can be seen within European countries that have, and are determined to maintain, a more clear-cut national identity. This can be seen within the next three chapters. In 'New approaches in the Danish education system' Chapter 5, Peter Bacher reviews an educational system that has traditionally been premised on very different grounds to those of much of the rest of the world, and which has often been a source of interest to outsiders. The system has always been highly decentralized; many different educational offerings, provided through very small units, take care of a particular educational speciality. It is an educational system which, until the present, has changed slowly. Yet pressures are being brought to bear on this system, too, and review suggests that debate is being fuelled by concerns similar to those of Britain and Australia. The current trend is that, on the one hand, educational institutions are gaining more autonomy; on the other hand, the State is intervening more and more. Parallel to these trends, there is an ongoing spirited discussion on: 'what are core skills?' This discussion can be regarded as a battle between two paradigms: that of the tradional and that of the labour market.

The context of the chapters so far has been one of comparative affluence. This is not so for the last two chapters in Part 1. Lithuania is a small country in a state of considerable turmoil as the new democracy attempts to find its feet. Chapter 6 argues that a core skill for Lithuanians must be the ability to use a foreign language. The learning or developing of a foreign language is often encouraged within higher education and many students, through Erasmus and other international programmes, attend courses at foreign universities or take up offers of work placements. Lists of core skills from a variety of sources have included foreign language learning, although this seems to be an area that is readily abandoned. There is also much rhetoric, often promoted in employer brochures, about the 'global workplace' and the need for foreign languages. However, Lithuania perhaps has a more pressing incentive than many other countries to promote foreign language learning. In Chapter 6, 'English language as a key to open society', Ligija Kaminskiene outlines emphatically the need for the learning of an international language – preferably English – by all those who will shape the future of that country both educationally and economically. It is argued that without a facility in English at the national level, wider growth in education will be hampered, knowledge will remain restricted and international relationships will founder. For each learning individual, a core prerequisite will need to be a language for the purposes of opening up further avenues of learning, and for contact with the world beyond Lithuania.

Zoran Jelenc in Chapter 7 ('Slovenia – The Learning Country: how to reach the pre-set strategic goal') briefly outlines how a small country has taken up the kind of national commitment called for in the preceding chapter, but in relation to the concept of 'lifelong learning'. It suggests that in the last few years, lifelong learning has been acknowledged as a world movement. However, the concept will only have an impact when it is accepted as part of every country's national policy, and even more so when it becomes indispensable for every learning community, every learning organization and every individual. This chapter is not specifically an account of higher education, but outlines an interdisciplinary long-term developmental project to include all aspects of education: 'Slovenia – the Learning Country'. Its basic elements are the elaborating and adopting of a national strategy for lifelong learning. The chapter suggests that adult education is the area of education that performs the leading role in the development of a learning society, through appropriate national programmes, through selected developmental projects and through the development of a suitable network of providers and sources of learning. However, despite optimism for change in Slovenia, the route to progress is long and hard. It is argued that concepts and strategies have to belong to a regulated national policy on learning – beginning in schools and continuing provision throughout life. Without national commitment, there can be no certainty that this will happen.

Chapter 2

Change in higher education: a learning society and the role of core skills

Elisabeth Dunne

Introduction

Over the past decade, higher education in Britain has been undergoing a period of intense reconceptualization and change. The rapidity and extent of restructuring in the system has had an effect on all aspects of university life. Much change has been premised on enthusiastically pursued and democratic principles, widening access to education and promoting a more diverse society of learners. The Government-engineered, wide-scale expansion of the late 1980s and early 1990s led to a broadening of the student population which now includes many more 'mature' students, more women and increasing numbers studying on a part-time basis. Expansion has also been accompanied by movement towards credit-based programmes and modularization, both of which offer flexibility of choice, and of time and duration of participation in higher education. There is a positive expectation that students will become flexible, autonomous learners who can select their personal pathways from what is on offer and who will develop the skills of lifelong learning.

Alongside, there have been pressures on institutions for greater accountability in the use of public funds and demands for the assessment of quality. Further pressures have been exerted by the need to compete for funding and for students, with tensions arising between the former polytechnics, or 'new' universities, and the 'old'. At the same time, students have been encouraged to take a more consumerist view of their education and this approach is likely to persist, given the increasing financial burdens imposed on them.

Traditional teaching methods, as well as a traditional curriculum and the role of knowledge within this, are being challenged. Academics are being expected to pay more attention to their teaching in order to satisfy demands for quality and to cope with the larger, more diverse student group, who exhibit a range of different expectations and learning styles. Academics are also being asked to address the assumed needs of society in the next century. Further, there has been a widespread shift of emphasis on 'who' should have the most influential voice in shaping the curriculum of higher education. There is pressure, often from those outside higher education and in particular from employer groups, to provide graduates who are well-equipped to cope with the demands of the world of work. It is in this context that the issue of core skills becomes important. It is also in relation to this move towards a functionalist or instrumental approach that Barnett (1990) perceived 'a particular crisis facing higher education which has largely been overlooked. It is a crisis to do with the way in which we understand higher education, the fundamental principles on which the idea of higher education has traditionally stood, and the way in which these principles are being undermined'.

Although this chapter deals mainly with the detail of the British context, the situation that is described, and the issues that are raised, belong to a far wider debate. Nations across the world are dealing with the same kinds of problem. The political and cultural context may be different, the emphasis on skill development may be different, but there is a shared need to respond to the requirements of a changing world and, specifically, to redefine the role of education within it.

Changes in the conceptualization of higher education

Well over 30 years ago, a review of the pattern of full-time higher education in Britain (Robbins Report, 1963) confirmed the traditional role of higher education, including the recommendation that 'what is taught should be taught in such a way as to promote the general powers of the mind'. It has been pointed out that the report articulated the contemporary assumption that the traditional autonomy of institutions and their liberal educational objectives represented an effective framework to prepare graduates to take their places in the workforce (Squires, 1990). In recent years this assumption has been challenged. Current interest in the nature of a learning society does not take for granted the established role of the universities.

Government papers on higher education (Department of Education and Science, 1987, 1991) cited the need for a body of graduates equipped to deal with the demands of a rapidly changing work environment. They asserted the necessity of 'core' skills, for example the ability to cooperate and communicate, which are assumed to transfer to other contexts. This was consistent with the Confederation of British Industry's view that 'the common denominator of highly qualified manpower will... be the ability to think, learn and adapt. Personal transferable skills – problem solving, communication, teamwork – rather than technical skills defined with narrow occupational ranges, will come to form the stabilizing characteristic of work. If higher education is to meet the needs of the economy and the individual it must seek actively to develop these generic core competences' (Slee, 1989). These aims were reflected in some of the major initiatives in higher education, for example the Department of Employment's *Enterprise in Higher Education* and the Royal Society of Art's *Higher Education for Capability* programmes.

A similar view was supported by Edwards (1994), then Chair of the Universities Committee of Vice Chancellors and Principals, who argued: 'the world we live in is highly knowledge intensive, and graduates will increasingly require core transferable skills. For certain, working life will be about continued learning, skilling and re-skilling to stay ahead'.

Surveys of employers strongly supported (and continue to support) such change. Reports highlight the desire for graduates with core or transferable skills, and continued concern at the lack of such skills, including dissatisfaction at the ability of graduate employees to express themselves, to make oral presentations, to write reports or business letters (Quality in Higher Education, 1993, 1994). QHE (1994) concluded that 'higher education has a responsibility for ensuring that students graduate with competences that enable them to work effectively in modern organisations'.

It is clear that there has been a growing demand for the role of higher education to be reconsidered. It is less clear what is preferred. Slee (quoted above) exhibits a lack of clarity in using the terms 'personal transferable skills' and 'generic core competences' in close proximity without specifying their exact relationship. Nor is it clear how these terms relate to Edwards' use of 'core transferable skills'. Both authors assert the centrality of the ability to learn or to continue learning, which is consistent in general terms with a notion of a learning society, but it is not clear how this relates to the acquisition of personal, core, transferable or generic skills (or competences).

What are core skills?

At this point, it seems appropriate to look more closely at what is meant by the term 'core skills'. Relatively unspecific definitions of 'core skills' abound. In general terms, they are usually conceived as being generic, non-disciplinary and transferable from higher education to employment. It is difficult to recognize a more detailed consensus among all the differing definitions and lists of skills that have been offered. Tribe (1996), seeking some coherence, proposes two models for core skills. Each of these reflects a competing extreme:

- the 'society-centred model', most akin to education as training, that focuses on preparing recruits for the labour market with the ultimate objective of economic growth and prosperity;
- the 'liberal model' that rejects a utilitarian view and asserts education as intrinsically worth while.

The former perspective is often found in authors or organizations with a vocational background, for example, 'Core Skills are central to education and training' (City and Guilds, 1993) and 'essential skills which are highly sought after by employers and educational establishments... are key to individual development' (Royal Society for Arts, 1997).

Hyland (1994) and Tribe (1996) suggest that the first publication to highlight the concept of a 'common core of skills' was that of the Further Education Unit (FEU, 1979). The list of core skills was complex and extensive. It included aspects of knowledge, skill and personal development considered essential to meet the basic demands of contemporary society, including competence in or the ability to develop the following: literacy, numeracy, graphicity; physical and manipulative skills; study skills; problem-solving; personal relationships; moral values; realistic decisions about own future; understanding of roles and status in society; political and economic literacy; appreciation of physical and technological environments; coping skills for self sufficiency; etc.

During the 1980s, as the concept of 'core skills' became increasingly popular, higher education tended to use the phrase 'personal transferable skills' (initially promoted through Enterprise initiatives) for a similar idea. The precise relationship between core skills and transferable skills remains unclear, although a statement from the Department of Employment (1995) suggests:

> The issue of transferability is key to the concept of core skills... there are some skills which are by their nature transferable to a variety of settings and... they are therefore the core skills – i.e. it is only skills which transfer which are core, all core skills are therefore transferable skills'. All transferable skills are not, however, perceived as core skills – especially if the definition of Jessup (1997) is used 'somewhat loosely... to refer to all knowledge, skills and understanding which are potentially transferable.

Some developments support the thematic and holistic approach of the FEU with this trend continuing into, for example, a list not of 'core' or 'transferable' skills but of 'self-reliance' skills, or more loosely: 'Skills for the 21st Century' (Association of Graduate Recruiters, 1995). Self-reliance skills, also subtitled 'Career Management Skills and Effective Learning Skills' are: self-awareness, self-promotion, exploring and creating opportunities, action planning, networking, decision-making, negotiation, political awareness, coping with uncertainty, development focus, transfer skills and self-confidence. 'Negotiation' includes the ability 'to negotiate the psycho- logical contract from a position of powerlessness'; 'political awareness' requires understanding of 'the hidden tensions and power struggles within organizations'. Such 'skills' are set on the same level as 'good telephone skills' for 'networking'. The complete inventory, though purporting to be premised on research, seems to reflect more of an employer wish-list coloured by the author's own persuasions. Coffield (1997c) suggests that this so-called 'stra- tegic assessment of graduates' future roles' is no more than 'a highly selective amalgam of untested speculations from focus groups and interviews with interested parties'. Overall, it could be that the world of employers, as out- lined within this particular document, and the world of traditional academics in higher education, are unlikely to meet, at least in the near future.

The majority of lists are more simple. But identical lists may in one con- text be labelled 'core' skills and in another 'transferable' skills. Many include 'communication', 'numeracy', 'IT (information technology)', 'personal' or 'interpersonal' skills, and 'problem-solving' – reflecting the requirement, especially in vocational contexts, for a grounding in basic (or even remedial level) knowledge and communicative skills. It could be argued that the nar- row list, reflecting the prevalence of these skills, best represents 'core' skills (it is similar to that in use for the national framework of 'core' – now 'key' – skills). However, a selection premised on commonality might ultimately be inappropriate, reductionist or meaningless, as well as philosophically and theoretically unjustified and unjustifiable. Further, the more basic lists of core skills, as conceptualized for vocational curricula, may be inappropriate for the complexity and breadth of skill development necessary at degree level.

The focus of attention may have been widened by the adoption of the term 'attributes' (Harvey et al, 1997). Attributes include the kinds of knowledge and skill deemed appropriate to graduates, as well as the personal qualities and attitudes which will be essential to continued and flexible learning and to a productive economic future. Skills which have previously appeared in lists of core skills, or personal transferable skills, are now subsumed in a different framework for categorization. Harvey et al (1997) incorporate employer re- quirements of graduates within the two strands of 'personal' and 'interper- sonal' attributes. The former includes 'knowledge', 'intellect', 'willingness to learn' and 'self-skills'; the latter, 'communication', 'teamworking' and 'interpersonal skills'. Although it may well be important to emphasize what is required of graduates in wider terms than traditional disciplinary knowledge and core skills, such lists confirm the continuing confusion. A major problem is that changing the vocabulary does not change the conceptual and practical difficulties. It is unlikely that such change will draw core skills more centrally into conceptualization of a learning society.

Nevertheless, the CVCP (Committee of Vice Chancellors and Principals) accepted the role of personal or core skill acquisition in higher education. This was illustrated by their joint declaration of intent with the Confederation of British Industry and the Council for Industry and Higher Education (1996). In this document, it was asserted that 'most British people, most educators, and most students now believe that it is one of higher education's purposes to prepare students well for working life'. A joint national effort was agreed to ensure that those in higher education are enabled to develop attributes thought useful for success in employment and future life. These attributes are 'general personal and intellectual capacities that go beyond those traditionally made explicit within an academic or vocational discipline'.

The most recent vision statement on higher education, *Higher Education in the Learning Society* (Dearing Report, 1997), continues to support the shift in purpose of higher education. It reiterates that external factors have affected the development of higher education, and that these will be even more influential in the next 20 years. The report restates the now familiar economic mantra: 'Powerful forces – technological and political – are driving the economies of the world towards greater integration. Competition is increasing from developing economies that have a strong commitment to education and training. The new economic order will place an increasing premium on knowledge which, in turn, makes national economies more dependent on higher education's development of people with high-level skills, knowledge and understanding, and on its contribution to research'. 'Key' skills – of communication and numeracy, the use of communications and information technology, and 'learning how to learn' – are claimed as necessary outcomes of all higher education, alongside knowledge and understanding, subject-specific skills, and cognitive skills such as critical analysis. 'Key' skills hence represent a narrow emphasis akin to comparatively lower-level disciplinary skills for all, and learning to learn fitting uncomfortably with them. In the latest framework for national vocational qualifications (QCA (Qualifications and Curriculum Authority)) 'working in teams' and 'problem-solving' are included in this list. This remains a list very different to the conceptualization of 'key' skills in Europe, outlined by Brown in Chapter 10.

However, the acceptance, indeed advocacy, of the role of the State and employers in the determination of a higher education curriculum, remains antithetical to some. A critical UK commentator, Barnett, decries the shift to a situation in which society is framing the character of higher education, arguing that the State now identifies the forms of knowing and development that it sees as worth while, a situation in which academics become State servants, fulfilling the State's agenda. He further claims that transferable skills are a means of disenfranchising discipline-based academics of their expertise (Barnett, 1994). He suggests that the issues are deep: 'The central argument is that one ideology, that of academic competence, is being displaced with another ideology, that of operational competence'. The shift, in extreme terms, is from higher education providing 'knowledge for contemplation' to that which equips students with a set of performance skills or competences which will prepare them to be instantly effective in the workplace. In other words, the mismatch rests on differing views of what might constitute a learning society within higher education. The dichotomy is between:

- a society in which study of disciplinary knowledge is seen as worth while in its own right;
- or another in which universities become providers of knowledge and skills to be used in multiple settings, and in which graduates are prepared in more specific and direct ways for employment.

Coffield (1999) argues that the language of human capital theory has 'hijacked the public debate and the discourse of professionals'. Education is 'no longer viewed as a means of individual and social emancipation', but as '"investment" or "consumption", as having "inputs" and "outputs, "stocks" which depreciate as well as "appreciate", and it is measured by "rates of return"'. In these terms, employers have been 'reinforced in their beliefs that the main obstacle to their success is the poor education of the workforce' (Levin and Kelley, 1997). The use or benefit of a higher education system is challenged. In this context, it becomes possible to ask: 'When push comes to shove, can higher education meet the demands of a changing workforce and a changing economy? One school of thought says that American colleges and universities already are being marginalised – that they now count for less because their products have failed to satisfy the demand for high quality, affordable, work related education and training' (pamphlet produced by the United States National Center on the Educational Quality of the Workforce, based on Zemsky and Oedel, 1994). Coffield argues that the 'overconcentration on one factor – improving standards in education – distorts both industrial and educational policy in ways that are unlikely to improve competitiveness and delays the advent of more comprehensive strategies'.

International perspectives

This outline of change, of issues and of pressures does not pertain to Britain alone. The USA have been grappling with such features over a much longer period. Australia, South Africa and parts of Europe are coming to terms with similar issues and debate.

For example a series of reports commissioned in Australia by the Business/Higher Education Round Table (1991, 1992, 1993), a body comprising 43 chief executives and 24 vice chancellors, demonstrate a commitment to joint initiatives that will 'advance the goals and improve the performance of both business and higher education for the benefit of Australian society'. Extensive surveys (see Chapter 4) highlight a perceived need for the development throughout education of thinking and decision-making skills and the ability to apply knowledge to the workplace. This same thinking is reflected at the national level in considerations of the competences required for employment by the Finn (1991) and Mayer (1992) Committees. The former asserted that there are certain essential things that all young people need to learn in their preparation for employment, which they labelled 'employment related key competencies'. It recommended that steps be taken to ensure that all young people are able to develop these regardless of the education or training pathway taken. The Mayer Committee followed this by developing seven key competency strands considered essential for effective participation in work and other social settings: collecting, analysing and organizing information; communicating ideas and information; planning and organizing activities; working with others in teams; using mathematical ideas and techniques; solving problems; and using technology — a list with obvious, and extensive, overlaps with those produced in the UK. As in the UK, these competences appear to lack a substantial foundation – 'a theoretical or empirical base for the establishment of the Key Competences is difficult to ascertain' (Beven and Duggan, 1996).

A list of 'generic attributes' from the University of Sydney suggests a slightly different emphasis, although the aim is similar. It is stated that graduates of the university will be 'more employable, more able to cope with change and more developed as people'. Their list of knowledge skills, thinking skills, personal skills, personal attributes and practical skills includes communication, teamwork, and so on, but also focuses on: the capacity and desire to continue to learn; striving for tolerance and integrity; and acknowledging personal responsibility for value judgements and ethical behaviour towards others.

Economic rhetoric is also driving educational reform in the USA. Stasz *et al* (1996) begin a review of the economic imperative behind school reform by stating that there is growing consensus that American education needs fundamental reform in order to adequately prepare youth for the current and future workforce. This belief is based on the view that changes in the workplace will require new and different skills of workers, and that America's competitive edge in the world economy will increasingly depend on the skills of its workers. It is also reported as common for scholars and policy-makers to assert that students are ill-prepared for the future workplace and that they need new kinds of skill. Marshall and Tucker (1992) sum up what they claim in the American context is the emerging consensus on the skills needed to power a modern economy: capacity for abstract thought; to solve real-world problems; to communicate well in oral and written forms, and to work well with others. Other reports such as that from SCANS (1991) present a broader conception of skills including, in addition to the above, those relating to information, systems and technology.

A report from the President of the newly formed Moscow External University of the Humanities (Khaladjan, 1996) outlines assessment criteria for students which, yet again, have many similarities with skills lists elsewhere. Alongside in-depth knowledge, students are expected to demonstrate an ability to:

- solve new problems;
- develop and express ideas and arguments;
- make prompt decisions and take responsibility for them;
- demonstrate the art of rhetoric through substantiating opinions and judgements.

Within Europe, there is again evidence of similar trends. Societal needs are perceived in terms of:

- highly specialized and professional skills;
- educational systems emphasizing learning skills and the maintenance of competence, rather than knowledge alone;
- efficient and cost-effective programmes making use of multimedia technology.

Alongside this, van der Vleuten et al (1996) argue that: 'Progression in educational theory requires educational systems to activate the learner and to critically reflect on traditionally accepted adagia of educational practice'.

Otala (1993), also arguing from a European perspective, presents the now familiar economic prognosis that: 'The output of education and training systems in terms of both quantity and quality of skills at all levels, is the prime determinant of a country's level of industrial productivity and hence, competitiveness'. The main conclusion is equally adamant: 'The workplace has a growing need for competence development that can only be filled by stitutions of higher education'. The shortfall in skilled labour is highlighted by Healy (1996) who presents recent analyses of labour market trends by the OECD (Organization for European Cooperation and Development). These show that new employment opportunities requiring higher skill levels are increasing at a rate of 10 per cent of the total labour force each year. However, the inflow of recently qualified young people from the initial education system is typically around 3 per cent of the total labour force in any given year.

It seems that an international consensus has emerged, at least in terms of rhetoric, with regard to the needs of the future economy, to the skills base necessary to confront it, and to the central role of higher education in developing that skills base. Many of the chapters in this book will illustrate and explore these issues further.

A list of skills which reflects a different political context and a somewhat different philosophy can be seen in those presented by an education minister from Estonia (Vanna, 1997). The new conceptualization of educational provision is premised on 'technical' skills and qualifications; 'cultural' qualifications (language skills, historical consciousness, social and sociological knowledge, public spirit and ethical knowledge; and 'personal' attributes: self-confidence, emotional stability, independence, a sense of occasion as well as 'your feet on the ground', communication, cooperation, logical thinking and understanding of process. A different philosophy can also be seen within the Nordic concept of *folkeoplysning* (explored in Chapter 5) wherein, for example in Finland, the principles of democratic behaviour, such as debating skills and defending one's views are paramount (Nordic Council of Ministers, 1996).

In Japan, skill development is central to education, although the concept of lifelong learning is perceived in different terms, not in any sense related to the instrumental approaches already outlined. Lifelong learning is conceived in terms of cultural, sport and leisure activities and policy statements focus not on contribution to the economy but on 'aspects of mental satisfaction with daily life, switching so to speak from "economic wealth" to "mental wealth"' (Trivellato, 1997).

What is a learning society?

The Dearing Report (1997) also argues that over the next twenty years the UK must create a society committed to learning throughout life, and that this should be realized through a new compact involving institutions and their staff, students, government, employers and society in general: 'We see the historic boundaries between vocational and academic education breaking

gly active partnerships between higher education insti-
s of industry, commerce and public service... There is a
lence between students, institutions, the economy,
te which needs to be recognized by each party'. Such
ning are beyond the scope of this book, but the notion
...eloping students in higher education who will be well-equipped with
the appropriate skills to be 'lifelong learners' is one that is addressed within
several of the chapters. Higher education cannot be disassociated from the
agenda for lifelong learning or for a learning society.

The concept of a learning society tends to incorporate notions of lifelong
learning within it. A learning society is often characterized as one in which all
members and groups of members are allowed and enabled to develop their
knowledge and skills and attitudes to learning. A 1998 discussion paper from
the Australian government (www) suggests:

> In the twenty-first century knowledge will be the most important currency of
> all. If Australia is to prosper in this new environment, and to continue to be a vi-
> brant, open and inclusive society, we must also become a learning society.
> Higher Education has a unique and vital contribution to make to the develop-
> ment of a learning society. Higher education should open, nurture and refine
> minds, and create independent learners who are able to grow intellectually
> throughout their lives and contribute fully and at the highest levels to society
> and the workplace.

Vision statements on a learning society have emerged from across the world.
One of the earliest came from Husén (1974). By the year 2000 he predicted
that a learning society would have been created:

- education would confer status;
- there would be equal educational opportunities for all, with no economic
  or social barriers;
- students would be involved in decisions affecting their studies; and
- communication of knowledge would be revolutionized by technology.

The vision of the future has often been associated with the 'technological revolution' and the possibility of 'creating a new form of electronic, interactive
education that should blossom into a lifelong learning system that allows
almost anyone to learn almost anything from anywhere at anytime' (Halal
and Liebowitz, 1994). However, Raggatt et al (1996) argue that the learning
society is 'not likely to be a Utopian society in which learning opportunities
are available to all without restriction but one in which fresh challenges and
new opportunities will be presented to those concerned with adult learners
and lifelong learning alongside older questions of justice and equity'.

In a paper first written in 1991, van der Zee (1996) states that 'defining a concept that has engendered a world-wide debate is tricky'. He outlines five criteria, or strategic issues, for the development of a learning society. These are the need to:

1. broaden the definition of learning (education as a dimension of society);
2. redirect the goal of learning (growth towards completeness);
3. go beyond learning and instruction (increasing collective competence);
4. foster autonomy in learning (self education);
5. stress a political approach to learning (the right to learn).

This approach is perhaps more useful than that of Husén. Rather than stating absolute and possibly unachievable goals, a broad thematic approach is apparent. However, this approach is more dependent on interpretation, both at the level of conceptualization and in terms of how these criteria can be achieved.

A different view, though not necessarily in discord with the above, is seen in the whole-life curricula suggested by Stock (1996). He outlines four areas to this:

1. life-enhancing education – cultural, physical, social, civic;
2. special needs;
3. earnings-related education;
4. life-stage changing education, including role education.

These, Stock argues, will contribute to the 'coherence of education... the health, happiness and growth of the people and the nation-state'.

The Delors Commission (UNESCO, 1996), in a report entitled *Learning: The treasure within*, also identified potential areas of tension to which special attention should be given in the context of lifelong learning:

- that between the global and the local;
- the universal and the individual, the spiritual and the material;
- the traditional and the modern;
- the long term and the short term;
- the contrast between the enormous growth of information and the ability of people to adapt to this;
- the need for competition and a concern for equal opportunities.

The problem in conceptualizing a learning society is that, as for core skills, much is again premised on rhetoric, and differing visions and perspectives. A similar issue is also apparent: to what extent should considerations of economic productivity outweigh all others in the promotion of a learning society for the future?

Rhetoric or reality?

In spite of the lack of precision, government and other initiatives related to core skills and a learning society do seem to be having some impact on higher education in Britain. Most universities now have modular programmes; some offer credit accumulation and transfer, or assessment of prior learning. A few universities are advertising competence-based approaches in response to the extant demands. Many universities have accepted the implications of the political and economic agenda, at least at the level of policy, the majority having central directives, policy and some form of strategy which assert their commitment to skills development (Drummond *et al*, 1997). However, Allen (1991) and Gubbay (1994) identified considerable scepticism about this trend among traditional university teachers, who believe it is not their role to provide skills for employment. They claim they lack the necessary skills and time to teach them, and cannot, or do not wish to, assess such skills. In the current climate of accountability, many see teaching for skills as a distraction from the drive for better research ratings. Findings from one university illustrate many of these features. Dunne (1995), reporting interview and observation data from staff and students in 33 departments, found that innovations in this area were few. Where the teaching of such skills was claimed, it was often not evident in course planning, teaching methods or assessment documentation. Discussions with students indicated that they characterized their learning predominantly in terms of disciplinary knowledge and not skill development.

Scepticism among academics in higher education also appears to pertain in the USA, where Zemsky (1997) reports on a meeting of personnel from 130 colleges and universities where most participants are reported to have grown tired of 'the clatter of the market'. Most institutions felt themselves under assault by a society that expects them to accept market demands as their own agenda. Consequently many faculties have been told to justify their practices by a set of criteria and a language that seem to them foreign, and even hostile to the values and professional purposes they profess.

Even when there is support for change, the issues are complex. Assiter (1995) argues that higher education in the UK cannot ignore the development of core skills simply because some see it as an initiative which is market-driven; further, core skill development is not incompatible with development for life. In the context of Europe, Tuijnman (1996) embraces a positive vision of the potential of a learning society. He describes how: 'The new belief in the positive outcomes of education stands in sharp contrast with the generally pessimistic view of the value of formal education of the 1970s and early 1980s'. Education is not just a social cost but a strategic investment. Workforce skills are elements in a strategy for promoting the economic and social well-being of nations. Nonetheless, he also warns that 'it seems doubtful whether the ideals of lifelong education can be given real meaning in the context of a training market model'.

A framework for analysis

The rhetoric and the practice, and differences between them, are examined throughout this book. A potential framework for analysis is provided at this stage, in order to enable the reader to make sense of the relationships between the chapters, and more easily to explore each chapter in the context of the issues outlined above. To this end, a lead is taken from Fulton *et al* (1982) who, in a discussion of the links between education, the labour market and employer policy, identified four fundamentally different, but interrelated, interpretations of the role of education. These connect strongly to the discussion above. The interpretations are, briefly, that:

1. Education's contribution to employment is discounted and its purpose is taken to be personal development.
2. Education is a progressive selection process.
3. Education develops general intellectual skills which are later brought to bear on the specific requirements of employment.
4. Education provides specific skills used in later employment.

These points largely summarize issues of the present day. Slightly modified and added to, they were used to provide the framework for a model of education (Dunne, 1992). The first two points were taken to represent the extremes of one dimension (x axis). The last two points were taken to represent the extremes of a second dimension (y axis). A third dimension (z axis) was introduced – 'centralized/decentralized' (Figure 2.1).

This model underpins much of the description and argument throughout this book and serves to outline continuing tensions. If extreme points of each of the three axes are taken together, one way of characterizing the purposes of higher education would be as:

- x axis – education for personal development;
- y axis – education for general intellectual qualities which can be adapted for future employment;
- z axis – decentralized control of the system.

In most ways, these three extremes could be said to characterize higher education as it was until recently, a 'stable' position, and one that is now often referred to as 'traditional'. The opposite ends of these axes represent a set of

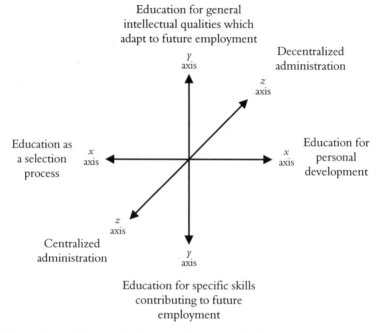

Figure 2.1 *A framework of analysis for aspects of influence on higher education*

extremes towards which higher education is steadily moving. The arguments and tensions remain in the decision-making processes – that is, with regard to the extent of movement along each axis; and in the implementation processes – that is, what it is that movement along any axis actually means, and how it can be effected in practice.

The pressure for core skills represents a strong shift in emphasis along the x and y axes, in a context determined by z: higher education is expected to provide specific skills for employment (with the implication that this will enhance national prosperity); individual success in these skills will determine access to employment (or so we are led to believe). The z axis is slightly more problematic, as what appears to be happening is that, *de juro*, universities remain decentralized; but *de facto*, they are becoming more centralized – bound by the 'new' hegemony in discourse which states that, for example, students must have freedom of movement and choice, they must be prepared for employment; they must become independent learners.

All the chapters in this book in some sense address the issues and tensions of movement along the axes, looking at both the decision-making processes, whether at national or institutional level, and at the implementation processes. Further tensions may also be apparent in the relationship between the notions of *individual* growth, the growth of a democratic learning *society* and the competitive growth of *national prosperity*.

Chapter 3

Perceptions of the importance of skills for employment

June Harwood, David Harwood and Kathryn Lamble

Introduction

In 1990, the EHE (Enterprise in Higher Education) was introduced to British Universities, with a view to developing 'enterprise' skills to ensure that graduates should be better prepared for working life. It embraced a wide range of approaches, including curriculum and staff development, innovative approaches to teaching and learning and the greater encouragement of partnerships between higher education institutions and employers. To support these initiatives, institutions were awarded contracts for up to £1 million over five years. The total expenditure for EHE and related projects between 1993 and 1999 will have been £60 million, within some 60 institutions.

The University of Plymouth's EHE programme ran from 1990 to 1994. The University is one of the UK's largest 'new' universities with 23,000 students and 2,100 full-time equivalent staff. It has a tradition of sound links with the industries within the region and a strong emphasis on teaching. The EHE project was dependent on a 'bottom-up' approach, seeding successful projects throughout the university, many of which, having been continually updated and developed, continue to bear fruit.

The need to respond to employers' needs for skilled graduates did not cease with EHE. A recent survey published by the Association of Graduate Recruiters (1996) reveals that employers are placing increasing emphasis on 'non-academic skills such as interpersonal skills and flexibility'. It also reports that academic high fliers are being 'bustled to one side by graduates with work experience'. A student thus equipped can earn three times as much money as a student with a first-class degree, but no relevant vocational experience.

Surveys on skills for employment

In 1994, shortly after the completion of the EHE programme, two surveys were conducted from the University of Plymouth. The intention was to take a snapshot of how far into student perceptions the proposed culture change had percolated. In 1997, funding from the Department of Education and Employment allowed a further in-depth survey to be undertaken within the Faculty of Science.

- *Survey one* was aimed at past students now in employment. Its intention was to gauge graduates' perceptions of the skills necessary for employment, and also how well they felt they had been prepared for employment by their course of study.
- *Survey two* was conducted among undergraduate students. The aim was to explore how much importance they attached to the development of the skills and abilities seen as necessary for employment. This was anticipated as giving some indication of how successful the EHE programme had been in conveying its messages to the student population. A further aim was to ascertain how well undergraduates perceived these skills to be encouraged and developed through their higher education programmes.
- *Survey three* examined ways of enhancing the relevance of the chemistry, environmental science and geological science first degree programmes to meet the needs of the workplace. In part, this was achieved through postal surveys of 850 employers of science graduates and 840 graduates completing their studies at the university during the five-year period, 1992–1996. The aim of the graduate survey was to assess how well graduates felt their degree programme had equipped them for the workplace; and to identify potential areas for improvement, with particular emphasis on scientific skills. The employer survey was devised to identify the transferable and scientific skills sought in the recruitment of science graduates and how they felt degree programmes in general could be enhanced to equip graduates more effectively for the workplace.

Survey one: ex-students in employment

A questionnaire was sent out to 400 ex-students, with a 30 per cent response rate. The questionnaire listed 14 core skills (including written and spoken communication, using IT (information technology), working independently, problem-solving and managing information) and asked respondents to com-ment on how frequently they were used in the course of their present job. They were also asked how well they felt their programme of study at Plym-outh had facilitated their development. In only 7 of the 14 areas did graduates suggest that provision matched or exceeded their perceived needs. In addi-tion, graduates were asked how relevant they felt their programme of study had been to their subsequent career. Overall, 50 per cent felt their programme of study had been highly relevant to their choice of career; 40 per cent felt it had some relevance, and 10 per cent felt their degree irrelevant to their subsequent career path. When asked whether the skills/content balance of their course had been appropriate, 74 per cent felt the balance was 'about right'; all others felt there was 'too much content'.

Survey two: undergraduates

Nine hundred questionnaires were sent to five faculties: Science; Technol-ogy; Agriculture, Food and Land Use; Arts and Education, and the Business School. This questionnaire listed 21 core skills. These were grouped under the headings of 'key skills' (eg communication, numeracy, use of IT, foreign language ability), 'career skills' (eg preparing a CV, conducting an interview) and 'professional development' (eg working independently, working as part of a team). All were skills perceived, through a review of literature, as giving cause for concern.

Students were asked to comment in three areas: the importance of core skills within their current programme of study; the success of their programme in enabling them to acquire these skills; and whether there was any other skill or area of knowledge they would have wished to see included. A second section asked whether a work placement was included in their programme and if not, whether they saw any advantage in work experience being made available. If they had undertaken a work placement, they were asked to comment on how relevant the listed skills had proved. In an attempt to gauge how seriously students regarded the skills issue, they were also asked whether they would be willing to undertake voluntary work during vacations in order to develop the skills that employers require. There was a high re-sponse rate (77 per cent) with almost 700 questionnaires returned. Mature students, that is over 21 years of age when beginning their course, provided 46 per cent of the sample (the percentage studying at the university is 53). Half of the respondents were in the first year of their studies.

University-based programmes
In response to the question: '*what additional skill or area of knowledge would you like to have seen included in your programme?*' most undergraduates appeared satisfied

with the broad balance of knowledge and skills in their curriculum. Eleven per cent of respondents commented that they would like more help in acquiring 'up-to-date or relevant' IT skills. Five per cent commented that a foreign language, as an elective or optional module, would be useful. Other comments included 'more practical experience', 'more maths and statistics' and 'more career skills'. Students were also asked whether they considered their programmes to have been successful, merely adequate or inadequate in the provision of the skills listed. Table 3.1 indicates student responses concerning the importance of skills within their subject area and the provision for the development of those skills within their programmes.

Table 3.1 *Percentage ratings for core skills – importance; success of acquisition; and adequacy of provision*

Listed skill	A	B	C
		%	
Communicating in writing	98	45	9
Listening skills	98	49	8
Communicating verbally	97	32	15
Working independently	97	56	4
Time management	97	28	20
Decision-making	97	30	12
Presentation skills	96	43	10
Problem-solving	96	30	11
Working as part of a team	95	44	10
Questioning skills	94	34	10
Report-writing	91	47	16
Using IT	90	32	28
Working under supervision	84	21	20
Being assertive	83	22	24
Writing a job application	82	16	49
Writing a CV	82	19	46
Interview skills	82	14	53
Negotiating skills	82	22	23
Mathematical ability	80	12	36
Managing a budget	72	8	53
Using a foreign language	30	3	82

Column A indicates the percentage of students considering the skills as 'vital' or 'important' within their programme of study

Column B indicates the percentage of students who said that their programme of study had been successful at enabling them to acquire these skills

Column C indicates the total number of students who felt that the provision for developing the listed skills was inadequate

The extent to which these skills are used obviously varies from course to course. Some of the skills are particularly important as they are used to assess discipline-based learning: for example, written pieces of work, oral presentations or working in groups. Forty-five per cent of students felt that written communication skills had been successfully developed; 40 per cent were satisfied with presentation skills; 44 per cent felt they had been well-supported in developing teamwork skills (seen as crucial by employers); 10 per cent felt their development had been inadequate within each of these areas. In terms of communicating verbally, 32 per cent felt satisfied whereas 14 per cent did not.

Of greater concern are the skill areas where students considered their programme provision to be inadequate. There were concerns over IT and mathematical ability was considered by 36 per cent to be inadequately developed. Given that numeracy is viewed as a core skill in science and technology and has been raised as a source of concern by professional bodies such as the Royal Society of Chemistry, this is an area which requires urgent attention. Managing a budget was seen as important, with 53 per cent feeling provision had been inadequate. Although 82 per cent of students commented that using a foreign language had been inadequately provided for, only 30 per cent of respondents considered it important, which in itself gives rise for concern.

The least satisfactory provision was for development of 'career' skills. Responses indicating adequate provision tended to be at the rate of more than 80 per cent. The career skills (writing a letter of job application, CV, interview skills, managing a budget) had a mean 'adequate response rate' of just over 50 per cent. Half of the respondents felt dissatisfied with their ability to write a letter of job application; 46 per cent felt preparing a curriculum vitae had not been adequately provided for, and 53 per cent were dissatisfied with the support they had received to develop interview skills. These results probably reflect the current system, whereby the university careers service provides assistance to students who make use of what is offered, rather than programme areas seeing it as part of their role to inculcate such skills.

The most successful provision appeared to be for working independently and for listening. Fewer than 4 per cent of students felt they had not had sufficient opportunity to work independently and only 8 per cent felt listening was something that required further development.

Work placements
Nearly 16 per cent of the respondents were engaged on a third year 'sandwich' placement at the time of responding, or had recently completed a placement. Given the current focus on the importance of work placements (Harvey *et al*, 1997), the fact that these students were the most articulate in terms of being able to assess the value of skills development and the part

played in their work placement makes their comments worthy of notice.

These comments almost universally reflected the importance of communication and presentation skills: 'Communication skills, both written and oral, are important – as I found out at a barrister's chamber'. They also reflected the view that the workplace takes good subject knowledge for granted and looks for additional skills and qualities demonstrating the application of specialist knowledge:

> [I am] currently placed at Toshiba, Tokyo. Skills from the course have, on the whole, been effective, although I feel that for people taking a foreign placement care should be taken to ensure the student has a chance to learn the language. I fortunately did. [You need to] make more publicity of the careers library and all of its associated facilities. This is one area in which it is more luck than design if you are knowledgeable about the services available (University of Plymouth Placement Student).

In response to whether they would be prepared to undertake voluntary work during the summer vacation (paid work not being available) in order to develop work experience, over half of the students replied positively. A minority said they would undertake voluntary work in any circumstances because it was rewarding and offered a significant boost to job prospects. The findings suggest that students are very well aware of the need to equip themselves with tangible evidence of using both skills and knowledge in a work-based context as a prerequisite for employment.

Survey three: Faculty of Science

Findings indicated that graduates universally recognized the importance of skills development (for a full report, see Lamble, 1998). Transferable or key skills were perceived as most important by those entering employment in an area unrelated to their programme of study: 'In my current employment I am more reliant on the skills developed on my degree programme rather than the knowledge attained' (Environmental Science Graduate).

There was general agreement with the previous survey, and also between graduates and employers, regarding the most important skills needed in the workplace: oral communication, written communication and the ability to work independently. Problem-solving, time management and teamwork skills were also viewed highly: 'We are looking for flexible, enthusiastic, hard workers who are prepared to put in the time to gain further opportunities. It is very important they work well with the existing team. Time management, organisation and business acumen are invaluable in ensuring we service our customers' expectations' (Food Science Research and Development Company).

Satisfaction with skill development

Overall, 60 per cent of graduates were satisfied with the development of skills within their degree programme. When asked to comment on the overall balance between knowledge and skills, 70 per cent of graduates felt the balance to be correct whereas 30 per cent perceived that too much emphasis had been placed on the acquisition of disciplinary knowledge: 'Too much emphasis was placed on knowledge, rather than skills that could be transferable between jobs and could therefore help graduates to get their first job' (Environmental Science Graduate).

The majority of employers responding to the survey were satisfied with the skills of the science graduates they had recruited. Greatest satisfaction was expressed for IT, managing information, the ability to work independently and oral communication skills. This is encouraging considering the latter two were classed in the top five most important skills by employers and graduates.

However, approximately a third of employers were dissatisfied with written communication, time management and business awareness skills: 'Universities should do more to ensure that high standards of literacy and numeracy are attained. Many bright graduates let themselves down because they can't communicate simple ideas in plain English' (Environmental Consultant). Considering written communication was classed as the second most important skill by employers, this is an area which needs immediate attention, a perception shared by many university academic staff. It is interesting to note, however, that the vast majority of graduates felt this skill to be developed well on their degree programme. Graduates were in agreement with employers regarding the need to improve business awareness and time management skills. IT, oral communication, mathematical ability, decision-making and presentation skills were also identified by graduates as areas for improvement. Thus for IT and oral communication skills their perceptions are in contrast to the views of employers.

To improve the development of skills, environmental science and chemistry graduates indicated a need for specific skills training by professionally trained staff, and some suggested that a specific module for skills development should be provided: 'Key skills were talked about a lot, but we were never taught or trained. No advice was given to improve one's own skills. It's a good job I didn't come to university straight from school' (Environmental Science Graduate). In addition, many graduates felt that more emphasis should be placed on increasing undergraduates' awareness of the benefits of skills development; how to promote skills to employers and how to apply the skills and knowledge learnt to the workplace: 'There was little specific advice on how we could best sell our skills/knowledge to gain employment' (Environmental Science Graduate).

Both graduates and employers suggested that universities should obtain

regular information from employers regarding the main skills and qualifications they require and that they should utilize this information more fully,
both to aid curriculum development and to increase undergraduate awareness. Some employers were adamant about the need for change: 'Most
courses I've seen need to be rewritten. You must get serious advice on what
we need and how we use graduates' (Environmental Advice and Training
Company).

Increasing undergraduates' awareness of the workplace
Strengthening links between higher education and employment was recognized by both graduates and employers as important. In particular, the benefits of gaining work experience were acknowledged by the majority of
employers. In addition, 77 per cent of graduates felt they would have welcomed the opportunity to undertake a placement as part of their degree
programme. Guest speakers, case studies, site visits and honours' projects in
collaboration with employers were also regarded highly. In addition, graduates suggested that the university should provide more detailed careers
advice, including training in job-seeking skills, for example, completing
application forms, CVs, interview techniques and interview-based tests,
and should give them more realistic expectations of employment opportunities after graduation: 'I feel that you need support when you graduate and
you need to be told realistically of the job prospects and how to obtain a job
that you want' (Geological Sciences Graduate). Graduates also called for the
integration of careers advice into year two of degree programmes to allow
ample time for career planning before the end of the degree programme is
reached.

Summary and discussion

These surveys provide a snapshot of how University of Plymouth students,
their employers and their graduates view the development of core transferable skills. They show that students in higher education are aware of the need
for a wide range of skills to be acquired and developed, both for successfully
completing their university studies and as a basis for subsequent employability. They reveal areas of student satisfaction; working independently scoring
most highly; with developing mathematical ability, communicating verbally,
report-writing, using IT and 'career' skills worryingly low. Students who had
experienced the world beyond the university in the form of a work placement
were clear that, in addition to subject knowledge, skills and experience were
important, so much so that many were prepared to engage in unpaid work in
order to further their development.

It was a common perception of graduates that the content of degree programmes must be more 'customer'-oriented. They felt that degree programmes must be developed with greater thought to the ensuing careers of students and to the employment opportunities available to them after graduation. The main suggestions, from both graduates and employers, for the enhancement of degree programmes – that is, making them more relevant to the requirements of the workplace – were the need for:

- improving links with employers, and increasing undergraduate awareness of the workplace, including providing more opportunities for work experience, site visits, projects in collaboration with employers and guest speakers;
- improving the development of transferable skills, and increasing undergraduate awareness of the benefits of so doing;
- improving careers advice and job-seeking skills, for example, completing application forms, CVs, interview techniques and interview-based tests.

To achieve the above aims, the promotion of links between higher education and employers and graduates is of central importance. It is paramount that both higher education and employers give priority to establishing, maintaining and utilizing these links more fully, and to ensuring that future curriculum developments focus on links with the workplace.

To conclude on a positive note, over the past year it has become policy at the University of Plymouth that all undergraduate programmes should make explicit both in their programme documentation and student handbooks where key graduate attributes and skills are developed, practised and assessed. There are increasing links with employers both at a consultative level and at the level of practical involvement of industrial partners in programme delivery. This two-pronged approach is a necessary part of increasing the profile of skills development in the undergraduate curriculum.

Chapter 4

The transition of graduates from universities to the workplace[1]

Kenneth E Sinclair

Introduction

The development and assessment of core skills and competencies in education has received a great deal of recent attention (O'Neil, 1997). In Australia there have been a number of influential reports addressing the question of core skills and competencies needed for effective workplace participation in the learning society (Finn Report, 1991; Mayer Report, 1992). In the Mayer Report, seven key competencies were identified:

1. collecting, analysing and organizing information;
2. communicating ideas and information;
3. planning and organizing activities;
4. working with others and in teams;
5. using mathematical ideas and techniques;
6. solving problems;
7. using technology.

The reports have fuelled a lively debate, but have also been influential in finding application at the school and post-school levels of education.

In the debate that has ensued, a generally agreed-on definition of competencies which can be used to guide curriculum development in school and post-school education has been particularly difficult to find. Two main conceptions of competence have been used (Hager *et al,* 1994). In one, competencies refer to discrete behaviours identified as being needed to perform the tasks and functions of a job with proficiency. In the other, competencies refer to generic skills, abilities, knowledge, attitudes and other attributes which together are needed for successful job performance. The second of the two conceptions appears to be gaining increasing support and is the sense in which the term 'competencies' is used in this chapter.

A number of studies and reports in Australia have focused on the transition of graduates from university to the workplace. The question of objectives for university education and the competencies and outcomes desired of graduates when they enter the workplace has been of particular interest to the Business/Higher Education Round Table, a group of university vice chancellors and CEOs (chief executive officers) from prominent business enterprises in Australia.

Four investigations have been conducted by the author of this chapter for the Round Table (Business/Higher Education Round Table, 1991, 1992, 1993, 1995). In the initial study, the views of Round Table members themselves were sampled about objectives of secondary and university education, characteristics desired of university graduates on entry to the workforce, and partnership possibilities between business and universities. This study was then replicated with a sample of lecturers from universities and managers from business who had responsibility for supervising newly recruited university graduates. The third study involved a national sample of business students and focused on their views about the objectives and outcomes of their university education. The final study examined factors influencing the career success and progression of a sample of university graduates in the first 10 years of their work experience. In that study, graduates discussed the outcomes of their university education in terms of its relevance for career success and the way in which competencies need to change as more responsible management positions are achieved.

Objectives of university education

A question common to all the studies conducted for the Round Table asked respondents to rank a list of objectives for university education in order of importance. The list included professional and general knowledge objectives, the development of generic skills, and objectives relating to business knowledge and work experiences. The results are remarkably consistent across the quite different samples of Round Table members, university lecturers, business managers, business students and university graduates working in business. The results are summarized in Table 4.1.

Table 4.1 *Ranking of objectives for university education in order of importance –*
responses across samples from four studies

| | Sample | | | | | |
	1a	1b	2a	2b	3	4
Learning thinking/decision-making skills	1	1	1	1	1	1
Learning communication skills (eg, writing and speaking)	2	2	2	2	2	2
Learning professional skills – practical studies	5	5	3	5	3	3
Learning professional skills – theoretical studies	3	3	4	3	5	4
Learning skills of cooperation and teamwork	6	6	★	★	4	5
Developing standards of personal and business conduct	4	7	5	6	7	6
Learning about work and career choice	8	8	7	7	6	7
Learning a broad range of general academic subjects	7	4	8	4	9	8
Receiving on-the-job work experience	9	9	6	8	8	9

Notes: 1a: Study 1 (1991) CEOs (*N* = 56); 1b: Study 1 (1991) Vice Chancellors (*N* = 17); 2a: Study 2 (1992) Business Managers (*N* = 147); 2b: Study 2 (1992) University Lecturers (*N* = 122), 3: Study 3 (1993) University Business Students (*N* = 535); 4: Study 4 (1995) Graduates in Business (*N* = 261); ★ response not available

With surprising consistency, the general skills of thinking, decision-making and communicating are accorded highest importance for objectives of university education, while the remaining generic skill objective – learning skills of cooperation and collaboration – is ranked near the middle of the list. Next in importance after the two highest ranked generic skills are professional studies at university, and after them (although still regarded as very important objectives) are objectives about work experience and knowledge and skills for the workplace. A notable difference between the business and university respondents, however, is evident with respect to the importance given to learning a broad range of general academic subjects as part of a professional education. This objective was rated as much more important by university vice chancellors and lecturers (ranked fourth) than by business CEOs or managers, who ranked it near the bottom of their list. It will also be observed that the business students and graduates in the workforce also ranked it near the bottom of their lists.

The result reinforces the view that, first and foremost, professionals need to be educated, at least in their first degree, in general skills and professional knowledge and skills. Those outcomes are consistently regarded as more important than outcomes focusing on business knowledge and work experience. Such a finding is consistent with the view that the workforce of the future needs to be adaptable and flexible to meet emerging challenges and changes. It is a finding that has been supported in a number of other reports as well (Higher Education Council, 1992; National Board of Employment, Education, and Training, 1992). For instance in the influential *Higher Education: Achieving quality* report of the Higher Education Council in Australia (1992), and after considerable consultation in the business and education communities, it is concluded that:

> Discipline-specific skills in many areas have only a short life, and what will be needed in even the medium term cannot be predicted with any great precision. The groups consulted were as one on this issue – while discipline skills and technical proficiency were seen as important... the so-called higher-level generic skills were seen as critically important, and sometimes lacking. While it would not be claimed that these characteristics are found only in graduates,... if universities are to add value, they must take responsibility for the specific development and refinement of these skills.

Desired characteristics of graduates

In the second of the studies (Business/Higher Education Round Table, 1992), university lecturers were asked to indicate what emphasis was being given in their programmes to developing particular graduate characteristics. Business respondents were asked to indicate what emphasis they gave each of those characteristics in choosing graduate staff. Responses were on a five-point scale: 1 (no emphasis), 2 (little emphasis), 3 (moderate emphasis), 4 (strong emphasis), 5 (very strong emphasis). These results are summarized in Table 4.2.

The importance of the capacity to make decisions and solve problems, the capacity to learn new skills and procedures, the ability to apply knowledge to the workplace and the capacity to work with minimum supervision are all rated highly both in course emphases and company recruitment. Some significant differences also emerged, however, in the responses of the two groups. It is interesting that, while recognizing the importance of developing communication skills as an objective of university education, the lecturers indicate that only a moderate amount of emphasis is given to it in professional courses. For business, in contrast, communication skills are clearly the number one criterion of those listed characteristics in selecting staff. The frequencies for this response are provided in Table 4.3. Similarly, capacity for cooperation and teamwork is ranked third by business but only eighth by university respondents.

Table 4.2 *Ranking of emphasis given to selected characteristics of university graduates –
business and university respondents*

	Business		University	
	Rank	Mean(%)	Rank	Mean(%)
Communication skills (eg, writing, speaking)	1	4.3	7	3.3
Capacity to learn new skills and procedures	2	4.2	5	3.4
Capacity for cooperation and teamwork	3	4.2	8	3.2
Capacity to make decisions and solve problems	4	4.2	3	3.5
Ability to apply knowledge to the workplace	5	4.1	4	3.5
Capacity to work with minimum supervision	6	3.7	6	3.3
Theoretical knowledge in professional field	7	3.5	1	4.0
Capacity to use computer technology	8	3.4	2	3.7
Understanding of business ethics	9	3.2	12	2.2
General business knowledge	10	3.0	11	2.3
Specific work skills	=11	3.0	9	3.1
A broad background of general knowledge	=11	3.0	10	2.9

Note. University respondents were asked: 'In educating undergraduates in your faculty...what
emphasis is given to developing each of the following characteristics?' Business respondents were
asked: 'In selecting newly-graduated professionals to work in your company...what emphasis do
you consider should be given to each of the following characteristics of applicants?'

On the other hand, for universities the greatest emphasis is given to providing
theoretical knowledge in the professional field followed by capacity to use computers, yet these are ranked only seventh and eighth by the business respondents
for purposes of staff recruitment. There are, then, some sharp differences to be
observed between university teaching priorities and the priorities business gives
to the outcomes of that teaching in selecting staff. Universities have traditionally
focused on knowledge outcomes in teaching. Furthermore, large lecture classes
in many undergraduate courses do not lend themselves particularly well to skill
development, and it is often assumed that important skills such as communication skills will be well-developed on entry to university.

Table 4.3 *Emphasis given to developing communication skills in university courses and
to the importance of communication skills in selecting company recruits*

	Little or no emphasis (%)	Moderate emphasis (%)	Strong/very strong emhasis (%)
Emphasis in university courses (university respondents)	21.5	38.0	40.5
Emphasis in business recruitment (business respondents)	0.9	6.3	92.8

As well as asking business and university respondents in the second study (Business/Higher Education Round Table, 1992) about the desired characteristics of graduates, a second element of the question asked them for an assessment of the current standards reached by university graduates in those characteristics (Table 4.4).

Table 4.4 *Current standards reached by graduates from universities – mean scores for business and university respondents*

	Business Mean (%)	University Mean (%)
Communication skills (eg, writing, speaking)	2.7	3.0
Capacity to learn new skills and procedures	3.7	3.5
Capacity for cooperation and teamwork	3.0	3.2
Capacity to make decisions and solve problems	3.2	3.4
Ability to apply knowledge to the workplace	2.8	3.4
Capacity to work with minimum supervision	3.2	3.2
Theoretical knowledge in professional field	3.6	3.6
Capacity to use computer technology	3.7	3.6
Understanding of business ethics	2.7	2.3
General business knowledge	2.9	3.3
Specific work skills	2.9	2.8
A broad background of general knowledge	2.6	2.5

Participants rated the standards achieved on a five-point scale: 1 (very poor), 2 (poor), 3 (adequate), 4 (good), 5 (very good). A mean score of 3 indicates that the responses cluster around the 'adequate' score, while a mean of greater than 3 or less than 3 indicates that responses tend towards a judgement of 'good' or 'poor' respectively. The lecturers and business supervisors in the survey judged most characteristics to be in the adequate range.

While no characteristics were assessed as being clearly good or very good (mean of 4 or greater), those judged adequate to good by both groups of respondents were:

- theoretical knowledge in the professional field;
- capacity to learn new skills and procedures;
- capacity to use computer technology.

The characteristics judged as being of poorest standard include:

- general business knowledge;
- understanding business ethics;
- communication skills (business but not university respondents).

The question about standards achieved in developing a range of desirable characteristics in graduates was asked of the business students who participated in the third study (Business/Higher Education Round Table, 1993) as well. The results revealed that a third or more of respondents considered that standards achieved by graduates from their faculties were poor or very poor with respect to:

- developing specific work skills (46.6 per cent);
- understanding business ethics (46 per cent);
- ability to apply knowledge to the workplace (43.9 per cent);
- general business knowledge (34.7 per cent).

It is significant that these characteristics are predominantly ones directly relevant to workplace career goals. It is also significant that as many as a quarter of the respondents considered the standards achieved by graduates in their faculties to be poor in relation to the highly regarded general skills areas of communicating, capacity to make decisions and solve problems, and capacity for cooperation and teamwork. The result confirms that views about lower than desirable standards of achievement among university graduates in areas of key importance are not confined to people from the university and business communities but are acknowledged by the students themselves.

Influence of home, school, university and work on workplace attributes

In the most recent study (Business/Higher Education Round Table, 1995) an attempt was also made to gauge the graduates' perceptions of the relative influence of the home, school, university, and workplace on the development of selected attributes chosen for their occupational importance (Table 4.5).

Table 4.5 *Influences attributable for present capacities (mean per cent)*

	Home	School	University	Work	Other
Ability to apply professional knowledge	8.4	7.9	26.9	53.0	3.9
Communication skills	24.8	21.6	18.5	28.5	6.6
Thinking and decision-making skills	20.5	17.7	27.0	30.7	4.1
Professional knowledge	6.7	10.0	32.9	46.7	3.7
Motivation to succeed	34.9	15.4	16.8	26.3	6.7
Skills of cooperation and teamwork	22.1	17.4	19.0	32.9	8.7
Ability to work independently	19.4	16.7	29.4	30.0	4.6
Ethical values	49.6	13.5	12.2	18.3	6.3

The results are very interesting and reveal that, at this point in their careers, the workplace was most commonly considered to be of greater influence than the home, school and university in relation to most attributes. This applied to the development of communication skills, thinking and decision-making skills, professional knowledge, ability to apply professional knowledge and skills of cooperation and teamwork. For instance, in the case of development of communication skills, 28.5 per cent of total influence was attributed to the workplace, 24.8 per cent to home, 21.6 per cent to school, 18.5 per cent to university and 6.6 per cent to other influences. The home was considered to be of greatest influence in developing motivation to succeed (34.9 per cent relative influence) and ethical values (49.6 per cent relative influence), while the university was considered to be of similar influence to the workplace in the development of ability to work independently (29.4 per cent relative influence).

The results stress the importance of learning and development that takes place in the workplace after schooling and university have been completed. For the most part such learning will occur through the experience of work, supplemented only to a small extent by workplace training. It is of particular interest that the respondents attributed, on average, 46.7 per cent of their professional knowledge to the workplace and only 32.9 per cent to university. This reaffirms the importance given by the business students in an earlier survey to the importance of on-the-job experience as part of their university programme (Business/Higher Education Round Table, 1993).

Graduate competencies for workplace success

Together, the studies assist our understanding of the competencies needed for graduate career success. Furthermore, the view that emerges receives wide support from such different perspectives as business managers, university lecturers, business students and university graduates in the workforce. Generic skills such as thinking and decision-making skills, communication skills, and skills in cooperation and teamwork are accorded highest priority. However, professional knowledge and its application are also considered to be of high overall importance, and of greater relative importance than business knowledge and work experience. Such a finding is consistent with the view that the workforce of the future needs to be adaptable and flexible to meet emerging challenges and a rapidly changing workplace. Given the increasing rate with which specific jobs in the workplace disappear, are modified, or are added to, staff will be expected to be particularly adaptable with well-developed general skills in learning how to learn and think and well-developed and up-to-date mastery of core professional knowledge.

This finding is at odds with the more behaviouristic approaches used to define competencies as discrete behavioural skills, but is consistent with the view that competencies should refer to generic skills, abilities, knowledge, attitudes and other attributes which *together* are needed for successful job performance. The finding also reinforces the importance of a career-long approach to learning. As we have seen, graduates in business responded that the workplace is responsible for a relatively greater influence than the school or university on such matters as the development of communication and thinking skills, skills of cooperation and teamwork, and professional knowledge and its application. Planned experiences encouraging such development in the workplace and through post-graduate study at university will greatly assist this process.

The findings also reveal that the emphasis given to competency development at university does not always coincide with the emphasis given to particular competencies in recruiting graduates for the workplace. Despite the importance given by both business and university respondents to the objective of developing communication skills and the importance of communication skills in securing employment, the amount of emphasis given to its development in university courses is considered to be only moderate to low. University lecturers give greatest importance in courses to providing theoretical knowledge in the professional field. The emphasis on knowledge outcomes has been a traditional focus of universities and one which they have performed with distinction. A sharper focus on being able to use that knowledge, and to use communication skills, collaboration and teamwork skills, and thinking and decision-making skills in both creating and using that knowledge is needed in preparing graduates for professional lives in the decades ahead. Recent implementation of problem-based learning approaches in such university programmes as medicine, business, nursing, and education demonstrate that universities are gradually moving in the needed direction.

Notes

1. Paper presented at the 7th European Conference for Research on Learning and Instruction, 26–30 August 1997, Athens, Greece. An extended version has appeared as a chapter entitled 'Workforce competencies of college graduates', in HF O'Neil (ed) (1997), *Workforce Readiness: Competencies and assessment*, Erlbaum, Mahwah, New Jersey. The studies reported were commissioned by the Business/Higher Education Round Table whose interest and assistance is gratefully acknowledged.

Chapter 5

New approaches in the Danish education system

Peter Bacher

Introduction

With its 5.2 million inhabitants, Denmark is a small country. Nevertheless it has, together with the other Nordic regions, been regarded as a pioneer country for adult education and popular enlightenment. The educational system in Denmark has always been decentralized, even at the level of higher education (unlike neighbouring countries). What follows is a description of an educational system which is in the throes of change and wherein discussion on the shape of its future is intensifying.

At present, educational institutions are gaining greater autonomy (becoming independent institutions) and the annual frame budget, the day-to-day decisions etc are being taken over by local boards. Yet the State is also intervening more and more, for example concerning the number of institutions within specific areas (higher education), or concerning the definition and delimitation of aims (general adult education). In the pipeline, besides regulation of grants (ie a certain grant to the institution per student full-time equivalent), are instruments such as quality control schemes and evaluation which will be carried out by a (soon to be established) national unit.

Parallel to these trends, there is an ongoing spirited discussion on: 'what is the meaning of core skills?' In the Danish context the key concepts are *qualifications* and *competences*. This discussion can be regarded as a battle between two paradigms:

1. The tradition of popular enlightenment (*folkeoplysning*) including its deep mistrust of measurable skills and expedient education; and
2. Socio-economic models of planning, which roughly regard education as a means of improving productivity, welfare and labour market conditions.

The second is a familiar scenario, but the first warrants some explanation. It is best summarized by a paragraph in a document entitled, 'The golden riches in the grass – lifelong learning for all', from the Nordic Council of Ministers (NORD, 1995):

> At its very core, folkeoplysning is a counter-culture. It arose as a protest against the dominance of the few over the many. One of its key features is voluntarism. The sole prior requirement for participation is the desire to participate. And the yield? That must be assessed by the participants themselves. In this context, curriculum requirements, tests and exam certificates are usually extraneous elements. Another characteristic feature is free initiative. This applies to the right to implement an idea, to the choice of subject and choice of teacher. In folkeoplysning, all are of equal merit, though they may not be equally knowledgeable. The basic assumption is that the single human being is a valuable experiment, and can develop his or her potential only when freedom prevails. A third characteristic is the spirit of liberalism. The folkeoplysning movement acknowledges that the different ideas and attitudes found among people must have an equal right to a platform. Each person must reach his or her own interpretation of the meaning of life and at the same time allow other people's interpretations to be considered. The right of other people to maintain their viewpoints must be respected, even though one need not respect the actual points of view.

This chapter focuses on three issues with regard to a lifelong learning perspective:

1. trends of current interest concerning the Danish system of higher education;
2. the 'competence-discussion';
3. a competence system for adult education.

Higher education – current trends

Since 1994, when the revised Act of Open Education came into force, all kinds of education have been available to adults who want to update their qualifications. All institutions for vocational or higher education are, in principle, allowed to provide any kind of educational offer – part time or full time, day or night etc. The participants can choose to follow classes in specific subjects, or follow modules or courses, or they can, for instance, complete a Diploma or Masters programme. The fees are relatively high, but they are very often paid, at least in part, by employers (Danish Ministry of Education, 1997). The colleges for trade and commerce at present provide the largest number of courses, but the five universities are now intensifying their activities.

Open education at higher levels for adults has existed in Denmark for about 100 years. The University extra-mural department (the People's University) was established in 1898, with the aim to disseminate knowledge about the methods and results of university research. At the moment (autumn 1998), a proposal for the merging of the institutions for higher education in Denmark is being discussed. The point of departure is the many and very small units, which according to the Danish Ministry of Education (1998a, 1998b) are not capable of surviving in the future.

Compared to other – in many other ways similar – countries, the figures representing the number of Danish institutions, students per institution, and so on, are quite different. This is outlined in Table 5.1.

Table 5.1 *A comparison of numbers of institutions and students in countries similar to Denmark*

Country	Number of institutions	Number of students	Students per institution	Number of inhabitants per institution
Sweden	34	227.000	6.676	258.823
Norway	30	170.000	5.667	150.000
Finland	36	188.000	5.222	141.666
Netherlands	82	507.000	6.183	187.085
Germany	326	2.113.000	6.482	203.503
Denmark	**195**	**161.235**	**827**	**26.153**

Source: Danish Ministry of Education, 1998b

Two models of merging have been suggested:

1. that medium- and short-term higher education should be merged in centres, while the universities carry on managing long-term higher education;
2. that long- and medium-term higher education should be merged into 10–12 units.

With the Minister of Research being responsible for the universities, and the Minister of Education being responsible for other higher education, it can easily be understood that it is rather difficult to obtain consensus about either of the two scenarios!

The higher education system is at present affected by quite radical demographic fluctuations. The size of the cohorts of young people will decline to a minimum level in 3–5 years time and then successively increase by 40 per cent towards the year 2010. Within the same period of time, a large number of teachers will retire. This could be regarded as a big challenge for the higher education system. A further difficulty can be seen in the *10-Point Programme on Recurrent Education* launched in 1995 by the Danish Ministry of Education and reflecting the ideas of lifelong learning. It is stated in the fourth point that: *The educational institutions shall be under an obligation to update the educational qualifications of graduates – to give them a recharge guarantee.* According to the higher education institutions, however, in practice, it has apparently been difficult to raise funds and to find qualified teachers for these tasks.

Core skills – qualifications and competences

The concept of *qualifications* – mainly inspired from German (Marxist) social researchers and German industrial sociologists – was commonly adapted in the Danish educational debate at the beginning of the 1970s. Since the beginning of the 1990s the concept of *competences* is used more frequently. In general, it can be said that the concept of competences is broader than that of qualifications, covering personal characteristics as well. In practice, though, the two concepts are often used as synonymous.

In 1997, the Ministry of Education launched the programme, *National Development of Competences*. The main objective of the programme is to place the Danish educational system among the 10 most outstanding systems in the world – measured in relation to OECD (Organization for Economic Cooperation and Development) analyses as well as to specific national targets. The initiatives to reach the objective can be divided into five areas (Danish Ministry of Education, 1997):

1. The Danish educational system shall belong to the world élite.
2. Personal qualifications shall be developed.
3. The partnership between educational institutions and working life shall be strengthened.
4. Lifelong learning and recurrent education shall be developed.
5. The role of the teacher and of the participant shall be broadened and the introduction of ICT (information and communications technology) shall be intensified.

The means to reach the objective are, among others, the development, assessment and evaluation of quality in all parts of the educational system. Two of the goals are, for instance, that the number of young people receiving general or vocational youth education has to be raised from approximately 80 per cent to 95 per cent, and that the number of young people taking a degree has to be raised from 35 per cent to 50 per cent.

In the report 'National Development of Competences', the different requirements for qualifications in the future are described in detail. Hence the report sums up well the concepts and classifications that are frequently used in the Danish debate. These concepts are now scrutinized. The conceptualization and operationalization of the terms 'competences' and 'qualifications' blurs the distinction between knowledge, skills, sentiments and character so that one or more of these elements may form part of a specific competence or qualification. The general framework of concepts has derived from current research, while the list of specific personal qualifications/competences is the result of interviews with key persons in 'spearhead enterprises'. Thus the report on the National Development of Competences is a 'spearhead report', aiming to intensify the debate about the educational system in the future. However, when it comes to the point, neither the Confederation of Employers or the trade unions, nor the different departments of the Ministries of Education, Labour, Social Affairs, Research etc, are eager to implement personal qualifications in the educational system. New approaches in the education system, such as Open Youth Education – where the young participants have to be responsible for their own education and have to combine several units of general education modules and carry them out individually – have been abandoned by employers' organizations as well as by the employees. The conception of *the good old industrial society* is still predominant!

The three main categories of qualifications used in the report are:

1. general qualifications;
2. professional and technical proficiencies/skills;
3. personal qualifications.

General qualifications include basic skills such as RRR (reading, writing and reckoning), language skills, international orientation, cultural understanding and empathy, and even ICT skills.

Professional and technical skills consist (besides vocational and scientific qualifications connected directly to the working process) of – at higher levels – the ability to plan, analyse and assess the working process. The most important *personal qualifications*, according to the interviewed enterprises, are:

- flexibility;
- cooperative skills;
- an ability to take a comprehensive orientation and overview;
- skills in project leadership;
- independence (originality);
- communicative skills and critical assessment (estimation) skills.

In particular, enterprises are claiming the following personal qualifications (it is not feasible here to quote the arguments):

- sense of responsibility (Illeris, 1998);
- awareness of quality;
- vigilance (carefulness);
- compliance;
- flexibility (skills for readjustment, readjustment abilities);
- initiative;
- creativity;
- readiness to take risks;
- overview (comprehensive or general view);
- analytical abilities;
- cross-disciplinarity;
- holistic (comprehensive) view;
- international orientation;
- skills for teamwork;
- qualities for leadership, organization and negotiation.

Would you like to have a very creative bookkeeper? No, we guess not. The enterprises distinguish between different qualification profiles (ie ranking qualifications in terms of importance), for example Danish Ministry of Education (1997):

- production: sense of responsibility, awareness of quality, teamwork skills;
- administration: vigilance, overview, communicative skills, analytical abilities;
- sales: initiative, creativity and communicative skills;
- R&D (research and development): initiative, creativity, readiness to take risks, communicative skills and analytical abilities.

The discussion in the above quoted report focuses on the usefulness or application of competences (mainly) in relation to the labour market. This is also the case in the recently released report on 'Quality in the Educational System', in which it is stated: '[It is not] possible to fix the economic gains of the non-economic profits, as for example increased welfare and a strengthened democracy. These gains may, however, be regarded as a positive contribution to the total return of education' (Danish Ministry of Education, 1998a). The 200-plus pages following this statement deal with the issue of whether it is possible to assess and measure quality.

A competence system for adult education

In 1996, the Ministry of Education published a discussion paper on a competence system for adult education. The basic idea behind this paper is to give all adults the opportunity to tailor courses of education to their own specific needs, and to give them credit for courses as well as for their work and life experience.

The three overall aims are:

1. to create a more transparent structure for specific adult competences;
2. generally to render the competences acquired in adult education more visible both to participants and to the employers;
3. to add a new dimension to the education system based on the job experience of adults and consisting of short courses of education primarily aimed at improving job competence.

The paper suggests four well-defined areas: Basic Adult Education, Further Adult Education, Diploma Programmes and Master's Programmes. Competences at the four levels are either obtained by piecing together credit-bearing courses or by completing a full programme.

The competence system is still being discussed between ministries, employers' and employees' organizations etc. The principles behind the system are well in accordance with the keynotes for an adult education system presented by the OECD (1998). However, important qualifications concerning quality of life, personal development and learning how to be an active member of a democratic society are unfortunately not included in the official reports in Denmark at the moment.

Chapter 6

The English language as a key to open society[1]

Ligija Kaminskiene

Introduction

In terms of education and learning, what happens in a state that restores its independence after 50 years of oppression and tries to catch up with the rest of the world? Where does the individual stand when the old political, economic and social system collapses, while the new one takes its time to appear from the debris? Actually, the individual does not 'stand' at all: the individual becomes stuffed, twisted, moulded and reshaped by the experiences that the new situation brings about. The processes in society affect everyone to such an extent that virtually nobody is protected from the crushing avalanche of the novelty of information. The gravitational field of all social processes shifts from East to West, and former knowledge and a hierarchy of values have to be subjected to severe revaluation. The whole country is in a frenzy of learning, as learning a lot and fast means being at the front line of opportunity. As never before, the individual places an expectation on the educational experience he or she is pursuing, and the motivation for learning as well as the requirements of educators are ever growing. For the first time in 50 years, the individual's needs rather than those of the system become the driving force of education. Variety, fragmentation, short terms and competition become the new reality of education.

The need for an international dimension in core skill development

If we assume that the above described processes do take place in Lithuania (and elsewhere in Eastern Europe) and that the central figure of education, the individual, plays a new role within them, then it becomes interesting to stop at one major aspect of the change: the 'space' of educational orientation in Lithuania. (By using the term 'space', we are referring to the abstract term indicating space in general, rather than any distinct geographical borders.) During the six and a half years of independence, a major shift of values has taken place in the mentality of the learning individual: it has been recognized that the skills required for a free market economy are *internationally* assessed and evaluated. The very first wave of business visitors to Lithuania in 1990 demonstrated that international contacts could be established so long as there was some knowledge of a *global international* language and (at least) minimal skills to meet the *international* standards of trade and industry. Many international contacts failed because of the absence of either the former or the latter. The result of that experience has been the growing awareness of learning adults that their career choices should be either internationally oriented or at least have an international 'fringe' to them.

This is already evidenced in the burgeoning language teaching industry in Lithuania, with attention to English, German and, to a certain extent, French, and the proliferation of communicative language schools which have gained a tremendous market for general as well as professional language skills. A number of private college-type schools offering attractive internationally oriented programmes (English or German language, Business Management, Auditing and Accounting etc) are proud of their great number of applicants. The most attractive curricula at State-run universities are those of International Relations Studies, English, German, French, Economics, Law, Sociology, Business and Management and Computer Technologies. Medical students, students of transport and flight logistics, students of history and philosophy, and so on, all have a number of courses read in a foreign language.

Thus, going back to the concept of space, we can assume that during the last 10 years the educational orientation of Lithuania has shifted from being targeted towards the closed Soviet Union market to the free market opportunities with neighbouring countries, and with an emphasis on future relations with the EU (European Union).

There has never been a moment of *national,* or *inwardly* directed, education. The 'space' of education was not, and could not possibly be, oriented towards a geographical spot on the world map called 'Lithuania'. All the major changes that have happened in Lithuanian education since Gorbachev's rule were directed towards European concepts, values and standards, as well as towards the world free market. For instance, the National Education Reform has revised the curricula of secondary schools, introducing the European dimension into the teaching and interpretation of Lithuanian history, culture, geography etc. The fact is that the success of National Education reform, especially at the level of post-compulsory lifelong education, is in its international orientation and the awareness of the international space within which newly acquired knowledge and skills are going to be used. The measuring rod of success will be the compatibility of the system with other educational systems of the world.

The English language as a prerequisite to growth and change

The next step needs to be recognition of the need for a means of international communication, the need for a language that would be recognized and used as part of our educational system at the post-compulsory level of education. This is the issue we would like to discuss: the concept of an *international language* or a *global international language* which should be recognized by law. Our personal preference lies with a *global international language,* or more specifically, *English.*

Why do we need it, and need it urgently? The factor of having an international language would allow the recognition and legitimization of a number of aspects of adult education. At present, both formal and informal education is in a period of transition, which, among other things, means that (depending on the curriculum, teacher and circumstances) the students are using Lithuanian, Russian, or English or German textbooks. Technological universities are still using Russian textbooks as the mainstay of education and they are dreading the moment when the new generation of students arrives – the generation that cannot read Russian. What is going to happen then? Where is the army of translators who will translate the books for the students? Will the students be able to use other, modern books written in the *global international language* we are discussing? As to the English textbooks in adult education, they will do no more harm than the Russian ones. It is better to have a policy about textbooks than to have none at all, the more so since Lithuania can simply not afford to publish the necessary variety of texts.

The recognition of an international language of communication in education would enable us to have model educational programmes, schools or training centres. This is extremely important at the non-university and informal levels of teaching. The young generation of today are facing a highly competitive job situation, and good knowledge of English might mean many more choices in the job market. The learner-oriented approach should promote the language as part of the educational skills package for the young professionals of the future. The private sector in non-university level education is, in a number of cases, using English *de facto;* its legal recognition would hardly affect the situation of State-run schools. The factor of a global international language would certainly promote a revision of the curricula of schools; it would stimulate the reform of the system of education and introduce the missing European elements into the system (eg BA granting non-university education); it would direct language learning towards much higher standards than they are today; and it would enable Lithuanian education more effectively to achieve its internationally oriented goals. The fact that English (or another international language) is used alongside Lithuanian would bring more international schools into the private sector of education which actually means variety and ideas in the educational market.

The opponents of such an approach would probably say that we are trying to push Lithuanian to the level of everyday usage; to deny the language the possibility of complex development, but we are not. In fact, Estonia has Concordia University which teaches in English only; there is the Stockholm School of Economics in Latvia and the Central European University in Hungary. The countries mentioned are small, their languages old and complex, and linguistically they are endangered to the same extent that Lithuanian is. However, they recognize that it is their international English-speaking schools that help them establish international links and gain international resonance in the world of education.

The international aspect of education is mentioned in a number of official State documents concerning education. However, experience shows that the lack of clear vision of Lithuania's position in the economically, politically and culturally interrelated world allows the provincial wishful thinking that a self-sustaining Lithuanian culture and education can be maintained. There is an unwillingness (or inability) to support the learning individual by providing an international dimension to education. Can these concerns be regarded as taboo just because we have to abide by the present State language law? A thorough analysis of the situation is needed, with the focus on the issue of language.

Notes

1. The ideas presented for the discussion were stimulated by the Report on Lithuanian Science and Research by the Norwegian Council of Research to the Nordic Council of Ministers (1998) and by six years of the author's educational management experience in adult education.

Chapter 7

'Slovenia – The Learning Country': how to reach the pre-set strategic goal

Zoran Jelenc

Introduction

The learning society is certainly an ideal for which we are striving (Jarvis, 1990; Field, 1996). It demands an integrated system wherein education takes place in a new social, economic and political context. This should be a society which guarantees any kind of learning, at any time, to any population throughout its lifetime (Jarvis, 1990). The characteristics of the learning society are as follows:

- continued learning throughout one's life;
- encouragement of the learner's responsibility for their own progress;
- emphasis on the positive aspects of learning;
- equal value attached to knowledge no matter how acquired.

This requires partnership and mutual help in learning, the use of numerous providers and sources of knowledge, accessibility of learning materials and technology, flexibility in learning and so on (Dohmen, 1996; Longworth and Davies, 1996). We should not close our eyes to the fact that currently there is no country capable of meeting the ideal of having a clearly outlined policy and strategy. It would be possible to single out Japan, which has been implementing such plans from the beginning of the 1990s and can demonstrate its endeavours in practice (Okamoto, 1994). Also in Germany, the north Rhine state of Westphalia set itself the goal of developing and achieving a strategy of lifelong learning within five years (Dohmen, 1996). However, and perhaps because of difficulties in the way of realizing the idea of a learning society, such change calls for intensive professional engagement, in cooperation with appropriate social developmental policy and strategy.

Higher, or university, education is not a specific focus of this chapter, but needs to be viewed within an overall context of creating appropriate circumstances and strategies for the development of a learning society. A learning society embraces education and learning of all kinds and at all levels and higher education is just one aspect of this. This chapter primarily focuses on how strategy and policy could be developed in partnership between professional workers and the State. We argue that the creation of a national policy and associated strategy is not possible without State support and approval but, on the other hand, it should be initiated from the professional side. In the case of Slovenia outlined here, we shall be talking primarily about work that has been done up to now and is still being carried out, but this must be seen in the context of a larger picture and ultimate gaol – the project known as 'Slovenia – The Learning Country'.

It is clear that each national policy and strategy is determined by the special needs and situations of the particular country; there are as many national policies as there are nations. The following characteristics of Slovenia are of crucial importance for its educational and learning policy:

- Slovenia is a small country with only 2 million inhabitants in an area of 20 thousand square kilometres.
- It is a young country that became independent from Yugoslavia in 1991.
- It is a country in transition with huge political, societal and economic change since 1989.
- It has a strong school tradition, but learning has never been a matter of public concern and policy; learning has always been pushed into the individual or private sphere and, as such, it was inhibited and not manifest in public life.
- The Slovenian people have good working habits, but nonetheless, they need stimulating circumstances and opportunities to promote learning; they must be pushed and challenged to start learning.

Among the characteristics mentioned there are positive as well as negative features. Some of these features will support progress:

- the ambitions of a young country reviewing its developmental needs can be harnessed;
- it is a small country with a relatively well-coordinated and still centralized administration;
- the people have appropriate working habits.

The long and strong school tradition is not so helpful in the context of life-long learning. Nor is the fact of being a country in transition with persistent economic crises.

In order to develop new learning strategies in such a country, it is reasonable to create policy and strategy in partnership. Two main partners are the professionals who can represent providers and employers; and the government and its representatives. Preparing and implementing any strategy requires a set of preconditions. On the one side, intensive and ambitious professional work, which started in Slovenia about 15 years ago, is gradually opening the door to those who are in a position to make policy decisions. On the other side, we need a wise and capable administration whereby professional aims can be identified with those of national policy. Systematic merging of both sides has partly taken place.

In the last 10 years, intensive work has been done on both sides. On the professional side there has been attention to the conceptualization and preparation of professional bases for systemic regulation of adult education and learning; that is, changes in administration, legislation, financing, infrastructure, networking and so on. A draft national programme of adult education has been prepared and there has been the launching of important developmental projects for adult learning and education. Finally, there has been the establishment of a research and development centre as an institution for the development and promotion of adult education and learning. This is known as the SAEC (Slovenian Adult Education Centre), which now has a well-educated and highly regarded staff of 31 persons.

On the State side, there has been an acceptance of the need for measures of systemic regulation of adult education, financing of development and research projects, and support for the functioning of a public network of providers and programmes. Such progress is not yet officially approved strategy. However, in spite of that, the State has substantially supported projects organized by the SAEC in the last five years.

The current situation looks promising, especially when taking into account that the basic documentation on the development of adult education has been drawn up. This includes:

- a draft strategy for lifelong learning;
- a draft of the conception and strategy for adult education;
- a draft of the national programme for adult education;
- several measures of systemic regulation of adult education, for example an umbrella law on adult education was approved in 1996, determining general statements about State support for adult education, mainly for non-formal aspects, and the national programme of adult education.

The national programme will be the determinant of public interest in adult education, and has to be adopted by Parliament. It was prepared as a result of research and is proposed by experts, but is being merged with the statements of State representatives in the final stages. The law on adult education is being used to determine general statements for the national programme (goals, priority areas, implementing etc) and the total scope of funds. It is being implemented through annual programmes which should be approved each year, the main objectives being:

- the raising of the educational level of the population;
- the development of the areas of knowledge deemed most important to the national interest;
- the improvement of access to adult education and learning;
- the increasing of public funds for adult education.

The priority areas are:

- basic general and vocational education;
- non-formal education for improvement of knowledge across the population.

The infrastructure consists of:

- information systems;
- research and development;
- education and training of adult educators;
- necessary services such as counselling and guidance facilities.

Since 1991, government support of adult education has been steadily, if slowly, increasing. From 1992, there is evidence of positive developmental trends and these are outlined by the figures relating to specific projects shown in Table 7.1. There are new opportunities for education and learning to be gained both from working at theoretical models, and by implementing them within practices that have been introduced. Currently, this is through development projects in areas such as study circles, open learning centres, learning exchanges, methods of assessment and accreditation of prior learning, programmes for quality assurance education, programmes for the development of democracy and project learning for the young people. Programmes for the development of information and counselling services and education needed by enterprises and employees (to create learning organizations) are also being promoted. When the national programme comes into force, various programmes of non-formal education will also be stimulated.

Table 7.1 *Development of projects*

Project	Implementation	Number of cases	Number of participants
Study circles	1992 1993	300	3500
Organized autonomous learning	1993 1995	18	600
Learning exchange	1992 1993	4	3000
Accreditation of prior learning	1994 1997		
Functional literacy	1991 1992	45	450
Programmes for the development of democracy	1993 1994	27	411
Project learning for young adults	1992 1993	1	20

Source: Adult Education Centre of Slovenia

Evaluation of some of the above projects indicates that the Slovenian people responded to them well, and this can be seen in the quantitative data as well as through other indicators, for example, the distribution of projects throughout the country. In addition to these, an appropriate network of providers and of sources of learning, for both public and private programmes, is being developed. All these go beyond traditional institutions and programmes of adult education (schools, folk high schools, education and training centres, universities etc).

In order to promote learning further, the Lifelong Learning Week has been organized since 1996 and it has already became a permanent national project of Slovenia, supported by the government. Given that in the first year it was carried out mostly on a voluntary basis, without State support, it had to be deemed successful: 58 providers organized 197 performances, with 456 events in 28 communities and on 40 different sites. In the second year, the activity for the Lifelong Learning Week doubled. For continued development and promotion of learning and education in local communities, a special project, the Summer Adult Education School, has also been established.

It is important to remain critical in an assessment of the current situation. Slovenian school policy is still not taking into consideration the principles of a lifelong learning strategy. Although it has featured in official documents, the general principle has not yet been incorporated into corresponding statements in legislation, which would make it possible for the principles and strategies to be put forward into practice. Lifelong learning has been treated in education reform as an administrative issue (whole school legislation, education administration and organization). It is also conceived solely as being relevant to adult education and not an activity for every human being from birth to death. It lacks any detailed concern with the whole of society. The current legislation merely suggests that a local community should support adult education. Hence, the manner of regulating and carrying out lifelong learning at this level is dependent more on the subjective forces in local communities than on systemic and legislative regulation.

On the State's side, there has been the passing and ratifying of all strategic documents not yet passed, these being:

- a strategy for lifelong learning;
- a concept and strategy for adult education;
- a national programme of adult education.

In further systemic regulation of adult education, in particular the delimitation of competencies between the State and local authorities (communes), it is important to increase the concern of local authorities for adult education.

Nevertheless, there is room for optimism. Policy and strategy has been prepared for public discussion And this will be proposed for approval through parliamentary procedures. Projects are still in the process of growing. There are also new ventures, for example, an information and counselling network; the organizing of work-based learning to promote the growth of learning organizations; and further structuring of learning in the community.

The direction for the future is certain: we need to become a learning country. At this stage of development, the term 'country' seems more appropriate than 'society'. It is a term which implies less structure, whereas systematic growth of adult and other forms of educational activity will enable the conditions for, and lead the country towards, becoming a learning society. For its survival, a country such as Slovenia needs knowledge as a basis of national development, and learning as a basis for creating and implementing knowledge. The major opportunity for development in the country is through the optimum use of its human resources. So, it is of greater importance for Slovenia (even more so than for some of the more developed countries of the EU) to take a lifelong learning strategy seriously.

It is intended that the current state should be continued as an integral and interdisciplinary development project named 'Slovenia – The Learning Country'. It is planned to become a mutual project concerning all branches, not only of education and labour, but on the national level, being implemented in local communities which accept lifelong learning as part of State as well as local policy. Lifelong learning is the concern of the whole society, thus, research and development must include all aspects of society and life, including the educological, economic, cultural, sociological, historical and the political. The implementation of the project 'Slovenia – The Learning Country' is a long-term one which is based on the stages that have already been achieved. The concept of lifelong learning, and the strategy, is changing the traditional views and approaches to learning and education. It is not entirely that it is a 'new' experience. It is, rather, an issue of new conceptions being built on the old and long experience of learning that is one of the main advantages of the human being. The new circumstances are a basis for creating core skills for living and learning in the learning society.

PART 2

STRATEGIES FOR TEACHING AND LEARNING – ISSUES AND THEORY

Chapter 8

Introduction

Whereas Part 1 of this book considered requirements of higher education largely dependent on vision and rhetoric rather than practice, Part 2 provides a set of perspectives that address more closely actual practices in higher education, and are largely critical of such practices. It also provides suggestions for ways in which learning and teaching, and core skills as an aspect of this, need to be reconceptualized to achieve required outcomes.

The second chapter in Part 2 (Chapter 9), 'Core skills: interpretations in higher education', by Elisabeth Dunne, Neville Bennett and Clive Carré, returns to the context within higher education. Evidence is provided of the difficulty of bringing about change, especially in a context such as that of the university with its history and culture of autonomy. Findings are presented from a major project on core skills in higher education, one of thirteen projects under the umbrella title of 'The Learning Society'. The context for the study was provided by contested notions of a learning society apparent in the mismatch between what employers state that they want (as outlined in the first few chapters of Part 1) and the skills and knowledge that universities currently provide.

The chapter provides a view of core skills as perceived by academics in four British universities. A sample of successful programmes of skill development was selected in order to describe and analyse appropriate practice. It was anticipated that findings could be used to illuminate and develop further practice. However, the area of core skill teaching was complex and it was difficult to draw out easy lessons, mostly because the concept of core skills has a wide range of interpretations and associated practices; and university teachers find it difficult to talk about how students learn and seem unused to examining their own beliefs about teaching, learning or the purposes of higher education. The multiple interpretations of skills are discussed, and the difficulties for higher education in meeting the demands of a learning society. Currently, there seems to be considerable incompatibility between rhetoric from outside higher education and practices and interpretations within universities. Suggestions that changes must be grounded in a more developed approach to the conceptualization of skill provision and an enhanced understanding of how students learn, are among issues taken up by further chapters in Parts 2 and 3.

Alan Brown, in Chapter 10 – 'Going Dutch? Changing the focus from core skills to core problems in vocational higher education' – suggests that part of the problem of change resides in the unresolved tensions in the conceptualization of core skills in the UK. Core skills were initially formulated as a developmental tool for work-based learning. They were then used to perform a remedial function of equipping 16–19 year olds with basic skills they had not fully grasped in compulsory education. Their association with the skills necessary for employment, within a narrowly framed vision of occupational competence, means they are seen as undermining the traditional model of education, with its emphasis on knowledge, understanding and cognitive development.

However, discussions about 'key qualifications' in Germany and the Netherlands had a completely different starting point and have developed as a way of giving greater breadth and depth to vocational education and training. The conceptualization of key qualifications is more multi-dimensional, encompassing knowledge, insight, skills and attitudes. In addition, attempts have been made to facilitate the development of key qualifications through a focus on occupational 'core problems'. These problems are characterized by conflicting considerations and interests, uncertainty, complexity and require the exercise of judgement. As such, their resolution is dependent upon the holistic use of key qualifications in interrelated ways. It is argued that a focus on 'core problems' may be a much bolder, more innovative and more acceptable way of progressing debate about the use of core skills in vocational higher education in the UK, rather than simply trying to add to current conceptions of core skills, which were developed for different purposes and for use in different contexts.

In Chapter 11 – 'How universities fail the learning society' – Peter Levin provides a highly critical account of the provision for learning in universities, both at the conceptual and the practical level. He suggests that problems arise from one specific failure: that higher education in the UK is not guided by a workable concept of learning. Further, the criteria by which student success is gauged are hidden from them, and indeed are not made explicit among academics themselves. The implicit criteria appear to be rooted in a concept of learning which amounts to learning to be, and to think, like one's mentors.

While in practice this is what successful students are rewarded for, they are not taught it specifically: it is not found in syllabuses, where the emphasis is on subject matter.

The dichotomy between what is taught and what is assessed is reflected in a further dichotomy, between the mental set associated with teaching and that associated with research and professional discourse. The consequence for students is that under the guise of education they are being subjected to mystification. This does not assist students to prepare for the world of work, and nor do two conspicuous mismatches between the academic world and that of work – one to do with culture, the other to do with skills. It is contended that, arguably, the UK already is a learning society, and universities have possibly not had a great deal to do with this. Considerable changes are necessary if universities are to make a worthwhile contribution to society and justify the funding they receive.

Peter Danby and Mike Rawlins borrowed the slogan – 'To change the thinking of the world' (Chapter 12) – from a great explorer who inspired them. Although having a background in industry and training in multinational companies, they are also committed to bringing about change within higher education. This chapter provides their perspective on the need for change, informed by their experience both outside and within universities. In their contacts with global corporations, business schools, universities and schools, they have worked with children, managing directors, undergraduates and managers at all levels and from many different cultures. As well as gaining strong impressions of the ways in which people learn, they have also come across what they perceive to be blocks to further development. In particular, they see the 'university culture' as one of the main blocks in any move towards a more open, learning society. They describe a learning process that provides opportunities for people to develop knowledge, skills and confidence, and encourages individuals and teams to take responsibility for their own development.

Taking responsibility for one's own learning, and independent learning, are phrases that are often uttered in the context of higher education. Much of European university provision has traditionally been, and still is, dependent on this kind of approach. Students succeed or fail; many drop out and little attention is paid to this. Successful students in British universities will always have been those who have been able to make the most of learning independently. However, these terms take on new connotations in the present climate. The implication is that students who can take responsibility for their learning, and who can learn independently, will be more cost-effective. There is a political agenda which demands larger teaching groups and less contact time with students, and an assumption that independent learning skills will enable students to cope.

The preceding chapter suggested the need for creating a learning environment which enables students to understand what it means to 'take responsibility for learning'. In Chapter 13 – 'Independent learning confronts globalization: facilitating students' development as learners' – Terry Evans and Alistair Morgan consider the need for creating a learning environment in relation to information and communication technology. This is an area which tends to be viewed as a panacea for the ills of higher education. IT (information technology) is seen as the 'provider' of the curriculum and the resource base for learning. Evans and Morgan critically consider issues of globalization and relate these to issues of independent and lifelong learning, raising matters and questions concerning educational practice in a 'globalized' field. The tensions which are generated by these matters are related to the need for a critical appraisal of the ways in which teachers, administrators and student-support staff facilitate learners' development. They argue that these ways will need to be consistent with the 'new times' – the emerging cultural and technological contexts. Facilitating student development as learners requires a consideration, not only of the diverse contexts and needs of students, but also of potential resources and strategies which are emerging as useful. These include forms of collaborative and peer group learning mediated through new information technologies.

Part 2 ends with Chapter 14 – 'A defence of teaching against its detractors'. Richard Dunne provides a critical view of some current assumptions: for example, that following investment in an appropriate course of study (probably including the development of 'core skills' or 'transferable skills'), subsequent learning would require minimal investment. Similarly the implication of 'lifelong learning' is that, appropriately prepared (with core or transferable skills), people can continue learning throughout their lives. This (comfortingly) suggests that students will be able to adapt not only to any currently known, but to any future, contexts. It is suggested that this is an inappropriate and inadequate view when higher education is under pressure to change its approach to teaching. This chapter argues that the nature of the changes have not been subjected to principled analysis. The major problem is that university teachers lack a model of teaching and learning which could be used as a defence against partisan arguments for unjustified reform. A model is described in order to clarify how it is possible to retain the essence of traditional, and successful, teaching with larger and more diverse groups of students.

Chapter 9

Core skills: interpretations in higher education

Elisabeth Dunne, Neville Bennett and Clive Carré

Introduction

The study of core skills reported in this chapter was designed in the context of the backdrop of change and development as outlined in Chapter 2. It was not based on any specific assumptions about, or visions of, a learning society, but took as its central premise that the attempted shift to operationalism through the acquisition and development of core skills was worthy of critical and independent exploration and evaluation. It was designed in the knowledge of tensions and confusion over terminology. To recap briefly: the term core skills is but one of several related terms, each of which has been used to label sets of skills or attributes deemed important by employers and government. These sets contain different numbers and combinations of skills, and are based on differing purposes, definitions and interpretations. What they have in common is that they are theoretically threadbare, and have rarely contained the perceptions of those staff who are expected to deliver these skills in higher education.

The aim of the study was to identify, describe and analyse ways of acquiring and developing core skills in both higher education and employment. In this chapter, the focus is largely on the voice of academics in universities – those who were recommended by their institutions for good practice in the teaching of core and transferable skills. Some feedback from students is also included. The practice of 32 university teachers in 16 departments was studied. They represent a mix of vocational and non-vocational disciplines, from four institutions of higher education in England and Wales. The sample of academics, being selected by their institutions for their good practice, was not controlled for gender or age, but a wide range of disciplinary areas were chosen. The findings reported in this chapter are drawn from interviews, observations, questionnaires and course documentation. Student responses were gained on the practices of these same teachers via questionnaires, and interviews with focus groups and individuals. The sample was again not controlled since it was dependent on those students who happened to be following the courses or modules of the selected academics.

Perspectives from university teachers

There is evidence of a wide variety of beliefs, conceptions and practices across each institution, reflecting features that are personal, social and intellectual. There is no obvious pattern to responses which would differentiate male from female academics, young from old, or distinguish teachers of vocational modules from non-vocational, or the new universities from the old.

Beliefs and conceptions

If, as has been suggested in the introduction, there is an imperative for a cultural shift in terms of the purposes of higher education, with a significant change in emphasis towards employment skills or employability, it might be expected that this view would be shared widely, and actively supported, by academics. Most, however, continued to talk in traditional terms. Few seemed accustomed to articulating their beliefs about the purposes of a degree. One believed 'Almost certainly [a degree] is to do with broadening the mind in a very general sense. I don't think it's to get people good jobs'. Others spoke in similar terms: 'it's education in the broad sense of the word. It's about developing the mind, about acquiring specific knowledge and critical abilities'; 'it's all about self-development and being aware of society and culture'; 'intellectual maturity'.

The most comprehensive rationale came from an academic who has devoted a considerable part of the last few years to the development of modules on transferable skills:

Clearly there are a variety of purposes which at one end can be personal agendas, individual development; but I suspect for society as a whole that the principal purpose of undergraduate programmes must be to enhance the skills of the students so that they can contribute more effectively when they enter the world of work. That, I am sure, is the government's principal agenda and I suspect that it is often very much the student's principal agenda too, in that they hope that having an additional significant qualification will enhance their marketability and ultimately improve their life chances in the job market.

A general wariness that skills-based, or competence-based, objectives could devalue higher education was reflected in views such as:

> If we teach people a lot of highly complicated mathematics in a very narrow area, then most of that is not transferable in any sense. What might be transferable is the essence of the process of understanding, that is, it's worth studying in depth in order to try and understand, rather than skate across the surface, and that's why academic disciplines are important in higher education. We shouldn't just be a training shop for all kinds of skills – which we could be. If you want to set up a training shop you wouldn't fill it up with academics because they are not actually very good at that.

There were also difficulties in discussing 'core skills'. The term was unknown to some academics. For others who recognized the term, there was a clear distinction between skills specific to a discipline and more general cross-disciplinary skills: 'As I understand it, personal transferable skills could relate to any discipline, they could be things such as capacity to take notes, organize yourself for study time… but core skills I would see as having an intellectual discipline element'. Core skills had a very wide range of interpretations in practice, but whether discussed in terms of 'personal transferable' or 'core' skills, the connection with disciplinary study remained firm: 'I see the ability to research, get their materials together, get their argument together and select their topic as an essential core skill which of course will be transferable, but I am thinking of it here in terms of the discipline.'

Most of the sample felt reasonably comfortable with the concept of transferable skills: 'Well I guess that they are skills that you can acquire in higher education that are transferable to the world of work, or indeed non-work, not discipline specific'; or 'things such as how to organize themselves when doing an oral presentation to time management, data handling and IT'. For a few, 'transferable' and 'core' skills meant the same thing.

The term 'learning society' was less well known. The majority of those interviewed had never heard the term and few were prepared to volunteer a definition. So far, just one reply has been clear: 'as an economic training nation, we have to have a learning society if we are to flourish in the world, we can't stand still, we have to constantly update ourselves'.

The term 'lifelong learning' was more familiar, generally expressed as 'we are going to have to keep learning in order to retrain for different jobs throughout our lives'; or 'you dip in and out of learning'. Lifelong learning was spoken about as if it is an acceptable idea, not controversial. Most prevalent was a sense of confusion: 'I tend to have all of those phrases together in my mind, lifelong learning and transferable skills and I don't in my head have a clear distinction between them'. A certain commitment to the concept was evident: 'I am not sure I used those terms until they started to appear in the press but I very much believe that they are important. I think that is probably the most important thing that we have to give to students, the ability to continue to learn. Life wouldn't be life if it wasn't continually learning'.

If the achievement of a 'learning society' is important, it may be problematic that academics are not familiar with the term. It might, however, be expected that they should talk easily, knowledgeably and explicitly about how students learn. A major problem in asking academics about student learning is that it is not, in general, an issue which they seem used to addressing. It was not unusual to hear in some form that 'I just don't think I know how people learn'. This was on occasion modified by 'I am quite persuaded that they learn in very different ways', or 'learning by doing, they learn more than by being told'.

One of the major recent structural changes in higher education, considered to be an important vehicle for wider change, including flexibility for the provision of core and transferable skills, is that of modularization. Although our sample comprised university teachers who in general support innovation and change, many believe modularization to be constraining, inflexible and inviting an ethos which works against learning. They claimed that modularization aggravates a situation in which students work only for the final assessment, where they are encouraged to move on to the next module with no consideration of its links with others, where assessment does not encourage or build links, where for example, core skills taught in compulsory modules, as an essential foundation for the future, may never be used again in the course of a degree, and where it is becoming increasingly difficult to plan for continuity and progression in teaching or learning. Nonetheless, some of the courses observed clearly did plan for learning and for transfer of learning between modules – in terms of knowledge and skills being developed in increasingly complex contexts, with more complex knowledge bases, or through the gaining and application of skills to give progression and development.

Teacher practices

As outlined above, the term 'core skills' has a variety of meanings to academics. However, the term most usually connotes skills which are central to the discipline, as distinct from personal transferable skills which are defined as cross-disciplinary and generic. Hence, for the purposes of this study, we decided to maximize ecological validity by using the word 'core' to refer to disciplinary skills, and the label 'generic' to represent the skills which can support study in any discipline, and which can potentially be used and transferred to a range of contexts, in higher education or the workplace.

A model of generic skills

A further difficulty in the description of generic skill acquisition lay in the variety of contexts for provision, and in the complexity of overlap between disciplinary learning and generic skills. A model was, therefore, developed in order to clarify analysis. It distinguishes five elements of course provision for skills in higher education: disciplinary content knowledge, disciplinary skills, workplace awareness, workplace experience and generic skills, as shown in Figure 9.1.

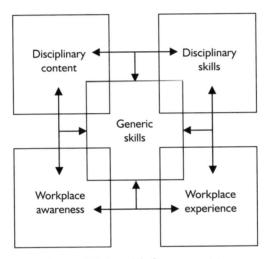

Figure 9.1 *A model of course provision*

Epistemological, psychological and curriculum analyses indicate that substantive and syntactic knowledge, although interdependent, can also be considered as independent in characterizing the nature of any discipline, and are so identified in the model. In some courses disciplinary content knowledge and/or generic skills are planned to be acquired through work experience, achieved either through direct placement in the workplace or through some other kind of experience of the world of work, or a workplace simulation. These are represented by the bottom two elements of the model.

The relationship between core and generic skills is complex, as is the relationship between generic skills and disciplinary learning. In some disciplines, generic skills may be seen as core skills. In other departments these same skills will be considered as generic and may be taught in separate 'bolt-on' courses. For this reason, the central element of the model (generic skills) is shown intruding into the other four elements, so that the relationships can be illustrated. In this model there is no assumption about directionality of learning. Thus disciplinary content, for example, can be learnt in the institution with the intention for subsequent use in the workplace, or vice versa, as in education degrees, for example, where much disciplinary knowledge is learned in classrooms.

Patterns of course provision
All the courses and modules observed for this study can be described in terms of the five elements of the model, but each 'fits' or overlays the model in a different way, according to teaching objectives, and the processes and contexts used for learning. The 'fit' of each module can be described, or mapped, as a series of patterns which can then be compared to identify different approaches to developing generic skills within the curriculum.

The practices of the teachers in the sample were ascertained by analysis of course documentation, interviews about teaching intentions, approaches, tasks and assessment procedures, together with several observations of the teaching of the selected courses. The outcome of analysis is a typology comprising six patterns (although potentially there could be many others) as presented below. The patterns (Figures 9.2–9.7), albeit briefly described, highlight ways in which modules from the different disciplines observed can be mapped on to the model. Most modules cannot be described with reference to one element alone, but may range over several. There is usually, however, one context that provides the major focus. (For more detailed description, examples and theoretical analysis, see Bennett *et al*, 1999.)

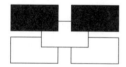

Planned learning outcomes:
major – disciplinary content, disciplinary skills
minor – generic skills

Figure 9.2 *Pattern 1*

Skills provision is within the distinctive substantive and syntactic knowledge of the discipline, with discipline-based skills seen by the course providers as the core skills of the subject. Generic skills such as those gained via groupwork, communication, library use etc may be used or encouraged to enhance the academic study, but are of an incidental nature.

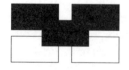

Planned learning outcomes:
major – disciplinary content, disciplinary skills, generic skills

Figure 9.3 *Pattern 2*

Substantive and syntactic knowledge of the discipline is developed through the acquisition and use of specific generic skills. The latter are the means by which learning of the disciplinary knowledge is encouraged and enhanced. Disciplinary and generic skills are considered of equal importance.

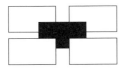

Planned learning outcomes:
major – generic skills
minor – disciplinary content, disciplinary skills

Figure 9.4 *Pattern 3*

There is an emphasis, explicitly, for students to acquire generic skills as an outcome rather than as the means to develop disciplinary knowledge. Disciplinary knowledge provides a context for learning.

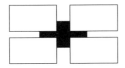

Planned learning outcomes:
major – generic skills

Figure 9.5 *Pattern 4*

The focus is exclusively on generic skills, to the extent that the disciplinary knowledge acquired or used could be of the students' choice, or could be only tangentially related to disciplinary study.

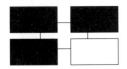

Planned learning outcomes:
major – disciplinary skills, disciplinary content, workplace awareness
minor – generic skills

Figure 9.6 *Pattern 5*

The focus is on substantive knowledge and its application, particularly in those subjects which are vocational. Insight into the workplace is through contacts with employers, visits to the workplace or through simulations. There is also some provision for generic skills.

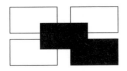

Planned learning outcomes:
major – generic skills, workplace experience
minor – disciplinary content, disciplinary skills, workplace awareness

Figure 9.7 *Pattern 6*

Here there is an emphasis both on generic skills and raising awareness about the requirements and constraints of the world of work. The context for skills utilization and development is 'real' work experience in a workplace setting. The focus on disciplinary knowledge and skills, or on generic skills, will vary depending on the purpose of the experience.

Observation suggested that skills courses were planned and taught with rigour and attention to detail. However, the extent to which the teaching of skills is effective depends, in part, on the attitudes and motivation of the student body. It was, therefore, important that data be acquired from students on their understandings of generic skills and the importance afforded to them, and on their perceptions of the quality of skills teaching, and their own learning.

Perspectives from university students

Students' beliefs and conceptions about generic skills were acquired from interviewing and observing individuals, as well as from focus groups of those who were studying the sampled courses, together with a questionnaire survey of 400 students taking these same courses. Data from the survey showed that familiarity with, and definitions of, terms such as 'personal transferable' and 'core skills' varied widely. Not surprisingly perhaps, students who had studied modules where these terms had been emphasized showed most familiarity. Nevertheless, even among this group definitions varied, and there was some confusion over differences between definitions.

When asked about the purposes of gaining a degree, almost 80 per cent cited job and career prospects. Few mentioned the importance of skills. Students seemed somewhat unsure about what employers thought were the benefits of graduate education. About a third mentioned the acquisition of disciplinary knowledge, and another third suggested cognitive development and personal management skills, which included maturity of thinking, the ability to argue, having commitment, self-discipline and aspirations. Few identified generic or transferable skills in this context, and only 15 per cent mentioned career or job-related skills as a perceived benefit to employers. Ironically, they did recognize that employers saw these skills as lacking in graduates.

All students reported a diet of lectures, individual work, and seminars/tutorials in their degree studies, and the majority also experienced teamwork or groupwork and project work. Far fewer had been involved in student-led activities. There was a strong tendency for responses to be conceived in terms of subject knowledge rather than skills, despite all the students in this study following skills-based courses. The skills that they believed they had developed most included presenting information, taking responsibility for their own learning, using appropriate sources, carrying out agreed tasks, managing time effectively, identifying key features of a task, gathering information, listening actively, respecting other viewpoints and dealing with criticism. However not all were deemed important. Managing time was seen as the most important of these skills, and listening actively the least.

Of importance to course developers is the finding from the interviews that, despite the perceived benefits of courses that included generic skills, students would not have chosen a skills-based module if it had been optional. Students report being committed to their chosen discipline and tending to opt for what was perceived as a traditional degree, although skills courses were likely to be more acceptable if introduced early in the degree programme. A frequent theme of focus group discussion was in relation to the nature of effective learning and how this can be promoted and supported. Since many of the skills courses required students to take on responsibilities beyond what they had anticipated, much debate covered the extent to which the pressure, stress and time commitment is useful to their learning. Retrospectively, they were positive about what they had gained and many claimed to have grown in confidence.

Assessment is likely to provide the main motivation for student involvement, whether the orientation is disciplinary or generic. This may seem a somewhat negative approach to learning, and was of concern to academics in the context of modularization (as outlined above). It is also possible to view the role of assessment in a more positive light. Assessment of skills requires teachers to be explicit about skill development and students to devote attention to it. If assessment is the most effective way to ensure that generic skills are recognized by students, then a powerful means of addressing skill-based learning outcomes is via an assessment-led curriculum – that is, the assessment is devised to drive the aims of the course. When assessment is of syntactic and substantive knowledge, students are less likely to perceive the significance of generic skills – even if skills processes have been emphasized by teachers. When skills remain embedded and implicit within disciplinary study, and are not assessed, students are least likely either to recognize skills or to be eloquent, or even interested, in their description.

Discussion

Problems of conceptualization

What is illustrated by this research is that there can be huge gaps between the rhetoric and the reality, or between prescription and practice. Stalker (1996) took, from the German philosopher Adorno, the notion of an 'unfulfilled concept', indicating one which 'is not sufficiently coherent in the abstract to be fully "realised" in practice'. Core skills, in their many interpretations, or with the lack of clear conceptualization by the academics interviewed in the four institutions under study, would seem to exemplify this notion. Elsewhere, two groups have openly abandoned such terminology: Industry in Education (1995) no longer uses 'core skills' as a descriptor because of the range of interpretations; the 'Graduateness' project (HEQC (Higher Education Quality Council), 1996) no longer talks of 'personal transferable skills' because of the difficulties associated with transfer and the connotations of skills.

Core skills belong centrally to a wider debate: what are the purposes of higher education and what kind of curriculum does it need? What kind of learning society do we want? One problem is that little is known about the relationship of learning provision in higher education to the ability of graduates to be effective in employment in later years. Further, little is known, beyond the rhetoric, about what economic productivity really requires. There is increasing recognition that a focus on skills may not represent the sole pathway to competitive advantage. Keep (1997) suggests that instead of viewing increasing levels of knowledge and skill as some form of magic bullet that can transform organizational performance, there is growing consensus that they represent one piece within an interlocking jigsaw puzzle that adds up to a high performance workplace. If post-modern society continues to emphasize 'operationalism' to the extent that traditional academic stances are eroded, then to what extent do we risk losing the demand on students for conceptualization of deep learning and understanding of a discipline which is the central purpose of a degree to many academics – including those who are open to change, and who do not discount the value of skills for employment?

Universities may well be considered guilty of ill-preparing students for employment, but what kind of higher education provision is actually the most effective, for now and for the future? How much is known about the relationship of changes in learning provision to the ability of graduates to be effective in employment in later years? Are those graduates who can demonstrate the performance skills required by employers actually those who develop and grow? Are these the same graduates who will be successful in personal terms as well as public? Many academics continue strongly to defend disciplinary study and the disciplinary skills deemed integral to such study as being the most important preparation for any future.

Problems of change

In the context of developing models of generic skills, Oates (1990) has argued that 'The process of generating a (skills) framework... must be accompanied by a firm statement of function, a sound theoretical base, and appropriate empirical evidence/validation. Without this there is a very strong risk of building a house of cards on a foundation of sand'. This study is intended as a step in the direction of providing a firm basis on which to build. However, substantial change, at individual, departmental and institutional levels, will be necessary if the teaching and learning of skills is to be successful. There remain considerable barriers to change. As explained by one academic:

> increasingly what we are asking them [academics] to do is to get interested in the psychology of teamwork or the assessment of verbal presentations and so on, or enhancing people's portfolios of interpersonal skills. They are just not the right people to do it, they have got no interest in it, they are not prepared for it, they are not trained for it. I think there is an enormous tension therefore between the kind of people that we have got in HE (higher education) and the kind of expectations that the government has of what HE ought to be delivering in terms of student capabilities.

Many departments have to contend with the explicit rejection of change by some staff members: 'How dare you assume that we all agree. I fundamentally and categorically do not believe that these skills have anything to do with a university degree'. In a prior study (Dunne, 1995), it became evident that staff providing skills-based courses often felt isolated, unsupported, criticized for attending to teaching rather than to research. In the present study, recognition is also an issue: 'I suspect lots of my colleagues would say there is very little recognition for teaching, you don't get Chairs for being innovative in the curriculum or for producing really successful programmes, but that is another big agenda'. A further problem is that individuals do not know how to go about promoting change. 'TQA (teaching quality assessment) gave us a terrible shock. We do actually want to better the way in which we teach'. The need for knowing about models of teaching and learning is discussed in this context, and their role in enabling colleagues to understand the necessity for change and how it might be attained. Members of the sample suggested there was a genuine desire to work at the issues and questions raised by the project, or to review their practice in the light of new ways of understanding. As an example, one academic asked if he could complete a questionnaire for a second time: 'I thought I would do it very quickly and then I realized there were some fairly deep issues here... what your questionnaire did was make me think about it'. Academics will need to become more flexible in their approaches, open to change (though perhaps maintaining a critical stance), and willing learners if they are themselves to become members of a society which values learning.

In the modules observed, an explicit focus on skills was often intended as providing a foundation to students that would be central to effective learning throughout higher education, rather than specifically as preparation for work. First-year students were introduced to skills so that they could use, practise, and develop them in new contexts, in particular within disciplinary study. Skills courses were seen as an investment by those who taught them, with the pay-off that they also provide what employers say they need. However, their rationale comes from within higher education, and its major purpose is the enhancement of student experiences within higher education. This may be of importance if the involvement of universities in developing a society of learners who are prepared for the future is to become a reality.

Chapter 10

Going Dutch? Changing the focus from core skills to core problems in vocational higher education

Alan Brown

Introduction

Debates about the purposes of education and training are currently framed around the necessity of equipping people for lifelong learning and of building a 'learning society', primarily in order to improve international competitiveness (European Commission, 1995). Interest has focused on whether it is possible to build up the core skills of individuals such that they can be effective and continuing participants in a 'learning society'. However, it is worth while reflecting on the meaning of 'core skills' when used in this way, as the term has been used in a variety of ways in different contexts over the last 20 years.

One of the key debates about core skills in the UK since the late 1970s has focused on the extent to which they needed to be contextualized: could they be separately taught or could they only be developed in particular contexts. It is perhaps ironic then that one of the pressing requirements 20 years later is that debates about core skills themselves need to be contextualized, as there are unresolved tensions in how they are currently conceptualized (Young *et al*, 1997). This is in large measure due to the legacy of how they developed in practice. It is noteworthy that the genesis of a national approach to core skills in the UK was in the idea that they could be used as a developmental tool to give structure and direction to learning in the workplace (particularly on Youth Training Schemes) (Evans *et al,* 1987). Secondly, when used within education, primarily for 16–19 year olds, core skills became identified with 'the more remedial function of equipping significant numbers of young people in each age cohort with basic skills and understanding that they have not acquired through the compulsory phases of education' (Young *et al,* 1997). Thirdly, their association with the skills necessary for employment was interpreted as part of a wider attack, in which an emphasis on skills was seen as undermining the traditional model of education, with its emphasis on knowledge, understanding and cognitive development (Jessup, 1991; Hyland, 1994).

The interesting point is that, when looking at the parallel development of 'key qualifications' in Germany and the Netherlands, a completely different conception has been formulated. 'Key qualifications' were associated with the need to broaden and deepen vocational education and training, in relation to development of an underpinning knowledge base and increased emphasis on logical analytical and critical thinking. As such, 'key qualifications' raised the intellectual demands within vocational education and training, rather than being viewed in any sense as remedial. Indeed, insofar as these related to the skills for employment, they could be seen as the education and training required to maintain an economy at a 'high skills' equilibrium (Finegold and Soskice, 1988). Finally, the German term *Schlüsselqualifikationen* ('key qualifications') has been thought to be broadly equivalent to the English term 'core skills.' However, 'key qualifications' does not imply any primacy being accorded to a skills-based approach. Indeed, Van Zolingen (1995), in her comprehensive review, identified 'key qualifications' in terms of knowledge, insight, skills and attitudes.

So although the term 'core skills' has a specific legacy within the UK, there is no conceptual reason why a consideration of core skills in HE (higher education) could not be broadened from how it has been historically treated in other contexts. A switch to the term 'key qualifications' is a non-starter, simply because the conventional English usage of 'qualifications' carries such different connotations in education. However, related recent ideas from the Netherlands may be of value in a UK context. In particular, the attempt to use 'core problems' as a focus for the development of 'key qualifications' (Onstenk *et al*, 1990; Onstenk, 1997; Van Zolingen *et al*, 1997) may have considerable value for the development and implementation of broadly framed curricula for 'vocational' HE in the UK.

The issues surrounding how core skills in HE in the UK should be conceptualized and implemented will be discussed later in the chapter. It has been outlined elsewhere that it is possible to broaden existing ideas about core (or key) skills, when seeking to apply them to HE (Brown, 1997). However, a bolder approach, which is more innovative and may also prove to be more acceptable to staff in HE, would be to shift the focus to 'core problems.' Before doing that, however, we must understand more about the initial framing and subsequent development of 'key qualifications' in Germany and the Netherlands.

Key qualifications

The term 'key qualifications' (*Schüsselqualifikationen*) was first used by Mertens (1974) who was studying the increasing requirements for flexibility in skilled work in Germany. He proposed that vocational education and training should focus on the development of key qualifications, as this would improve students' labour market prospects (as they would be able to apply for a wider range of jobs) and equip them to be 'better able to react to future developments that are not wholly predictable (for example, when there are changes within a job)' (Van Zolingen *et al*, 1997).

Mertens argued that there were four sets of key qualifications. First, there were those aimed at giving depth to fundamental skills: 'for example, logical, analytical, structured, associative and contextual thinking; critical thinking using argumentation and discussion; co-operative behaviour by employing social rules and techniques' (Van Zolingen *et al*, 1997). Second, there were qualifications with an extensive horizontal transfer value: for example, being able to gather, understand, process and use information. The third set of qualifications provided breadth: for example, knowledge of technology that underpinned broad occupational groups. The fourth set related to the need to be able to continue learning, so that as experienced workers they would be able to update their skills and knowledge through access to adult education and training.

The whole thrust of Mertens' argument was that there was a need to broaden and deepen vocational education and training, and that this entailed paying greater attention to cognitive and meta-cognitive skills. From 1974 onwards, however, the meaning of 'key qualifications' was extended in various ways, and Van Zolingen (1995) sought to provide a new coordinating interpretation of 'key qualifications', based on European experience, mainly in Germany and the Netherlands. By this time, key qualifications were not limited to the cognitive dimension and were more closely tied to an occupational context, whereby key qualifications specifically involve qualifications that are necessary to practise an occupation. Van Zolingen *et al* (1997) provide a comprehensive definition of key qualifications as 'the knowledge, insight, skills and attitudes that are part of the durable core of an occupation or a group of related jobs, with the possibility of transfer to other, new jobs within that occupation and of innovations within that occupation, which contribute to the development of a person's occupational competence and facilitate transitions within the career'.

Van Zolingen *et al* (1997) produce an extensive specification of the knowledge, insight, skills and attitudes that make up key qualifications. This includes:

- technical knowledge;
- general knowledge of languages and computing;
- interdisciplinary knowledge;
- cognitive and meta-cognitive skills (identifying and solving problems; abstract thinking; intellectual flexibility; learning to learn; tacit skills);
- communication skills;
- ability to work with others;
- ability to plan and organize work;
- personal attributes such as self-reliance, perseverance and creativity;
- ability to adapt oneself to the corporate culture;
- acting as a modern citizen;
- showing a critical attitude to work and one's own interests.

It is apparent that this type of listing is not a restricted set of skills that should be incorporated into programmes of VET (vocational education and training), but rather it is a challenge to the way VET is organized and delivered. One response to this challenge has been to make use of 'core problems', those problems and dilemmas that are central to the practice of an occupation (Onstenk *et al*, 1990), as a way to broaden and deepen VET in practice.

Core problems

The crucial lesson from a consideration of the development of key qualifications is that it is important to maintain a broad curricular focus and not get sidetracked into thinking of core (key) skills in a narrow or exclusive way. Any new approach should, therefore, be pedagogically driven, with proposed activities considered within an overarching conceptual and theoretical framework. Hence any approach to vocational HE should address not only the development of the requisite skills and technical knowledge base, but also be underpinned by a commitment to continuing learning and professional development as a reflexive process, acknowledging the importance of critical reflection as a basis for learning. Such an approach to learning would also be collaborative with a particular emphasis on the use of problem-based learning.

Almost by definition, it is desirable for vocational HE to be closely related to the work context. One way to achieve this is to focus on the 'core problems' of groups of practitioners. Core problems are central to the performance of roles of particular groups of practitioners. They are characterized by uncertainty, complexity, conflicting considerations and require the exercise of judgement. These problems may have organizational, occupational and technical dimensions, and their solution may require knowledge, insight, skills and attitudes related to these dimensions, as well as interdisciplinary knowledge, the application of high-level cognitive skills and the interrelated use of communication and other core skills. Such an approach does link to the increasing use of problem-based learning within medical, legal and engineering education. From a core skills perspective this is important as this approach leads to the integrated application of these skills in a way that aligns with progressive curricular developments that are already taking place. Core skills development fits naturally within a curricular approach that utilizes core problems as a key learning strategy.

A more fully developed rationale for this type of approach, which focuses on 'core problems', would highlight that it is a learning environment making use of problem-based learning such that:

- it provides authentic contexts for learning with a focus on real (complex) problems;
- it is collaborative and dynamic, enabling learners to develop shared understanding and a sense of belonging to a dynamic community of practice, which they are helping to change and shape;
- it is participative and fosters active engagement as the learners determine for themselves the issues that need to be addressed when facing core problems. They can draw on the knowledge and skills of others in facing these issues and also create their own learning agenda to fill any gaps in their knowledge and understanding;
- it supports learning which is highly relevant, because the learning is focused on issues which are perceived as pressing by practitioners;
- it gives (possibly isolated) individuals the opportunity to think through problems as part of a team;
- it supports the development of creative and flexible approaches to problems;
- it supports the development of contextualized critical learning;
- it supports reflection on and review of the learning process as well as of the outcomes.

Reflection on core problems can give insight into current practice and provide ideas as to how they might tackle similar problems in future. Such reflection is critical in two respects. First, it is necessary if learners are to look beyond current practice and to help shape how such problems are tackled in future. Second, it can act as a stimulus to creativity and innovation, not least because the learners have learnt the value of applying a reflective approach to the development of their own practice and expertise. Such an approach not only increases the likelihood of significant learning, it also provides a framework for subsequent continuing professional development in which it is likely that processes of new knowledge creation may be facilitated. In this sense it helps those who are learning within vocational HE to feel they are moving towards assuming a full position within particular 'communities of practice' (Lave, 1991), and a subsequent continuing commitment to explore, reflect on and improve their professional practice (Schön, 1983, 1987).

The explicit linking of processes of learning and reflection within vocational HE to 'core problems' at work does not, however, mean that this type of work-related learning is the sole curriculum driver: not least because the essence of competent professional practice is that the practitioner is able to respond intelligently in situations which are sufficiently novel that the response has to be generated *in situ* (Elliot, 1991). The collaborative dimension, too, needs stressing (Lave and Wenger, 1991); as the concept of work-based learning sometimes at present relies heavily on individualistic processes of reflection (Winter and Maisch, 1996). Further, Eraut (1994) highlights how a focus on workplace practice cannot necessarily be equated with a capacity to understand the ideas and concepts that inform such actions. Work-related learners should seek to ensure that significant intellectual development takes place. One way of raising the intellectual demands is to make use of problem-based learning where the focus is on core problems of groups of practitioners (Onstenk, 1997), acknowledging the contribution theoretical concepts can make to assist individuals to understand what they are doing and why work practices are subject to change (Engeström, 1995). Another advantage of a focus on 'core problems' is that it highlights the way professionals working in one sphere increasingly have to deal with issues that are not necessarily within a single disciplinary compass, and that they have to be able to work with colleagues and in groups with different kinds of expertise (Engeström, 1995). Young and Guile (1997) argue that increasingly professionals need to possess a connective, rather than an insular, form of specialization, which stresses the ability to look beyond traditional professional boundaries.

The focus on core problems can help draw attention to another aspect of developing expertise which lies in the ability of the professional to handle the complexity and interrelatedness of issues. This has at least three dimensions. One is the form of the representation of knowledge structures into mental models (Soden, 1993) or networks (Simons, 1990), which are capable of handling increasing complexity and interrelatedness of issues. The second dimension relates to the way an individual is able to hold and interrelate ideas from different spheres (practice, research and theory) to get a fuller, deeper contextualized understanding of professional issues, which affect policy and practice. The third dimension then revolves around the capability to apply that contextualized understanding to particular situations and, if appropriate, to translate that understanding into action.

Core problems can be used as a facilitator of both practical and theoretical learning: that is, rather than becoming locked into current modes of practice, 'theoretical learning' is also developed through applying the concepts for analysing the problems that arise for professionals at work and for making explicit the assumptions underlying existing practice (Guile and Young, 1996). This conceptual knowledge can then be used to underpin reflection on practice at a deeper level than just 'theorizing' practice. Such conceptual knowledge can have both explanatory power and be applied to (changes in) practice. It, therefore, complements the development of practical learning, based on reflection on practice. Crucially, however, the development and application of theoretical learning also facilitates a forward-looking perspective: enabling thinking about how practice *might* be developed in future. Indeed, a base is laid whereby the subsequent application of the processes of research, review and reflection in new contexts can lead to the creation of new forms of knowledge (Engeström, 1995). The use of core problems within vocational HE can, therefore, act as a springboard for the:

- exploration of and reflection on professional practice;
- development of skills, knowledge and understanding (of critical reflection) necessary to evaluate and review professional practice;
- need to understand processes of change (as practice increasingly takes place in complex and dynamic contexts);
- ability to create new knowledge;
- development of theoretical knowledge to underpin and complement reflection on practice;
- study of the interplay between theory and practice;
- need to be able to transfer skills, knowledge and understanding from one context to another;
- ability to handle complexity and interconnectedness of issues (including through the formulation of mental models, schemas or networks);
- development of contextualized understandings;
- translation of understanding into action, as appropriate;
- further development of communication skills.

Discussion

Some of the unresolved issues associated with the way the core skills debate has been framed in the UK in the past have to be tackled if a more productive way forward is to be found. It is unfortunate that in certain contexts an emphasis on core skills has been interpreted as downgrading the value of technical (subject or occupational) knowledge. This association is not present in debates in other European countries about the development of 'key qualifications', and the polarization of arguments around whether curricula should be primarily about the development of knowledge bases or process skills is unhelpful, not least because mastery of a substantive knowledge base is itself an important process skill. The obvious solution is that core skills development should be integrated into and contextualized within the development of disciplinary (or vocational) bodies of skills, knowledge and understanding. However, it should be recognized that this has often proved problematic in practice in the past (Wolf, 1991). This leads on to issues associated with questions of scale: a number of curricular innovations work well in particular contexts or with relatively small numbers, but give considerably less benefit when applied across the curriculum as a whole. This links to pragmatic considerations.

Advocates of the application and integration of high-level core skills should recognize that to do this well is demanding of time and human resources. Hence they should not seek to impose this approach on all areas of the curriculum in a standard way, and they should initially concentrate their efforts in subject areas with a strong vocational orientation. The latter choice is not only because this is the area in which the benefits are greatest, but because this goes with the grain of other curricular developments in such subject areas, including interest in problem-based learning, project work, industry links and so on.

The lessons from Europe are that where 'key qualifications' are broadly defined with an emphasis on increasing cognitive and meta-cognitive skill demands in vocational subjects, then there is no implicit reproach to more academic subjects, such as history, because such subjects have traditionally concerned themselves with cognitive skills development. The whole development of the 'key qualifications' debate has been that the closer HE programmes get to vocational areas, then the more appropriate an emphasis on occupational key qualifications becomes. In vocational HE, learners can benefit from increasing exposure to core problems of the profession, which draw on occupationally relevant knowledge, insight, skills and attitudes in an integrated way. Such a focus on core problems can be part of a powerful learning environment, which is drawing on ideas about the value of problem-based learning, joining communities of practice, situated learning and collaboration.

That key qualifications elsewhere in Europe have been much more broadly drawn than core skills in the UK has had a paradoxical effect. The breadth of key qualifications has meant that particular combinations of key qualifications are interpreted as applying to much narrower (occupational) fields of action: that is, if key qualifications comprise knowledge, insight, skills and attitudes, and have substantive cognitive, meta-cognitive, personality, strategic and socio-communicative dimensions (Van Zolingen *et al*, 1997), then the combination and application of these only make sense in particular occupational contexts. In contrast, the more narrowly defined core skills in the UK were initially regarded as general skills applying across a much wider variety of contexts. Subsequently, core skills have been developed in a number of different contexts, and fundamental tensions about what they are remain. Renaming core skills as key skills has not resolved this tension, and debate continues over their function, definition and appropriateness in different contexts. One resulting problem is that there is pressure to produce overambitious prescriptions, whereby attempts are made to apply 'key skills' in a similar way to too many contexts. We favour the logic underlying the use of 'key qualifications' elsewhere in Europe, whereby the conception is broader and the application is narrower, because their use has to be contextualized, whether in a disciplinary or a vocational sense.

However, the use of 'key qualifications' is a non-starter in the UK and, for good or ill, the current debate is about the application of core skills to HE. Core skills should, therefore, be broadly defined (following the approach of Van Zolingen *et al*, 1997) and should be embedded within a broad, developmental approach to vocational education and training at higher levels. This should be done in a way that complements, rather than undermines, other progressive developments within education, such as the use of problem-based learning, situated cognition and collaborative learning. Additionally, core skills development would need to be integrated with the development of technical knowledge, skills and understanding and, if this is the purpose, then it could be more effectively achieved by focusing attention on 'core problems' rather than 'core skills'.

The attractions of this are manifold but two benefits stand out. First, the most appropriate arenas of action are those areas of vocational HE, which have already been using complementary parts of the teaching and learning 'mix'. Second, the importance of contextualization, whereby core skills have varying relations and combinations with the technical knowledge base, means that subjects should not be judged one against another as to how well they cover a particular core skills specification. Indeed the notion of core problems is transferable in an unthreatening way, as each disciplinary or vocational area would have to define these for themselves. Shifting attention from core skills to core problems could, therefore, act as a stimulus for a reflexive curricular review, with each curricular area being expected to own the process of review, as they search for an appropriate way forward. This broader, developmental and more inclusive approach to core skills in HE would also provide much greater continuity with subsequent learning in other contexts. This approach would, therefore, have much clearer links with the inculcation of positive attitudes towards lifelong learning and underpin moves towards the development of a 'learning society'.

Chapter 11

How universities fail the learning society

Peter Levin

Introduction

The Dearing Committee heard from 'prominent researchers specializing in learning in higher education' that learning at that level 'can be defined as the development of understanding and the ability to apply knowledge in a range of situations… Learning also involves acquiring skills, such as analysis and communication, but these in isolation do not constitute learning' (Dearing Report, 1997). This is all that the Report says about learning as a process (as distinct from learning as something that one possesses).

How do people out in the real world use the word 'learning'? Manifestly, different people use the word 'learning' in different ways, and differently in different situations. For example, they use it when they mean:

- *memorizing,* like learning your multiplication tables by heart;
- *discovering,* like learning something you did not know before;
- *developing skills,* like learning how to be really good at playing a game, or working a piece of equipment, or leading a team of people;
- *getting a grip on a subject,* like learning everything there is to know about it and being able to talk and write about it in your own words;
- *making sense,* like learning why something happened that you did not expect, or learning to fathom the motivations behind other people's puzzling behaviour;
- *gaining understanding,* like learning how a machine, or an organization or system works.

- *acquiring expertise,* like learning how to think and approach problems in the ways that experts do, becoming able to recognize particular situations, to suggest what actions might be taken within their context, and to forecast with accuracy what the outcomes would be of taking such actions.

All these, even simple memorizing, have in common that they involve people in using their minds (and arguably the job of schools, colleges and universities is to help them use their minds to better effect). However what is significant is the striking contrast between these down-to-earth but quite precise meanings – whichever one is used, it enables us to recognize learning when we see it – and the abstract, general 'definition' espoused by Dearing and his 'prominent researchers'. Precisely because it is abstract and general, it allows for a multitude of interpretations and for flexibility or looseness in how it is applied.

Success in 'learning'

The Dearing Committee was told that a successful student will be able to engage in an effective discussion or debate with others in his or her field, relying on a common understanding of terms, assumptions, questions, modes of argument and the body of evidence. However is there evidence on which to base this statement? On the basis that a successful student is one who is awarded a 'good' degree – a first or upper second, say – we would need to know what a student is awarded a good degree *for*. And for this we would need documented evidence of what actually takes place in examiners' meetings.

Such evidence is in very short supply. However, two years or so ago, the History Faculty Board at Cambridge, concerned that women were under-represented among those gaining first-class Honours, enterprisingly set their students a mock finals examination and then held a mock examiners' meeting on it. As a mock meeting it was not subject to the normal confidentiality restrictions, and indeed it was video-recorded and extracts from the recording were broadcast (BBC2, November 1996).

One of the questions set for the mock exam was on wars. A televised extract from the mock examiners' meeting revealed some of the criteria being used for assessment:

- [The] range of wars discussed was terribly impressive… all sorts of wars I'd never heard of were here;
- I liked some of the allusions to the literature… [such an allusion] always spices up an essay;
- Bringing up the trade wars was, I thought, a very neat idea;

• There was no mention of theories about war, and that might well be a significant failing.

On this evidence, successful students had not merely mastered 'terms, assumptions, questions, modes of argument and the body of evidence': they not only remembered to bring in theories where appropriate, but they found ways of *impressing* and *surprising* the examiners – with the lateral thinking they had brought to their reading, their imaginative interpretation of the question, and their skilful deployment of spicy allusions. (It also appeared that male students were more likely to do this by virtue of being more adventurous in their approach, forcefully pursuing an argument rather than presenting a balanced consideration of a range of points of view, and venturing further in their reading.)

To a considerable extent, what the successful students had done was to get themselves taken seriously by their teachers: their writings were treated as worth paying attention to. They had learnt to be – and established their credentials as – 'historians', and were effectively being assessed on that basis. However the criteria being used were to do with impressing and surprising, with lateral thinking, using their imagination, making neat allusions. These attributes were not, it appears, consciously *taught* to them.

We can now see that Dearing's definition of 'learning' is a remarkably narrow and superficial one. To conceive learning as merely the developing of understanding and of the ability to apply knowledge, is to conceive it merely in terms of the mechanical application of intellect. Drawing on the above example of history at Cambridge, a deeper definition is suggested: that is a successful student of physics, say, is not merely acquiring knowledge and understanding; it is that someone who genuinely takes to the subject *is learning to be a physicist, and in particular to think how a physicist thinks.* This entails developing the intuition of a physicist, the imagination of a physicist, the 'feel' for the properties of matter and energy in their various forms that a physicist has, a physicist's *alertness,* and a physicist's attitude to observation, experimentation and the formation and testing of theories. (Inevitably it also entails developing the loyalties of a physicist and possibly, too, the blinkers of a physicist – so far as the approaches of other disciplines to matter and energy are concerned.) Likewise a historian learns to be and to think like a historian, a lawyer learns to be and to think like a lawyer and so on.

Why conventional teaching is not conducive to learning

How does a student learn to be and to think like a physicist or historian or whatever? What part does the teaching that he or she receives play in this process? A useful approach to answering these questions is to compare the modes of thinking that academics propound to students in their teaching with those that they themselves adopt in their research and their professional discussion and debate.

A historian enquiring into the causes of an event or development works backwards in time. However the results are delivered to students as a narrative going *forwards* in time. A physicist starts with puzzling observations and asks: 'Why is this the way it is?' but succeeding generations of students then carry out experiments, not to address the puzzle but to demonstrate the truth of the theory formulated to explain it. Economists present their subject to students as an analytical one, making use of graphs and equations, but the debates among themselves reveal economics to be a subject rooted in *argument,* not pure analysis. (One's suspicions are aroused by the fact that the material presented to students by the authors of elementary economics textbooks is often not 'real' data drawn from statistics on economic activity but fictitious data on the supply and consumption of butter, or fictitious scenarios: 'Imagine you are running a squash club...'. To a scientist, the idea of presenting fiction in a textbook is preposterous.) To medical students, anatomy is taught in lectures and textbooks as a matter of memorizing the names of parts: they are not taught to think themselves into the minds of the surgeons who did the original naming, or to do the detective work which would reveal the logic behind names. The chemistry teacher who described his subject as a 'factual' one clearly has no notion of teaching his students how chemists think and how they approach problems. Law students find themselves being taught 'the law' rather than how to reason as a lawyer. A student opening a standard text on government or public/social policy will find a definition of 'policy' which is so general and abstract as to be quite useless for research purposes because it doesn't enable you to recognize a policy when you see it.

We do not assert that these generalizations apply to every teacher, every course and every textbook. However there does seem to be a pattern and it does seem to be widespread and deeply entrenched, not least in the gulf that has grown up between teaching and research. These have competing demands on academics' time and attention, and on the company that an academic keeps as a member of a research group and community as opposed to a teacher. Increasingly undergraduate students are taught by postgraduates in order to spare academics for more important work. Dearing attests to the strong influence of the Research Assessment Exercise in deflecting attention away from learning and teaching towards research. The book review section in *The Times Higher Education Supplement* concentrates on scholarly monographs and ignores textbooks almost completely.

What seems to be happening is that academics are using very different 'mental sets' in their teaching, and in their research and professional discussion and debate; and – without telling their students – using the latter, not the former, when they assess students' work and decide the class of degree that a student is to be awarded. Unfortunately the *mental sets that underlie conventional teaching do not help students to learn 'to be' and 'to think like' their mentors.* Students are taught 'subject matter' and left to themselves to acquire their mentors' ways of being and thinking. It follows that a student who gets a good result, who is adjudged to have learnt to be a physicist or historian or whatever, has done so intuitively, by a process of 'osmosis' that comes about through being exposed to physicists and historians – to their ways of being and thinking, to their enthusiasms and methods of inquiry. (Students at Oxbridge and other institutions that operate a system of one-to-one tutorials in the essay-writing subjects will clearly have a head start in this respect.) But these 'successful' students may well not comprehend what they have done or how they have done it. (These are the ones who will provide the next generation of teachers who assess what is not taught.) Dearing's 'successful student', who is able to engage in an effective discussion or debate, will do so despite the teaching that he or she has received, not because of it.

For other students, the failure of conventional teaching to help them to learn 'to be' and 'to think like' has calamitous consequences. This is especially so for all the middling students whose results do not do justice to the work they put in, and who do not have the faintest idea why. Such students end up with a 2:2, which in some institutions has now become stigmatized, a situation reinforced by advertisements for jobs and courses inviting applications from people with a 2:1 or better. So graduates with a 2:2 all too often regard themselves as failures (and decline to attend graduation ceremonies, for example). It is ironic that universities have succeeded in reproducing in higher education the divisive effects of the old 11-plus.

The discomfort that students currently feel emerges clearly in the Dearing Report. Dearing noted that 'fewer than half the students responding to our survey were satisfied with the feedback they got from staff about their work'. Feedback is of course *a means of conveying expectations* – not merely, *pace* Dearing, a means of transmitting information – and dissatisfaction with feedback is a clear indication that expectations and criteria are being concealed from students. Academics are refusing to tell them and to show them what they need to do in order to achieve good results.

The relationship between teacher and student can be characterized in several ways. For example, it can be seen as a relationship between a transmitter and a receiver of information, or as a relationship with a built-in ambiguity, in which the teacher is on the one hand guide, philosopher and friend, and on the other hand judge and assessor. The Cambridge history experiment offers us another characterization: the relationship prior to the experiment is revealed as a game in which students have to work out for themselves what the teacher's expectations are when it comes to exams, what approach, style etc will be rewarded and what will be penalized. The fact that the Higher Education Quality Council's 'graduateness' programme, which had as one of its objectives the making explicit of educational outcomes and criteria, met with considerable criticism from academics and institutions, can be interpreted as an indication that those academics and institutions are attached to preserving this game and its rules.

Several recent developments are perpetuating this unhealthy situation. Students taking fashionable modular, cross-departmental degrees that invariably lack an overall integrating framework, do not know whose ways of being and thinking they are meant to absorb. Nor do students despatched to learning resource centres to teach themselves by means of one of the computer-assisted learning packages into which funds have been poured. And the principle, endorsed by Dearing, that students should manage and take responsibility for their own learning, will inevitably hinder the process of 'osmosis' that appears to be essential to 'learning to be' and 'learning to think like'. Unfortunately Dearing's 'prominent researchers' do not appear to be atypical in their overlooking of 'learning to be' and 'learning to think like' as necessary elements of learning.

The consequence is that the so-called system of higher education is also a system of mystification. It leads to questioning the intellectual integrity of the university system. It is indicative of a widespread and deep-rooted malaise in higher education, of which students are the victims.

Mismatch between the academic world and the world of work

Subjecting students to mystification in the guise of education is but one way in which the university experience is 'mismatched' to the world of work. We contend that there are two other important and indeed damaging mismatches, both again overlooked by Dearing. One is to do with culture and the other is to do with skills.

Culture

A culture can be recognized by, among other things, the attitudes and ways of thinking and looking at the world that it engenders. Among academics, there are, we suggest, two cultures (shades of CP Snow (1959)!) that are particularly noticeable. These are termed 'thematic' and 'analytic': they are commonly found in the humanities and sciences respectively. Within the thematic culture the 'focus' of one's work is a *theme* of some kind. The definitions that are used are abstract and all-encompassing, and the very goal of one's work is to generalize, to arrive at generalizations. The material used comprises views and metaphors, with the addition of a selection of facts, survey data etc, juxtaposed to form a kind of 'collage'. The mode of discourse is argument, commentary, deployed in an attempt to persuade others of the correctness of one's point of view, and those others will apply the test of plausibility, which rests essentially on an appeal to intuition. A best-selling study guide for students which is rooted in this culture describes 'the classic structure for a short essay' as (1) introduction, (2) points against the proposition, (3) points for the proposition, (4) conclusion. Another section captures the essence of the thematic approach with the unforgettable opening: 'What if you want to support your arguments with evidence?'

In contrast, within the analytic culture the focus is a *phenomenon,* not a theme, and definitions are concrete, to enable you to recognize something when you see it. The goal is unification in the sense of mutual consistency – of theories (notably about mechanisms) and observations, and the mode of discourse is the non-judgemental report of findings and discussion of their implications. The material is 'evidence' (even the one-off finding that is elsewhere dismissed as 'anecdotal'), and the test of validity of one's conclusions is not plausibility but consistency. (For more on thematic and analytic cultures, see Levin, 1997.)

In the world of work, however, there is a third culture, different from the two found in the academic world – the practical, issue-oriented culture. Here the focus is neither a theme nor a phenomenon, but an *issue,* a 'what shall we do?' question. Here the purpose of definitions is to establish a common language among those concerned with an issue, so that 'we all know what we're talking about, and we're talking about the same thing', and the goal is to decide on a course of action and make sure that it gets implemented. The mode of discourse is to construct and debate alternative 'scenarios', centred around the perceived need and scope for action, problems and opportunities. Much of the material is to do with the particular circumstances of the issue – that is, it is 'new' – while another major input is the collective experience of those concerned with it. The test of 'validity' is 'Can we do it?', 'Will it work?', 'Will it be acceptable?', 'Will it sell?'

It follows that when they enter the world of work graduates transfer to a practical, issue-oriented culture which is very different from the thematic or analytic culture to which they have hitherto been exposed, albeit – as argued above – in an incidental, mystifying fashion. Are there ways in which they can be prepared for this? Dearing suggests work experience as most useful, but this by its very nature takes place outside the university. It can, therefore, be added on to students' programmes without introducing changes to the curriculum, teaching methods or assessment – that is, with minimum inconvenience to academics and no cultural change whatever within the university. What is needed, are ways of actually 'embedding' preparation for the world of work into curriculum, teaching methods and assessment. In part, this involves giving students an awareness and consciousness of cultures, which will require the teachers themselves to possess such awareness and consciousness of them; in part (and in parallel) it also involves introducing students to skills that are of value in the world of work.

Skills

Dearing sets out four skills 'which we believe… are *key* to the future success of graduates whatever they do in later life'. These four are 'communication skills', 'numeracy', the 'use of information technology', and 'learning to learn', the last being included 'because of the importance we place on creating a learning society at a time when much specific knowledge will quickly become obsolete'. (It can be questioned whether universities are the ideal institutions to inculcate these skills. Not only do academics fail to comprehend 'learning': the PhD thesis as we know it is arguably not the highest form of written communication, and future generations may regard our present-day notion of information technology skills as we would regard the notions of 'typewriting skills' and 'use-of-the-telephone skills'.)

The four skills that Dearing lists should be compared with the list of six core skill areas identified and used by the National Council for Vocational Qualifications: communication, application of number, information technology, improving own learning and performance, working with others and problem-solving. Dearing has manifestly adopted the first four of these and rejected the others. In other words, *Dearing has consciously not included 'working with others' and 'problem-solving' in the category of skills 'key to the future success of graduates… in later life'*. This is extraordinary. It is in remarkable and diametric opposition to the views expressed by employers and the Council for Industry and Higher Education. We take it to demonstrate both the dominance of academic views in determining the content of the Dearing Report and the extent to which those views are out of touch with the world of work. *This section of the Dearing Report actually demonstrates the gulf between the cultures found in universities and the practical, issue-oriented culture found in the world of work* (though it is acknowledged that people in employment need to be able to work in teams). We begin to understand, perhaps, how 'academic' has come to be commonly used as a pejorative term in the world outside the university.

The skills of working with others and of problem-solving are indubitably linked, since in the world of work it is a common experience that it takes teamwork to solve problems. In higher education, by contrast, the emphasis is very strongly on *individual* learning and achievement. Students may find themselves competing *against* each other, and have incentives not to share the results of their efforts, while cooperating with others may lead to charges of copying and even plagiarism. In effect, they are socialized into *resisting* teamwork and collective problem-solving: the university experience actually erodes their value to prospective employers.

There are ways of giving students experience of working with others and of problem-solving, other than sending them away from the university for work experience. We mention two, both of which have been seen in action. One is the TDIU (Team Development in Universities) programme initiated and supported by BP, and organized by *Chalybeate,* a small independent team of personal and professional development tutors. The other is the IIM (Insight into Management) programme organized by the University of London Careers Service. Both of these provide two-day courses in which groups of 5–8 students are given a sequence of tasks to carry out or problems to solve. After each one, tutors assist the groups in looking back at how they worked and in seeing what lessons they can learn. In the TDIU programme, the tasks are physical, outdoor ones, and the tutors are drawn from the *Chalybeate* team, from BP and from the participating universities. In the IIM programme, the tasks are in the form of personnel, marketing, production and advertising games, based on case studies drawn from company training programmes, and the tutors are junior managers drawn from a wide range of companies and government bodies. At the conclusion of either course, despite the brevity, students can invariably see how they developed from a group of individuals into a team, and have become much more aware of the feelings that teamwork engenders in them. These courses have been remarkable because of the enthusiasm and energy generated and for the quality of thought stimulated, as well as for the benefit that students say they derive from them. There is no doubt that elements of this way of working could be introduced widely into degree courses. (Manifestly, the same cannot be said of work experience.)

How universities must change

There is self-evidently a pressing need for research into the nature of learning and what is learnt that is better directed and more sensitive than the research on which Dearing had perforce to rely. It should address the fact that learning at the level of higher education crucially involves learning to be and to think like practitioners of one's discipline, and that this entails the inculcation of particular attributes such as intuition, imagination, 'feel' for one's subject matter, alertness and certain attitudes of mind. Teaching needs to be viewed as 'inculcation' as well as the imparting of knowledge and understanding. And there are implications here for *standards:* the Quality Assurance Agency must appreciate the nature of the inculcation process in different disciplines before rushing into setting and imposing 'standards'.

The discrepancy between the 'mental set' purveyed to students in the course of teaching and that employed by academics in their research and professional discussion and debate must be addressed and resolved urgently, in all disciplines and subjects. This discrepancy, and the fact that academics use the latter, not the former, when they assess a student's work and class of degree, subjects students to mystification when they should be receiving education. It should not be tolerated any longer. The different mental sets need to be made explicit and faced up to. Bridges need to be built between teaching and research. For example, every taught course should have a methodology component of some kind, be it on methods of enquiry, methods of reasoning or methods of argument, whether the subject is an analytic one or a thematic one (and especially in the social sciences, where there is a tendency for thematic approaches to be presented by teachers as analytic). Modular degrees, where teachers from different disciplines may never meet, except at examiners' meetings, and possibly not then, need to be carefully examined. It may be necessary for them to incorporate methodology components that provide integration and an overview. It should be a requirement that all degree programmes incorporate group project work, which offers exciting opportunities for inculcating intuition, imagination and so on.

Emphatically, teacher–student relations should cease to be a game in which students do not know the rules. The need for rapport-based social relationships between teachers and students should be acknowledged, and teachers should receive training in initiating and sustaining them. Students are customarily viewed collectively as 'workload' and (at exam time) as 'artful dodgers': respect for students as fellow-members of learning communities, and indeed as customers, is long overdue.

Effective learning – to be and to think like – is surely a social process, and one that goes beyond merely engaging in 'learning conversations'. Effective learning in universities seems more likely to come about where there is *rapport* between student and teacher. Certainly some teachers will testify to the fact that a successful seminar is one in which there is social interaction among the participants: involvement is stimulated, energy is generated. However the 'prominent researchers' appear to have overlooked this aspect of learning, too. Although many teachers enjoy a good discussion (however, it is known that many are in the habit of turning seminars into lectures), the idea that they should receive training in developing rapport between themselves and students will be a novelty in academic circles.

Another suggestion: learning is a process that necessarily involves 'building' on past experiences and observations – such as when we compare new observations or accounts of those made by other people with memories and recollections of our own. It is also dependent on approaches ('mental sets' or conceptual frameworks) that we have previously used in 'making sense' of experiences and observations. The implication of this is that, if the increasingly diverse cohorts of students, bringing with them correspondingly wide ranges of experiences and approaches, are all to have the opportunity of effective learning, it will be necessary for universities to find ways of discovering what individual students bring with them, so they may relate new materials and ideas and approaches to it. This would involve 'reaching out' to students – the establishing of rapport between teachers and students would be a natural part of this – and possibly redesigning many courses, especially first-year ones, to incorporate at their outset a diagnostic component. This is a far cry from seeing teaching primarily in terms of transmission of information, which Dearing concluded is the way in which many staff still operate. This is a far cry, too, from the experience of mature students who have felt themselves devalued and belittled, sometimes publicly, by their teachers.

There is an unfortunate academic tendency, when considering the question of *participation and access*, to pigeon-hole people by socio-economic group, ethnic group, age and gender, as Dearing demonstrates (despite socio-economic group not being unambiguously ascertainable: when does a child acquire his or her own socio-economic status rather than their parents', and which parent?). We need market research that will identify groups of people in terms of their position in relation to the education market – the spheres of life in which they have experience, and the extent to which they have progressed in making sense of that experience, and the scope for them to develop along these dimensions.

There are profound cultural mismatches between universities and the world of work, and the Dearing Report itself is one piece of evidence of this. Employers seem to be more aware of these mismatches than academics, although they have not been able to put their finger on precisely what is amiss. Academics need to become more aware of their own cultures, and enter into a dialogue with employers on this subject and build bridges with them. It is crucial to embed problem-solving and working with others in university courses – and it can be done – to help graduates make the transition to employment and to help employers to realize the value of universities. If, at the present time, the university experience socializes students into *resisting* teamwork and collective problem-solving, and thereby actually *erodes* their value to prospective employers, this is damaging to society, to the economy, and to students and graduates. It cannot be allowed to continue.

As to *funding*, mechanisms are required that encourage individual academies, departments and institutions to follow the above principles. If these are to be market mechanisms, then the purchasers, both direct and indirect – students, employers, the taxpayer – should have the best possible information about what goes on in universities, in order that they can make informed choices. This is another argument for the demystification of higher education.

Finally, Dearing makes much of 'the importance we place on creating a learning society'. We would argue that *the UK already is a learning society,* and that universities have possibly not had a great deal to do with this. An enormous amount of learning takes place in the 'real world' – in the workplace, in leisure activities, in people's home lives and in their personal relationships. In this world people, individually and collectively, are continually facing up to problems and opportunities, learning ways of dealing with them, and digesting their experiences and trying to make sense of them. The onus should be on universities to reach out to, and learn from, the real world and the people in it, and build bridges between it – and the learning that already takes place within it – and themselves.

Chapter 12

To change the thinking of the world

Peter Danby and Mike Rawlins

Introduction

In this chapter we look at the concept of a learning society from a background of leadership and team development that has taken us into global corporations, business schools, universities and schools. We also work as healers and students of esoteric philosophy and our perceptions are coloured by our understanding of the principles and values of those teachings, particularly by the idea that the very purpose of our lives in this world is to develop and to learn. For us, the balance between material needs and spiritual values is the test for any society or organization that wishes to call itself civilized.

If we follow this 'middle' or balanced way and develop an understanding of how and why we learn, then the learning and growth will follow naturally. We will have created a 'learning society'. We believe that the balance in our modern world is not right and our work is to do with restoring it and to enable people to learn more effectively about themselves and the world around them. We will explain how our work can contribute something to the development of a learning society.

The learning society – what it means to us

When we work with individuals or teams we start by defining the purpose. We believe that there needs to be a clear and common purpose for a learning society too – to enable the lifelong and 'whole' development of each person within that society. That development must be for personal growth but also for the development and evolution of our society towards a common and agreed set of values. In the past, that set of values has been provided by a shared religion. The problem is that the values have been replaced at all levels in our society by words such as share dividend, instant wealth and efficiency.

If the focus of our society is to be learning rather than bank balance, then the leaders of our society must find and express that purpose, and the common and shared values that will lead to it. Where there is no clear purpose, then problems occur at every level. If the departments within a business are working to different agendas, then the sharing of information and ideas that is vital to learning and improvement will not occur; the individual sales team may benefit but not the company as a whole. In the universities, too, blocks in the learning process occur because people are working towards different goals. Some argue that academic excellence is the sole purpose of the university, others seek to develop students for their future work and environments. It leads to friction and waste. And so it is with a society; we become fragmented and isolated.

Why change is important

We believe that too narrow a focus within an individual or a society leads to imbalance and stress. For example, too strong a focus on spiritual purity can lead to unnecessary hardship. Too strong a focus on the instinctive drive for material wealth can lead to an enormous imbalance of wealth but a spiritual vacuum. The distress that we come across in our work would suggest that wealth or personal reputation may not bring long-term and lasting fulfilment. In the companies and groups that we work with, we hear a growing call for greater emphasis on quality of life and social responsibility.

To create a learning society that is prepared to look beyond immediate profit and instant success, there has to be a change in attitude from the self-seeking to the sharing, from selfishness to a sense of responsibility to the community. The implications of this are great – fundamental changes in the values and principles that underpin our current way of living. There are many who could influence or initiate changes but who will resist. There are those who will agree to the need for change 'in principle' but withdraw support as soon as it threatens their own way of life. There are many who would influence changes but have no voice. The people who sleep in cardboard boxes have no voice; the people who earn thousands of pounds a week to play football or gain millions of pounds a year for gambling with our money over a telephone do have a voice. The students who are searching for the tools to help them through life have no voice; the professors whose status and position is based on maintaining their personal level of knowledge above those around them do have a voice. The result is no change.

'No change' is not an option if we are to become a learning society. However the need for change is more than an intellectual argument about learning; it is a battle for our survival and to give our society a soul. The urgency of this need for change was driven home to us by the polar explorer, Robert Swann. He was the first human to walk, unassisted, to both poles; he now works to raise awareness about the environment in the business world. He talks graphically and with such passion about the obscene damage that we are knowingly doing to our environment. It is hard to ignore the message; we can see, hear and smell the evidence all around us. He states his own purpose in life quite simply as 'to change the thinking of the world' and we have been inspired to take up that challenge.

Learning in society – our picture

As tutors and coaches of leadership, management and personal development, we have helped to develop people from every continent (except Antarctica), of every age from schoolchildren to pensioners, and from every position from junior managers to chief executives and board members. The core of our work is a focus on learning. We have developed a model of learning and development incorporating a philosophy and guiding principles that we use for individuals, teams and organizations. We believe that it also reflects the needs of a learning society.

It is easy to sit and pontificate about the state of society; to make sweeping statements and concentrate on what is not perfect. That is not constructive. In much of the business world where we mainly operate, an increasing emphasis is being placed on the development of staff and the development of systems that enable the company to evolve and move forward – to learn. There has been an increase in the idea of coaching to encourage individuals to take responsibility for their own development, and to gain an awareness and understanding of personal and group behaviour. There is a clear incentive, of course, in the perceived need to stay one step ahead of the competition or to find new opportunities and markets.

In the schools that we have been involved with, too, there is a clear impression of a commitment to innovation and constant improvement to give the best possible education with the limited resources available. Part of that drive has come from the 'quest for efficiency' that was born in the Thatcher years and has so shaped our society. Part will have come from necessity and the squeeze on resources that this culture has brought. Part too, though, comes from the dedication, innovation and positive attitude of the people who work in this field. We see a great emphasis being placed on the development of the 'whole child' both inside and outside the curriculum. Only rarely do we see this kind of emphasis in the universities that we have worked in.

We have worked in 10 of the older universities and in a number of departments, in a project sponsored by BP as part of their work in the community. The aim has been to provide opportunities for students to develop certain non-academic or job-specific competences – a knowledge of ourselves, of others, and how to work and live together more harmoniously and productively. These are the 'core' or 'transferable' or 'life' skills that the Dearing Report (1997) mentioned and that employers increasingly look for in their new recruits.

In some of these universities, we have worked with people who have been open to new ideas and learning and recognized the benefits of our work. We have seen, since our programme began three years ago, a great increase in the amount of groupwork in different departments – we hasten to add that this has been as well as, and not because of, the work that we do. We have worked with group projects, and know of examples, in subjects as diverse as history, chemistry and law, where students are marked on their performance in the 'team' as well as on academic results. They are also encouraged to learn about themselves and about group dynamics. Our own programme now forms a compulsory part of certain courses; academics have been quick to seek opportunities to use and expand on the ideas that we introduced.

In other places the reaction has been very different. At one university we were described by a senior member of staff, responsible for innovative teaching, as 'typical arrogant businessmen, coming in and telling us what they think we should be doing'. We are well used to a certain amount of scepticism and questioning. There is a difference, though, between a healthy challenging of new ideas coupled with an open mind, and a closed mind and negative attitude toward changing the status quo. We have seen a strong resistance to the idea that the role of universities might include wider learning and the development of the whole person rather than maintaining a narrow academic focus. Far from providing the role model of a learning organization, these universities seem to present the very blocks which prevent the development of a learning society.

Removing the blocks

Many self-reliance and transferable skills can be developed alongside and during other, more specific, kinds of training or education. This requires teachers or tutors to have an awareness of, and skills in, the learning process.

We suggest that this is an area of weakness, particularly in the older universities where the focus is very much on the academic subject. This, again, is a real problem in the development of a learning society. Academic excellence is important, but neglect in what are known as the softer skills – of behaviour, social responsibility and communication – not only lowers the quality of our lives but also endangers our prospects of enjoying the fruits of that academic excellence.

A similar narrow focus can be seen in businesses where 'growth' has become equated with share price and bottom line. The lack of respect and responsibility for the individual as a person and for the needs of a wider community, or for the environment outside a narrow field of interest, has led to social and environmental problems at local, national and global levels. It is not a case of returning to live in caves or to horse-drawn carriages, but there is a need for balance to be restored. It will be helped greatly by recognizing the importance of understanding the learning process as the core skill for all of us. It will encourage us to see our own work and lives in a different and wider perspective, and respect the thoughts and needs of others. It is particularly important in the universities, which should be the role models of learning in our society.

From personal memories and our observations of working with some 2,000 students at different stages in their university education, this is a period of life when a great deal of development occurs. Many of the students whom we have worked with are taking their first steps in an adult society; there are opportunities to develop social skills in a relatively safe environment. At a time when their contemporaries on different career paths may be experiencing hard lessons about behaviour in the workplace, they are living in a world that is in danger of becoming isolated from the needs of the rest of society. Here we see great potential for change – creating in universities a more open learning environment with academics who encourage learning rather than just the accumulation of disciplinary knowledge.

Creating the learning environment

Underpinning all our work is a recognition that to get the best from any individual, they must first understand and develop the learning process. There are certain principles of learning that we consider to be essential and these manifest in a set of ground rules that provide the practical guidelines for behaviour and standards that have to be present for the components of the learning process to work. These ground rules reflect, for us, the requirements (at a much higher level) for an organization to be considered a learning organization, or a society to be considered a learning society.

In our work we encourage people to draw on their own experience and test what they see, hear and feel against their own logic and their own sense of what is right, and not be restricted by anybody else's view. We draw on theoretical models to help give meaning to what is happening to an individual or a group, but we push people to relate all the models to their own experience.

By encouraging and enabling people to learn from experience, we introduce an emotional dimension, the emotion that goes with taking risks and attempting new challenges. These risks might include the fear of failure, of looking a fool in front of peers or strangers, of losing dignity or respect. By recognizing that learning is more than just an intellectual exercise, and by enabling people to adopt this approach, we offer the opportunity to develop a deeper level of understanding about the subject and themselves, alongside the confidence that comes from accepting a challenge, and facing and conquering fears.

The work that we do provides development at different levels, depending on the individual. There is a skills element but there is also an opportunity to reflect on personal behaviour and deeper levels of self. What will characterize a learning society is when the responsibility for learning is taken by any individual throughout life. At present it is a random and sporadic process with few opportunities for the vast majority, once school days are over. Larger companies invest in the development of self-reliance skills. This encouragement to take personal responsibility for learning does not have to be separate from other education, it is part of it. The concepts of Records of Achievement at school and Continuous Professional Development in the workplace highlight the developments in this area. It is, once again, in universities that we have seen a gap in this development.

Whether it is in the academic world, in the business environment, in religious circles or in the highest levels of government there is a danger of becoming entrenched in one view. Bigotry, alienation and polarity are just some of the results and these are threats to our society. We believe that people should be encouraged to challenge, and for this challenging to occur requires a step change in thinking and attitude. There has to be open government and not just the promise of one where members of parliament are not disciplined for challenging the party line. Professors have to encourage their students to challenge their thinking – and the only way to do that is by example and challenging their own thinking, attempting to show themselves to be less than the absolute authority. Our leaders in all walks of life have to become masters of learning rather than masters of safeguarding their reputation.

Guiding principles

We express our guiding principles as a set of ground rules. The first ground rule is that each individual must take personal responsibility for their own learning. As trainers, we may be able to create a learning environment, but we cannot force anybody to learn. That must be the personal decision of each individual. It may sound like common sense but it does take people at all levels a while to come to terms with. We grew up with the idea that it was the teacher who was responsible for our education. We would be given a body of knowledge and be expected to learn it and to prove that learning by regurgitating it in some exam. As a society, we still place great store in that method, and it has its place. Again from our experience in working with schools, there seems to be a good balance now between the necessity to learn, by rote if necessary, but also to develop an inquiring mind.

Through other ground rules, we encourage openness and honesty. This is not just openness in the sharing of ideas and information but also in the expression of thoughts and feelings. If we are to learn about the impact that we have on other people, then it is vital that we hear from them what that impact is. This is not a comfortable process. In the business world, companies have devised all manner of ways to give and get feedback without upsetting people. We encourage constructive feedback. This is accepted practice in many parts of the business world, but not encouraged from our experience in universities. Here, it seems, criticism is often the tool to enhance personal status at the expense of another. If we are to become more aware of ourselves in relation to others, and adapt our behaviour, then we need feedback. Even on short two-day programmes, an awareness of personal potential within a team can help build confidence and enable individuals to reach decisions on their personal development or careers. There are visible changes in people as a consequence of the programmes. It can be something of a shock to the system – or a sharp reminder – that they have a personal responsibility for their own development.

We introduce rules that encourage constructive and supportive behaviour in a confidential and safe environment. We are looking to create an atmosphere in which people are prepared to take risks. A major problem lies in transferring skills and new habits; people are prepared to practise with us, in our environment, but not back at work. The environment is vital for any learning whether in an organization or in society as a whole and the ground rules of personal responsibility, honesty, openness, and constructive and supportive behaviour are missing in many areas that we work. It is a slow process but it can be changed. Where we have worked in a team or an organization, then changes can be seen and people recognize the value of creating this type of organization – it impacts on performance and on the quality of life.

A final ground rule invites individuals to 'respect the thoughts, feelings and needs of others'. It is a rule based on the 'Golden Rule' and is an example of applying the simple but hard rules of ancient wisdom. Respect for the ideas, feelings and values of others is the very heart of a learning society, but is so often missing. The behaviour of our leaders in the House of Commons, the behaviour and words of all forms of the media, set the tone for our social order. Lack of respect for people of all ages and cultural backgrounds and the environment pervades our world. In our programmes it often requires constant reinforcing to ensure that individuals are aware of the impact that their behaviour and words have on others. We have a sense that there is a growing wave of discontent with this behaviour and find both students and managers seeking to restore the balance. It is easy to think that we can do nothing at our level, that it is someone else's responsibility. That is not the way to change. Yes, we can encourage each individual to put their own world in order and influence those close to them. However to create the right conditions for a learning environment, the example has to be set by the leaders, and they must feel the pressure to change. That is our responsibility.

The way ahead

To create a learning society requires the commitment of the leaders and people of that society. There need to be champions of change for things to happen and to drive through the barriers. We have talked in general terms about society and the need for a clear purpose, shared values and a way of working together to achieve the common goal. Change can be driven from below as well as from above. We see that as the responsibility of each individual, to make the choice as to what they do with their lives and whether they view it as an opportunity to develop and grow.

Developing people is no longer the remit of just schools and universities and we have to compete with a growing number of agencies in this 'business'. That element of competition leads to improvement and many of these lessons have been taken into the academic world. There is scope for much more of this exchange. It seems strange that the business world has picked up on the idea of learning rather than teaching, and universities – perceived as the centres of learning – resist it so strongly.

We now have some 2,000 evaluation forms, which tell a very powerful story. Quite apart from the team skills and the confidence that the programmes encourage, students have valued the style of tutoring that encourages them to contribute in a safe environment. They have learnt a great deal about themselves and others – unlike many tutor groups that are together for longer but where no effort is made to draw lessons from the way that people interact or work together. They have also learnt something far more important, and that is how they can learn more effectively. They will be better prepared to learn from any experience and to use that process to improve performance in any competence area.

At one university a tutor who has worked with us asked to conduct research into the potential of the described learning process. She was refused because the work was not discipline-specific. To us, that is an example of the attitude towards learning that we need to change. In other universities there has been a cutting-back of teaching staff and a focus on research, with less contact time between tutors and students. The universities are being forced to focus on research at the expense of teaching and learning because that is where their funding comes from. By using more groupwork and encouraging personal responsibility for the learning process, the teaching load can be reduced. There is a temptation to pass the buck upwards and to call on the government to increase funding and to change the system to encourage teaching rather than research. However, changing attitudes may be easier than changing government policy, even in universities.

Changes *are* occurring. Universities are obliged to respond to pressures from society, employers and students. Change is also being forced by the increased workload on university staff. As in any change of style or approach, there needs to be an investment of time and energy to make the change work. Through induction programmes for new teaching staff, through programmes to encourage research supervisors to balance research with learning, and through the persuasion of professors to let themselves be challenged by their students, things will change. Having the sponsorship of BP enables us to help in that process. Our solution is to focus not just on providing students with the skills and awareness of learning; it is also our aim to provide tutoring skills for academics, so that they become the role models for the future.

In the business world, there is much to feel good about. The concepts of continuing professional development and of personal responsibility for career development are widely applied. The development of people is a key strand in business strategy and opportunities are increasing all the time, but there is still much to be done to restore the balance. Changes have occurred, not through any shift in thinking, but rather because companies see this as the best way in beating the competition – of mobilizing all their resources to keep the 'bottom line' growing. We do not believe that we can build a learning society on those values and it can lead to incongruence between 'the inspirational words' and 'the unchanging actions'.

We shall continue to encourage people to take responsibility for their own learning and to apply the principles and ground rules that we use on our programmes. While adhering to the principle of respect, there is also a need to make a few waves and ruffle a few well-groomed feathers. If we are serious about building a learning society based on the principles and behaviours discussed here, then we cannot afford to wait for the lead to come from the higher echelons of our society. We must apply them ourselves and encourage those around us to do the same. It is our personal responsibility and we cannot push that on to others. The guiding principles that we encourage are not meant to be recited, but translated into our work and our lives. If we each take that responsibility, then we will not only have a learning society but a world in which it will be worth while learning.

Chapter 13

Independent learning confronts globalization: facilitating students' development as learners[1]

Terry Evans and Alistair Morgan

Introduction

As both researchers and teachers we are concerned with issues of student learning. Especially we are concerned with research and teaching in the adult ODE (open and distance education) sector, where the majority of students are 'mature age' and part time (Evans, 1994; Morgan, 1993). The university contexts in which we work, as is the case for many other colleagues in other educational institutions, have been influenced by the rhetoric and realities of new technologies. In the case of our work in universities, there is a concern for constructing what might be called the 'new educational technologies' in ways which encourage and sustain educational dialogues between teacher and students (Evans and Nation, 1993a; Morgan, 1997). Most of the new educational technologies are based on computer and communications equipment, and the technologies which surround them, in the world at large. The surge of computer and communications technologies is said to be 'globalizing' economic, social, and political relations, and drawing educational institutions and systems into the fray.

Our aim in this chapter is to consider critically issues of globalization and relate these to issues about independent learning and lifelong learning, and to raise matters and questions concerning educational practice in a 'globalized' and/or 'globalizing' field. The tensions which flow from the above matters will be related to the need for a critical appraisal of the ways in which teachers, administrators and student support staff facilitate learners' development. We argue that these ways will need to be consistent with the 'new times' – the emerging cultural and technological contexts. Facilitating student development as learners requires a consideration, not only of the diverse contexts and needs of students, but also of the potential resources and strategies which are emerging: these include forms of collaborative and peer group learning mediated through new information technologies.

Globalization

The term 'globalization' abounds in the popular press and, particularly, in the rhetoric of government and business leaders. Despite, or perhaps because of all this popular rhetoric, settling the term conceptually is not an easy task. Often, it seems, in education and elsewhere, the terms 'globalization' and its derivations are used interchangeably with the term 'internationalization' and its derivations. However, the terms cannot be synonymous, logically, although they have some important shared elements. We can clarify the position by drawing on some of the collected work of Bartlett, Evans and Rowan (Evans, 1995, 1997; Evans and Rowan, 1997a, 1997b, 1997c; Rowan and Bartlett, 1997; Rowan et al, 1997). They have recognized the problematic nature of the concepts of globalization and, for them, its corollary 'localization'. It can be seen that the process of globalization is derived historically from the development of transport and communications – specially those involving electronic, digital, satellite and/or computer-based systems. This has contributed to what Giddens (1991) and others have called a 'time-space compression' to the extent that people may now 'feel' connected to remote and distant events by virtue of the immediacy of the mediated representations they can experience of those events. For example, satellite or Web-based news and information services connect people in one geographical location with events which occur in other 'connected' parts of the globe irrespective of the distances involved. Although the rhetoric of globalization is usually expressed in economic and financial terms – there is no doubt that these are very significant elements – we contend that, for educators at least, it is the social and cultural aspects which turn 'globalization' into a meaningful entity for people in general. It is in this sense that they become citizens of the 'globe' and interact, usually virtually and often vicariously, with their fellow citizens.

Globalization and forms of ODE

It can be understood that forms of ODE are both potentially, and evermore actually, players in globalizing education. Traditionally, these forms of education have often seen that their 'distances' included ones of an international kind which render them amenable to global practices. Likewise, their 'liberation' from having to see their practices as being bounded by the walls of an institution, or the boundaries of a campus, means that they often have educational and administrative practices and values which are adaptable and amenable to global operations. However, it is important for us to state that we are not only addressing institutions which call themselves 'open universities' or say that they are distance teaching organizations. We contend that, partly due to the technologies and consequences of globalization, all universities are shifting some of their practices into forms of ODE education. They are all doing so partly to use computer and communications means to create their institutions into, at least partially, 'global' educational entities (Edwards, 1994; Evans, 1989, 1995, 1997).

Evans and Rowan have argued that:

> The non-dependence on contiguity of the educational practices of ODE institutions – coupled with the increasing pressure to find 'new markets' and sources of income, and the 'competitive threats' of other institutions in 'their marketplace' – has led these institutions to contemplate policies and actions which can be seen to operate simultaneously on two levels. At the first level they respond to the processes and procedures of a concept widely defined as globalization. At the second level they negotiate contextual issues associated with both their own location and the site(s) and context(s) of their educational activities – 'localization'. They, therefore, respond to a need to be 'globally competitive', as well as racially, culturally and 'locally' sensitive (Evans and Rowan, 1997c).

We wish to take this position a step further by considering the needs and contexts of learners within globalizing forms of education and relating this to ideas from independent and lifelong learning. Our reason for so doing is that, if we recognize that there is a need to be 'racially, culturally and "locally" sensitive', then this implies that understanding the needs and contexts of learners is crucial, and yet it appears to be an extremely problematic matter for those who wish to teach globally. It is not merely a matter of the global expanse itself, although this in itself is daunting, but rather, the fluidity and diversity permitted or encouraged by the new technologies that are intensely problematic for those who advocate forms of, for example, student-centred learning. It seems that, on the one hand the new educational technologies permit greater capacities for interaction and communication (at a distance), but at the same time they sweep into the virtual classroom a potentially bewildering array of learners with whom most educators would find it perplexing to deal with.

At this point we should say that the conclusion we have just made about educators is based on our views about teaching and learning (Evans, 1994; Evans and Nation, 1989, 1993b; Morgan, 1983, 1993). These views eschew notions of behaviourist forms of programmed learning or instruction as being appropriate for the ways we like to teach (and learn) in the sorts of educational context we are discussing here. One of our motives for writing this chapter is that it seems probable to us that, given the difficulties of coping with a globally distributed and diverse student body, institutions will encourage or require their staff to look to forms of instruction which use only the conceptual and knowledge elements of their courses as the basis of their pedagogies, and ignore the students' needs, contexts and meaning-making capacities. In this sense, we fear that there is a danger that global forms of education will become 'programmed instruction' based entirely on the instructing institution's cultural, economic and political location and interests. Not only will this be an inferior education, but it will also contribute powerfully to a cultural hegemony which will crush local languages and cultures (George, 1997; Guy, 1997; Thaman, 1997; Wah, 1997). Given these concerns it seems appropriate to consider how the theories and practices of independent and lifelong learning can be marshalled to construct forms of global education which value and incorporate the diversities of students, needs and contexts.

What is independent learning?

What is independent learning? Is it a coherent educational philosophy or is it such a broad term with so many meanings, a slogan even, that it offers little for theorizing our practice and improving our practice? Independent learning means all sorts of things; people use it with very different meanings and assumptions about the nature of learning and the aims and purposes of post-compulsory education.

For some people, independent learning means the separation of the teacher and learner, with the learner studying at home, in libraries, using new technology sources of information etc. Independence in this sense is a basic characteristic of ODE. Course teams in ODE put considerable effort into the design of self-instructional materials which are supported by various forms of tuition and counselling provided at the local level. With this meaning, any debate about a move towards independent learning is usually as a disguise for financial constraint and the worsening of provision for tutorial support. Financial cutbacks in conventional institutions are also likely to drive this notion of independent learning.

For other academic staff, independent learning means something very different. Students are taking greater responsibility for *what* they learn and *how* they learn it and are developing autonomy and self-direction in their learning (Boud, 1981). A move to greater student autonomy in learning raises questions of curriculum and assessment and particularly issues of power within educational institutions.

With these contrasting meanings of independent learning, ranging from a teacher-centred curriculum followed by a student in isolation, to a student-centred curriculum and lifelong learning, the term needs to be used with care if it is to be of any value for critical reflection on our practice. The discussion of variations in project-based learning (Morgan, 1983) around the dimensions 'curriculum construction' and 'control of learning' would seem relevant for examining the widely differing practices adopting a label of 'independent learning'. Curriculum construction, derived from the work of Bernstein (1971) on the classification and framing of educational knowledge, refers to whether the curriculum and learning activities are structured within academic disciplines and subject areas or around 'real-world' problems and issues. Additionally, the dimension of control of learning relates to whether students or teachers (or in negotiation) decide the content of the independent study, how it is to be tackled and how it is to be assessed.

A recent example of an independent study module, from a study of changing assessment practices in Scottish higher education, gives some idea of how a degree of learner autonomy can be designed into a university curriculum.

> The Independent Study Module... provides students with an opportunity to design, with support from and in negotiation with a specialist tutor, their own module. The module proposal, which includes learning outcomes, rationale for undertaking the module, pattern of study, resource requirement, has to meet formal requirements in terms of level of study, coherence and relevance to the rest of the student's approved degree programme. It does mean, however, that the student has the opportunity to negotiate a set of learning outcomes which they can show evidence of achieving, through agreement of the kinds and forms of evidence that will be produced and the ways in which these will be assessed by the specialist tutor. After approval of the proposal the student works to produce the evidence required by the jointly designed assessment specification (Hounsell *et al*, 1996: 23).

In this case the student is taking some responsibility for the learning within a broad framework of the institution. In practice, most learning within institutional contexts will be some form of interdependent learning, certainly where assessment and accreditation are involved. If we look further towards Candy's (1991) notion of self-direction and lifelong learning, he suggests the term includes personal autonomy, the capacity to manage one's own learning, a context to allow control by the learner and the independent pursuit of learning outside formal institutional settings. Hence, for Candy, independent learning in the complete sense can only be established outside formal settings.

The concern or 'drive' for independent learning comes from a diversity of sources; these range from a long tradition of autonomy in learning in philosophy of education, to curricular reforms in the 1970s and demands for student-centred relevant curricula. In the late 1990s this concern comes from discussions about transferable skills, graduateness, vocational considerations and in the UK, the Enterprise in Higher Education Initiative.

Students' development as learners

How do students change and develop as a result of their studies? How do they develop autonomy in learning and how can this be facilitated? The research of Saljo (1982) on conceptions of learning and the longitudinal studies of Perry (1970) and Morgan and Beaty (1997) provide insights into the complex area of student development. The changes identified are that students move from holding absolutist conceptions of knowledge towards developing more relativistic conceptions of knowledge. There are changes in confidence, competence and control in learning. Students are changing from relying on the institution (or teacher) for control of their learning to exercising more of their own control over their learning. As students feel more confident and competent to make decisions for themselves, so they develop more independence from the teacher; they feel able 'to go it alone'.

The crucial question is how can we as teachers facilitate these changes? Carl Rogers' book, *Freedom to Learn*, still provides important insights for critical reflection on our teaching/learning practices. Rogers stresses people's natural potential for learning and how this is realized when there is a personal intrinsic motivation and when external threats are at a minimum. And to quote Rogers (1969) 'Independence, creativity, and self-reliance are all facilitated when self-criticism and self-evaluation are basic and evaluation by others is of secondary importance'.

Research using approaches to studying and course perceptions' questionnaires (Entwistle and Ramsden, 1983; Ramsden, 1992) shows strong relationships between good teaching, freedom in learning, openness to students, realistic workloads and students adopting a deep approach to learning. So teaching learning activities which embody these characteristics within a supportive learning milieu or departmental style (Parlett, 1977) are likely to encourage reflection in learning and development of students' independence in learning.

Independent learning and new technology

There are many claims that learning with various forms of new technology will transform the quality of teaching learning and encourage student interaction in learning and help develop independence in learning (Mason, 1998). These forms of technology may be with multimedia instructional materials on CD-ROM or with CMC (computer mediated conferencing) between students and tutors or students selecting their own programmes on the WWW (World Wide Web) from the 'virtual universities'. There are even predictions of a new paradigm for education, as Collis (1996) explains: 'Tele-learning, connecting to resources and people via telecommunications, will be an important instrument of a new paradigm of educational organisation and of a new social conception of learning, in ways similar to the paradigm shifts accompanying the printing press and the popularisation of books some centuries before'.

New technology certainly provides challenges for students to engage in independent learning from the range of meaning associated with this term. However what are the realities of students' experience of learning with these new technologies when viewed from the learners' perspective? It seems far from clear that aspirations of teachers and course designers will be met if we look at students' learning experiences in more depth.

A recent study of resource-based learning on CD-ROM with Open University students (MacDonald and Mason, 1997) highlights the problems some students encounter of being overwhelmed with vast amounts of information and unclear about their task as learners. Similar problems are likely to exist for students in conventional institutions as they are required to make greater use of global databases and electronic libraries available on the WWW. At one level these students could be seen as lacking certain information handling skills. However, the underlying issue seems to be about how they perceive learning and their development as learners. These students seem to be constrained by a conception of learning which is concerned with a reproducing orientation to study, rather than seeing learning as a process of constructing meaning and going beyond the information provided.

If we look to virtual communities and collaborative learning on-line, what sorts of issue confront the independent learner and what are the learners' experiences? Is there the potential for local CMC groups to resist the globalizing pressures we suggest may occur? And how do on-line learning communities develop? These are, of course, complex questions which will be difficult to answer. The research of Wegerif (1995) into collaborative on-line learning identified that the 'construction of a community with a shared communication style' was the crucial factor for the success of collaboration on-line. This may suggest how local communities could develop on-line and thus challenge globalizing tendencies from a global educational institution.

Conclusion

In this chapter we have raised some of the current concerns about globalization and localization and to what extent learners can both participate in a 'global university' as independent learners, as well as using the potential of computer-mediated conferencing to counter tendencies of cultural hegemony. As educators, in designing our practice under the label of 'independent learning', we need to be aware of the assumptions we are making about the curriculum and who controls it. Learners will need 'just enough support' to enable them to move on and develop a degree of autonomy in learning, and competence and confidence as lifelong learners.

Notes

1. An earlier version of this chapter was presented at The Improving Student Learning Symposium, University of Strathclyde, Glasgow, September 1997.

Chapter 14

A defence of teaching against its detractors

Richard Dunne

Introduction

Universities in the UK are under pressure to change their approach to teaching. I want to describe those pressures, argue that they derive from lack of attention to a model of teaching and learning and describe an appropriate model. It is clear that changes in university teaching can be attributed in part to increases in student numbers. Successive governments in the UK have pursued a policy of expansion for higher education so that, currently, around 30 per cent of school-leavers continue studying beyond the age of 18 (planned to rise to 50 per cent). This expansion has created new challenges for teachers in universities who now have to work with less homogeneous groups of students. The situation is made more difficult by reduced funding with its consequent larger teaching groups.

The combination of these factors (wider range of students in larger groups) has provoked an interesting response. Courses are increasingly designed to be 'self-directed' so that students become 'autonomous' or 'independent' in their learning. In one respect, this is simply an administrative response to diminished resources, but there are other factors. Methodological change has coincided with the imposition of a new vocabulary by government agencies as well as groups of educators. These encourage the framing of educational objectives in terms of 'core skills', 'transferable skills', 'lifelong learning' and 'employability'. It has also become fashionable to plan courses as 'modules' so that relatively short, discrete units of work are successively assessed. This has the perceived advantage of tracking students' performance, consistent with demands for quality assurance.

Contemporary emphasis on core and transferable skills in higher education has raised questions about whether these are best developed in addition to subject study or as part of it. There is also substantial literature about their identification and assessment. In fact, there are more fundamental questions to be asked. It is not clear that the pursuit of these 'skills' is justified. It is an example of how it is too easy to lapse into what I will call 'cognitive diagnosis'.

Cognitive diagnosis

Educators have come too readily to assume both that knowledge resides in individuals and its current state can be diagnosed, in categories, from observations of performance. On the basis of a particular performance an individual is credited with understanding a rule that is then assumed to be the cause of the original performance. The danger in this view is that linguistic practices, which are, in fact, social constructions, are mistakenly thought of as mechanisms of individual cognition. Social practices that have been learnt in connection with, perhaps, problem-solving, are confused with abstract principles that can be used to describe those processes. This is the myth of cognitive diagnosis.

Cognitive diagnosis is associated with a distinctively individualistic tradition that is compelled to assert cognitive performance (or students' understanding of certain concepts) as deriving from an inner competence or ability. Cognitive development, in this view, is associated not with concrete practice but with abstractions. Successful *performance* on tests is supposed to indicate the learner's 'having' the corresponding cognitive structure, and this assertion has gained innumerable adherents in spite of a host of conceptual and practical difficulties. The more recent manifestation of this asserts that identifiable performance implies the possession of a 'skill' that is independent of context: it is 'transferable' or 'core'.

There has been a plethora of experimentation that is interpreted from the 'mental diagnosis' viewpoint. Very few authors have attempted a principled analysis of the same phenomena from a social constructive view of knowing. This neglect has itself contributed to a widespread way of thinking about how children come to know and, therefore, what should happen in classrooms, and this same mode of thinking intrudes into course design in higher education. Course design in higher education exhibits the mistake of formulating descriptive categories and assuming that they are explanatory: the error of mistaking social practices for mechanisms of individual cognition; and the mistake of assuming that principles are somehow able to define their own future application.

This dangerous set of faulty assumptions has been incorporated, without analysis, into the overwhelming majority of curriculum materials, classroom practices and testing technology. What is missing in this account is any persistent attention to the nature of the external objects with which people interact, and this is the problem that besets current reforms in higher education. Although the past three decades has seen a changed perspective in developmental psychology, it has not entered the collective consciousness of course planners in higher education. The new perspective goes beyond simply recognizing the learner as a social being who learns through interactions with others: there is instead an appreciation of how such social life provides a framework for interpreting experience. Some aspects of the new perspective are comforting and *have* been incorporated into the collective consciousness. To begin with, it seems to legitimize social talk, so students who work with materials for self-directed learning are encouraged to discuss their work with others. This is then interpreted as a core skill, offering the (mistaken) opportunity to diagnose the skill of, say, teamwork or communication. Discussion among students is assumed to contribute to learning in ways that were previously associated with tutorials conducted by university teachers. What is lacking in this conversion is how the university tutor, in fact, expresses culturally significant ways of examining important objects that are not available to novices working alone.

The academic disciplines

The academic disciplines are culturally determined ways of looking at the objects that have been selected as being significant for that discipline. Practitioners are inducted into those ways of understanding the subject. Experts continually demonstrate to novices (their students) how to think in relation to the significant objects. Novices persistently model those ways of knowing. When traditional university teaching has been successful this has been its essence. This approach is not negotiable: it is fundamental. It can be modified in new circumstances, but the essence must be retained. What has happened is that course developers have not appreciated the significance (for teaching) of knowledge as a social construction. In fact, they have tried to remove 'teaching' from the curriculum to replace it with 'learning', failing to see that learning simply cannot take place without teaching. They are making the mistake of assuming that knowledge resides in materials. They are also making the mistake of 'cognitive diagnosis'. When they see students learning, they note, say, that it involves communication. They then assume that communication is the cause of their learning and attempt to install it as a core skill to be developed and identified across subjects. They fail to recognize it is communication utilizing the technical language of the discipline about objects that have been selected as significant in that discipline, that is, the concrete practice of the discipline.

Education is a process of induction into coherent ways of perceiving the world. This does not imply that there are a fixed number of such disciplines: new ones can emerge. However this, in turn, does not imply that any random collection constitutes a discipline. A discipline is characterized by the agreement of its practitioners about what constitutes appropriate theoretical constructs (explanatory ideas) and tests of truth (see Kuhn, 1970 for a discussion of 'paradigms'). The process of induction involves demonstration by the expert and modelling by the student, a process I will call *assisted performance*.

Assisted performance and explanation

Induction into an academic discipline is achieved through a cognitive apprenticeship that can be formalized as *assisted performance*. A sound understanding of *explanation* is a predicate for assisted performance in teaching. That the word 'explanation' is part of everyday vocabulary tends to suggest that the term is unproblematic, but when people (including teachers) claim to explain something, they are rarely doing so. Most often they are describing, not explaining. They may be describing in a different way from that which caused confusion, and it may be helpful, but this does not make it an explanation.

In order to establish some important ideas about explanation, I will imagine that I have a bottle in front of me and I will tell you something about that bottle. It is green. This is an observation statement: I have told you about something that I have observed. I have given you a description (not very exciting but even so a description). I will now assume that you ask 'Why is it green?': a question that prompts me to *explain*. I now make a choice from a number of different approaches. I may say:

Light is comprised of all the colours of the rainbow; clear glass allows all these colours through and your eye is affected by all of them together and recognizes the result as white. But glass can be made so that it stops many of the colours going through – it absorbs many of the colours, and the only light that reaches your eye is that which goes through. In the case of this bottle, it is made in a certain way that all the colours except green are stopped, so only the green light hits your eye (you see only green light) and you say that the bottle is green.

There are, of course, many other possibilities (green bottles protect wine; the manufacturer wants a distinctive bottle for marketing purposes) but I want to concentrate on just one. I have adopted a particular *orientation* to the problem of why the bottle is green: one taken from physics. We can think of it as a story, and this is a reasonable label to use because it is not a question of whether it is true but only of whether it is engaging, helpful and productive. Some stories are better than others; some have greater credibility with a given community; but each is chosen for reasons other than 'truth'. It is not that they are untrue, but that 'truth' does not exist in any absolute sense (see Kuhn's (1970) account of the nature of science). For my explanation to be worth while, I have to do something to enable you to adopt my point of view. I have to instruct you in the essential features of the story and to convince you that this is a story that is worth adopting as a way of approaching the problem (although I do not pretend I have done this adequately in this purely illustrative example). In fact, I will not stick with the word 'story' because I want to use vocabulary that is more technical than this. I will refer to it as a *theoretical construct*. So I can now say, rather than I must persuade you of my story, that I must orientate you to my theoretical construct.

I am, of course, assuming that the situation I am referring to is well known to the listener. This assumption is quite reasonable in such a trivial case (people tend to know what a bottle is). As long as the problem is known to the listener and provided the orientation has been established strongly, the listener will locate the problem as an example of the wider perspective given by the orientation: connections will be made between the problem and the new orientation. This making of connections is stimulating: I will refer to it as *energizing*.

In classrooms it is most often necessary to give students experience of the very item to be explained, so that there is something for the theoretical construct to connect with. This is the role of the teacher in formal education: to focus learners on the nature of the problem, orientate them to a theoretical construct and assist them in energizing. This process of explanation, appropriately carried out, is what I refer to as *assisted performance*. It is illustrated in Figure 14.1 with a horizontal plane and a vertical plane. The horizontal plane represents the set of activities that were designed to focus learners to the nature of the problem; the vertical plane represents the theoretical construct. Connections must be made between these two aspects. The initially separate planes need to be connected: I refer to this as *energizing*. However this assertion is too easily made and does not do justice to the complexity of how people learn. It is for this reason that I want now to develop these ideas in some detail in the following sections:

1. Instructional representation and mental representation.
2. Focusing on the problem.
3. Orientation to the theoretical construct.
4. Energizing.

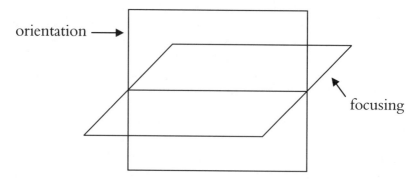

Figure 14.1 *The intersecting planes of focusing activities and orientating activities*

1. Instructional representation and mental representation

What do I do when I engage with a problem? The easy answer is that I think about it: that I make connections with other ideas; compare things; put things in categories; look for similarities; calculate; and so on. I want to suggest a slightly different way of talking about this: I want to suggest that it is not the problem that I engage with, but it is some mental representation of the problem. Why not just be satisfied with saying that the learner engages with the problem? It does seem that if I do not suggest that the initial act of coming to know something involves a mental act, then there seems to be an even bigger difficulty. To deny this mental act means I have to accept that every experience (touching, seeing, hearing) is a new one: that is, that there is no possibility of economically organizing my experiences and building on them. So, although the acceptance that some mental act takes place gives us a difficulty, it is one that I prefer to struggle with rather than the difficulty I have to confront if I insist that the learner engages with the problem or the actual experience.

Let us begin by characterizing every task as having two aspects, each of which is cognitive. The first aspect, which I have begun to discuss above, is 'getting to know what it is about'. This involves getting access to the nature of the materials or the problem or the presented situation. The second aspect I might call 'thinking about the problem', which is acting on the initial representation by placing it in a framework of more general ideas by comparing things, putting things in categories and so on. The initial act of getting to know the nature of the task does not involve just some simple act of touching, seeing or hearing: it involves some kind of mental representation of the situation. The manner in which the learner encodes the experience, that is, the representation from all possible representations that is actually adopted, depends on how it is presented. The purpose of schooling is to design and present the activity or problem in a manner that makes it amenable to further analysis. This further analysis is, of course, the application of the theoretical construct – and this also needs teaching

In Figure 14.1 the horizontal plane in the diagram is to be identified with the initial instructional representation. It is not simply that the teacher provides experience of the problem; it is that attention must be paid to the choice of an appropriate instructional representation for the problem. The instructional representation is a combination of a range of experiences, activities, discussions, phrases, pictures, diagrams, apparatus and so on.

Where does this leave us with respect to the vertical plane in that diagram? There is a further need to give direction to the learning by putting equal emphasis on the process of orientation to the theoretical construct. The theoretical construct needs teaching effectively, and so it, too, needs careful instructional representation. The theoretical construct is taught in order to place the learning experience (that is, its representation) in some wider context. This is summarized by Hausman (1982):

> A good explanation reveals the extent to which the happening to be explained is linked to some other more general phenomena. The more extensive and systematic the linkages (and thus the more general the phenomena to which the happening is linked), the better the explanation.

I need now to pause in order to clarify the above. The role of the teacher is to provide instructional representations so that learners will construct corresponding mental representations. The instructional representations can be thought of as having two distinct purposes. One is to enable learners to make sense of the nature of the problem (this I call *focusing on the nature of the problem*). The other is to provide learners with an appropriate theoretical construct (this I call *orientation to the theoretical construct*). It is important to appreciate from this section that it is the *instructional representations* that are designed by the teacher; and the purpose of these is to enable the learner to make corresponding *mental representations*.

2. Focusing on the problem

Let us now look carefully at the horizontal plane in Figure 14.1. In my discussion of 'explanation' I assumed that the learner had sufficient grasp of a problem that it was possible to ask some questions seeking explanation. For instance, the question 'why don't I fall off the Earth?' would be asked by someone who was aware that I don't fall off the Earth and that there was some reason to suppose that I might. It is this specific teaching of the problem that I call 'focusing the learner on the nature of the problem'. In order to provide focusing, the teacher must construct an integrated set of focusing activities that, together, constitute the instructional representation for focusing. It is as a result of this work that the learner achieves a mental representation of the problem (or task) which will be the subject of further action.

I can summarize how an *instructional representation* for *focusing* on the nature of the problem $[IR]_F$, produced by the combined effect of a number of focusing activities (f_1, f_2, f_3 etc), is designed to achieve a *mental representation* of the nature of the *problem* $[MR]_P$. This is the meaning of equation 14.1:

$$[IR]_F = \{f_1 + f_2 + f_3 + \cdots\} \rightarrow [MR]_P \qquad (14.1)$$

3. Orientation to the theoretical construct
The theoretical construct that is selected by the teacher for the learners to use in explaining the phenomena on which they are focused needs specific teaching: I say that the learners need orientation to the theoretical construct. This orientation is achieved by the provision of an integrated set of orientating activities which, taken together, provide the instructional representation for orientation. The purpose of this is to enable the learners to achieve an appropriate mental representation of the theoretical construct.

I can summarize how an instructional representation for orientating to the theoretical construct $[IR]_O$, produced by the combined effect of a number of orientation activities (o_1, o_2, o_3 etc) is designed to achieve a mental representation of the theoretical construct $[MR]_{TC}$. This is the meaning of equation 14.2:

$$[IR]_O = \{o_1 + o_2 + o_3 + \cdots\} \rightarrow [MR]_{TC} \qquad (14.2)$$

4. Energizing
The idea of energizing, being the act of bringing the theoretical construct to bear on the problem, is the third component of my model for designing instructional tasks. The above discussion clarifies how, to be more accurate, I should refer to energizing as being that mental action that brings the mental representation of the theoretical construct $[MR]_{TC}$ to bear on the mental representation of the problem or task $[MR]_P$. However this is not a one-way process. In doing this, both the nature of the problem and the theoretical construct are further clarified. This is the meaning of equation 14.3, and especially the two-way arrow in that item:

$$[MR]_P \Leftrightarrow [MR]_{TC} \qquad (14.3)$$

The model for designing instructional tasks

The conjunction of the three items above, understood in relation to Figure 14.1, constitutes a model for designing instructional tasks. It indicates that planning for teaching requires specific attention to the two instructional representations as separate events. It denies the prevailing assumption that theoretical ideas should be generated (in some ill-defined way) by sufficient concrete experience, and asserts that the theoretical construct should be sufficiently rehearsed to be applied to the problem which itself has been made sufficiently familiar for it to be further clarified. The theoretical construct, then, is not some spontaneously generated personal construct (which is likely to be unfruitful) but a construct that is known to produce powerful insights. Careful attention must be paid to the manner in which the instructional representation for orientating is designed: it must be amenable to energizing, and not only by those students who are popularly described as 'creative' or 'able'. The representation must be designed so that 'energizing' can be demonstrated by the teacher and the students can be enabled to model it. The several activities that make up the instructional representation for orientating must be designed in anticipation of the instructional representation for focusing. This is the purpose of emphasizing Figure 14.1: the two separate planes (the vertical and the horizontal) are not intended to be for ever separate: the whole point of the careful design of the programme is for them to be connected.

This approach to teaching can be identified in successful, traditional approaches in universities. It was not universally successful because it was not consciously planned. I have designed a model to capture its essence so that it can be used for planning and for advocacy in the face of competing demands. What it allows is for the organization of university teaching to be analysed in a principled manner. When pressure of numbers demands a reduced amount of contact with students, we can specify what it is that can be offered as self-directed learning and what it is that demands contact with tutors. I am reluctant to specify this absolutely, but it is clear that a substantial part of 'focusing' can be undertaken with a minimum of supervision. It is this experiential work that demands lengthy engagement with ideas, apparatus, models, text and other objects – and this can be done alone or in meetings of groups of students. It can also be tested in straightforward ways, sometimes with single word answers, multiple choice items or short descriptions.

Orientation, on the other hand, needs contact with tutors, but it does not need small groups. This is where the large lecture, meticulously prepared and delivered, comes into its own. Energizing is different again. It is not possible without a defined level of mastery of the focusing material and orientation to the theoretical construct. When these have been mastered, energizing requires relatively small groups: but these will not necessarily take place very often. Nor will it necessarily be possible to specify exactly when they will occur in pre-course planning. Their timing will depend on an assessment of students' performance in focusing and orientation.

Both orientation and energizing may be planned to refer to more than one module of work. It can be seen, then, that any demand for each module to be of the same level or same type should be resisted. Modules could be specified for a series of focusing activities without the particular intellectual activity implied by orientation and energizing. Focusing can include a substantial amount of rote learning or routine laboratory work. It is not less important: it is crucial. However it is different, and universities must retain the flexibility and autonomy to be able to design courses that deliberately provide assisted performance.

One of the most important points being illustrated here is that learning can be thought of as effective only when it involves linking experience with an explanatory theoretical construct. It is clear that those students who we judge to be 'able' are those that do this with minimal teaching. Faced with students who are less obviously 'able', educators have become used to the idea that there should be a reduction in the demands of the task with there being a consequent emphasis on 'focusing activities' via experiential learning. This is wrong-headed. It is these students who need a greater emphasis on orientation to the appropriate theoretical construct and on energizing. The wider range of students entering universities should be an incentive to design courses that are more obviously theoretical, not for them to be more practical. This does have implications. The theoretical content must be very carefully taught: it cannot be left to chance whether or not the students 'pick up' the theoretical construct and apply it. Theoretical constructs must be meticulously taught by those who are expert in the methods of 'assisted performance'. University teachers need to study pedagogical science to understand how close to being right they were in their traditional approach to teaching.

What is important here is that meaning and understanding are facts of public life and that cultural patterns (of how language and objects and practices are linked) provide a template for human action. Skills are developed in the context of specific cultural patterns; the most significant cultural patterns are those provided by the established disciplines. Skills are not transferable simply by wishing them to be so. Nor are they transferable because they can be referred to with a single label (like 'communication'). They are transferable to the extent that 'transfer' is part of the extant cultural patterning. However they remain skills that are learnt in a specific cultural context. The challenge is to plan for them to be taught in such a way that they are more widely accessible.

PART 3

STRATEGIES FOR TEACHING AND LEARNING – IN PRACTICE

Chapter 15

Introduction

The first three chapters in Part 3 are written by professional educators and researchers. Although each chapter has a research-based approach, they offer arguments and strategies for changing and developing specific areas of practice. They also offer practical ideas for ways of achieving change and managing student activities.

In Chapter 16, Alex Radloff and Robert Fox describe the need in Australia for 'Unstuffing the curriculum to make room for lifelong learning skills'. They describe a familiar picture, with higher education facing major challenges – a move from élite to mass education, an explosion of knowledge across disciplines, the need for accountability to stakeholders, competition between universities for students, globalization of education and work, rapid technological development and resource constraints. They argue that one outcome of these challenges is the 'overstuffed curriculum' – courses which have too much content and not enough opportunity for learners to develop transferable, lifelong skills. These include critical thinking, problem-solving, communication and interpersonal skills, all of which are demanded by employers, and are needed and valued by students. The chapter is based on a number of workshops, presented in Australia, South Africa and the UK, that address the consequences of the overstuffed curriculum for learning, that examine some of the symptoms and suggest strategies to help instructors who are 'clinging to the content' to rethink the way they plan and teach their courses.

Teamwork or groupwork has already been suggested as an important aspect of higher education, especially as many employers regard teamwork as central to activity in the workplace. Gaining the ability to work effectively in teams will, therefore, be a good preparation for future employment. It can also be a powerful method of learning within higher education, both for the acquisition of disciplinary knowledge and skills and for the strengthening of core skills such as writing or oral communication. In Chapter 17, Jim Cooper and his colleagues consider the topic of 'Promoting core skills through cooperative learning' from a North American perspective. A number of core skill areas are identified, such as appreciation of diversity, critical thinking, development of teamwork and developing a sense of community. The chapter includes an examination of the research base indicating that small-group instruction has a powerful effect on these and other outcomes, and explores how small-group (cooperative and collaborative) learning can be used to foster these skills.

In Chapter 18, Dai Hounsell and Mary McCulloch report and reflect on 'Assessing skills in Scottish higher education' – the findings from a recent survey of 21 higher education institutions in Scotland. This provides an illuminating picture of initiatives to assess students' skills. These skills include communication and presentation skills, the interactive and interpersonal skills associated with group and teamwork and skills relating to student involvement in assessment. The chapter, although reporting research findings, has a highly practical emphasis and provides ideas for those wanting to know how to monitor and assess the skills of their students, and what the problems are likely to be.

Chapters 19–22 are provided by academics providing skills-oriented courses for undergraduates. They were specifically selected because of their interest in writing about their own practice and also because of the detailed attention that they gave to it. Although each chapter is set in a disciplinary context, it is the focus on planning for specific, and different, skills outcomes that is important. Hence, all these chapters should be of general interest to anyone who wants to understand more about the rationale of university teachers for attending to skills, or who wants to develop their own practice.

'Teams in Law on trial' (Chapter 19) by Sue Prince, provides an overview of changes that were made to teaching and learning within the first-year Law curriculum at the University of Exeter. The main objectives of the changes were to make more efficient use of staff time and to develop the acquisition of communication skills in students. First-year courses were modified to incorporate a series of workshops which replaced traditional tutorials. The chapter looks at how the teaching of processes such as teamwork affected the curriculum. More importantly, it examines how these skills were integrated into the curriculum, and analyses the ways in which they were transferred to the learning of law, through the device of written group projects, in order to enable students to become more effective, independent learners.

South Africa has recently emerged from an oppressive political and educational system and many students who had been educationally disadvantaged by the previous system are now entering the field of higher education. For most, English is a second, if not a third language, although it is the language of learning at the University of Zululand. Such students have a narrow history of passive rote learning. In Chapter 20, 'Self-evaluation as a tool for developing lifelong learners: a South African perspective', Lee Sutherland describes a writing programme for a first-year course in Historical Studies. The programme aims to promote greater meta-cognitive awareness in students, with a view to developing their capacity to learn more efficiently and to producing lifelong learners. Despite the particular background, many of the issues of pedagogy will be familiar elsewhere.

In Chapter 21, 'Professional studies and career development: attitudes to learning in Fine Art', Heather MacLennan describes how providing learning experiences to satisfy needs in the world of work has become a priority in planning programmes. Graduates need abilities that enable them to manage their own careers, show confidence, communicate and deal with people. There are also many aspects of the liberal studies arts programme that students and staff would defend as vital for future lifelong learners. For these reasons, work experience programmes focusing on enterprise skills as part of professional studies provision have been carefully integrated with the more esoteric aspects of the subject-based Fine Art programme. However this has not been without some tension which, in turn, reflects conflicts of values within the wider culture.

The overarching demand placed on students in schools of architecture is to design. For an architect the skill of design is a *sine qua non*. Chapter 22, 'Teaching architects', by Simon Unwin, presents the methodological background of a course called 'Analysing Architecture', offered as a module by the author in the Welsh School of Architecture and published in 1997 in a book of the same title. The aim of the course is to help students understand architectural design, and thereby be better equipped to take on design themselves by analysing examples in a structured way. The course extracts some of the underlying conceptual themes (intellectual patterns and strategies) evident in works of architecture, providing the beginnings of a framework for categorizing the powers of architecture as a creative activity, and for generating a repertoire of seminal ideas that may be explored and developed in design. In doing this, the course aims to produce students intellectually equipped to continue increasing their understanding of the workings and the potential of their discipline throughout their professional careers. In this way, they will be well-prepared as members of a learning society.

Chapter 23, the final chapter of the book, 'Drawing together the threads', provides a discussion of some of the central issues and arguments and considers what these might mean overall to a learning society in higher education.

Chapter 16

Unstuffing the curriculum to make room for lifelong learning skills

Robert Fox and Alex Radloff

Introduction

There is growing recognition by governments and industry that knowledge is the passport to prosperity and social stability and that, if countries are to survive and flourish as part of the 'global village', they have to become learning societies. The creation of a genuine learning society is dependent on all its members working together to create and use knowledge for the benefit of all. 'Lifelong learning' is an essential requirement for a learning society and, for economic, social and personal reasons (Candy *et al*, 1994) a growing number of adults expect to learn in formal or informal settings throughout their lives. The catch cry that learning must continue from the cradle to the grave or, more accurately, from womb to tomb, is now well accepted by educators, employers, professional bodies and the general public. And the focus of such lifelong learning is the development of the core skills needed for effective membership of a learning society.

Skills and attributes needed for lifelong learning

Learners, whether they be first-year university students straight from high school or mature-age students returning to formal study or embarking on it for the first time, need to have the skills and attributes which will help them become effective lifelong learners. Research on student learning in higher education has identified a range of learner skills and attributes which are linked to success in learning (Boekaerts, 1993; Janssen, 1996; Pintrich and Schrauben, 1992; Radloff and Styles, 1997; Thomas, 1988; Zimmerman and Martinez-Pons, 1992; Zimmerman and Paulsen, 1995). Skills for lifelong learning include the ability to:

- set realistic and personally meaningful learning goals;
- identify and use appropriate resources to help them achieve their goals;
- have well-developed reading, writing and study strategies;
- have effective information retrieval and selection skills;
- use computers and information technology appropriately;
- plan and monitor learning and adapt strategies if needed;
- reflect on and evaluate the outcomes of learning;
- recognize and deal effectively with obstacles to learning.

Attributes for lifelong learning include:

- a belief in the self as a competent learner;
- meta-cognitive knowledge of personal strengths, weaknesses and preferred ways of learning;
- persistence in the face of difficulties or obstacles;
- a desire to continue learning beyond the immediate requirements of formal study.

Thus, for effective lifelong learning, learners should be self-directed and self-regulated with a wide repertoire of learning strategies and the willingness to 'learn how to learn'. Many students, however, do not have these skills and attributes and, therefore, need help to develop them.

Learners need help to develop lifelong learning skills

The need to include the development of lifelong learning skills as part of university study is well-recognized. According to Candy et al (1994), lifelong learning skills and attributes should 'form part of the core of all undergraduate courses, clearly articulated in course aims and objectives'. McKeachie et al (1986) state that 'every [university] course should help students become aware of strategies for learning and problem solving. An explicit goal of education throughout the curriculum should be to facilitate the development both of learning strategies and problem solving skills and of effective strategies for their use'.

Such help is most effective when it is offered as an integral part of university study (Chalmers and Fuller, 1995) rather than as stand-alone or 'remedial courses' (Kaldeway and Korthagen, 1995). Indeed, in a recent review of learning skills interventions, Hattie *et al* (1996) conclude that, for intervention to be effective, it should occur in the context of the discipline and use learning activities which are directly related to the content being learnt. This view is supported by the literature on situated cognition which stresses that knowing and doing cannot be separated since all knowledge is the product of the activity, culture and context in which it is developed (Brown *et al*, 1989). It follows, then, that lifelong learning skills should permeate the whole curriculum rather than be isolated in a single or specialized course. They are also best developed 'just-in-time', when learners have actual need for them in response to particular learning or assessment demands (Tate and Entwistle, 1996).

All too often, however, lifelong learning skills are squeezed out of a course as the discipline content increases and fills the available time. Candy *et al* (1994) suggest that one way to avoid this squeeze is by placing these skills in the centre of the course, as illustrated in Figure 16.1. Radloff (1996), on the other hand, in line with the notion of situated learning, proposes integrating discipline content and lifelong learning skills, as shown in Figure 16.2.

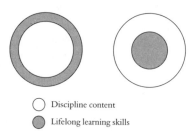

○ Discipline content
● Lifelong learning skills

Figure 16.1 *A representation of the need for change in the content of higher education provision*

Source: Simplified after Candy *et al* (1994)

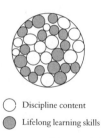

○ Discipline content
● Lifelong learning skills

Figure 16.2 *A representation of the need for change in the content of higher education provision*

Source: Radloff (1996)

The obstacle of the overstuffed curriculum

Unfortunately, despite the growing evidence that lifelong learning skills are best developed as an integral part of discipline study, instructors often assert that there is no room in the curriculum to help learners develop such skills because discipline content must take precedence. As a result, many students struggle (and sometimes, fail) to meet the intellectual challenges of university study because they have not been provided with the opportunity to learn how to learn. Moreover, as instructors attempt to 'cover' more discipline-specific content, they may actually make it more difficult for students to master the material. For example, a survey of over 4,000 first-year students from seven Australian universities found that 40 per cent of them considered that the course workload made comprehension of the content difficult (McInnis *et al*, 1995). Faced with too much content, students may resort to surface learning, making little attempt to understand concepts and ideas. Indeed, overstuffing the curriculum may put students off learning altogether, thereby making it less likely that they will continue learning beyond the end of formal study and thus become lifelong learners.

Suggestions for unstuffing the curriculum

In order to overcome the obstacles to effective learning caused by an over-stuffed curriculum, instructors must address the following questions: 'How can we ensure that students are self-directed learners – active and reflective about their work and responsible for their own learning?'; 'How can we encourage learning for understanding and transfer?'; and 'How can we encourage students to develop positive attitudes to, and skills for, lifelong learning?'

Our suggestions are based on our own teaching experiences and our work in academic staff development, instructional design and distance education. They are also supported by research on student learning and tertiary teaching (Angelo, 1993; Gibbs and Lucas, 1995; Ramsden, 1993; Shuell, 1990). Underlying our suggestions is an assumption about the general approach to teaching which instructors adopt. Effective instructors are systematic in the way they conceptualize and plan their courses and teaching, have a reflective approach to their work, and seek and value feedback about their courses and teaching.

We focus on ways in which we can 'unstuff' the curriculum to allow for the development of lifelong learning skills under two broad headings: course planning and design; and instructional activities and strategies.

Course planning and design

Know your learners

Develop an overall map or 'thumbnail sketch' of your students. The main categories to guide you are:

- age range;
- gender mix;
- cultural backgrounds and diversity;
- student expectations of the course;their expectations of their role and that of the instructor,
- previous learning and study experiences, especially within the subject area and discipline culture of the course;
- the numbers taking the course and the mode of study (full or part time, on-campus or off-campus).

This sketch obviously becomes more complex as variations in students increase. Rowntree (1990) provides a useful sample thumbnail sketch.

Gauge the workload of the course

You need to consider what the course is worth in terms of its study load and time you expect students to devote to this course in relation to their total study load. A useful guide is to match the number of similar or equivalent courses students are required to take per semester. In very general terms, a full-time equivalent undergraduate student will take four courses of study per semester. How many hours of study on average do you expect students to be doing per week? Divide these hours by four to gauge the hours per week your students can be expected to spend on your course.

Another guide is to match the credit points the course is worth to find a benchmark for study load. In some universities, dividing the credit points by two will provide a general guide to hours of study expected. It is interesting to note that a number of research findings suggest that we poorly match our expectations of workload with the time students require to study (Svinicki, 1990; Chambers, 1992; MacDonald-Ross and Scott, 1995). Feedback from distance education students at our university also supports this view.

It is also important to consider how realistic the expected workload is not only in relation to the course objectives, assessment and credit points but also in terms of students' other commitments. Research into how students spend their time outside class (de la Harpe *et al*, 1997) points to a worrying trend, with many students reporting spending more time in paid work than engaged in study-related activities.

Clarify the rationale and context for the course

Ask yourself these questions and answer them in three or four sentences:

- Why is this course worth studying?
- How does it fit into the course(s) of which it is part?
- How does the course relate to other courses in the programme(s)?
- Are there prerequisite courses to this course?
- Is this course a prerequisite to other courses?
- Are there other courses that parallel this course and that should be taken at the same time?

By answering these questions you get a clearer idea of the underlying rationale for the course and where the course fits within a larger context.

Identify the learning outcomes

Ask yourself what you want your students to know and be able to do after completing this course and what you imagine or believe students will want to know and be able to do when they have finished this course. Write no more than three or four outcome statements in terms of knowledge, skills and attitudes. By sticking to a few key statements on outcomes, you will find it easier to maintain a firm grasp on the general focus of the course. Ensure that learning to learn and lifelong learning skills are included in learning outcomes.

Match assessment tasks to learning outcomes

The assessment tasks should match the learning outcomes you have identified. The weighting of the different assessment tasks should also reflect the importance of the corresponding objectives and outcomes.

Develop a marking scheme which outlines how you will assess student learning. Clarify the main levels of marking based on overall objectives and outcome statements. Later, when you develop details about the course, you will be able to elaborate on assignments and the marking scheme. At this stage, however, generate a series of key concepts/issues/skills and so on that make up the core of the course.

Decide what to include and exclude in the course

It is often difficult to determine what to keep in and what to leave out of a course. Try writing a list of all items, issues, topics, concepts etc you would want to include in the course, taking into account the three or four outcomes you have listed for the course. Divide your list into three columns: essential, recommended and supplementary. The limitations of a semester course mean that despite your desire as the subject specialist to include more than is realistic, your main task is to pare down the curriculum to its essential elements to make room for the development of learning to learn skills.

Determine the conceptual framework

Develop a conceptual framework to show how various components in the course interrelate and how the overall course relates to other courses and the programme(s) of which the course is a part. Look for unifying or fundamental concepts, skills and ideas and make these explicit in your outline. Develop a strategy that enables you to refer students back to this conceptual framework frequently during the semester. One useful way of doing this is to produce a visual representation of the course, such as a flowchart or 'mind map', and refer to it regularly throughout the semester.

Structure the content around key concepts

Review your list of essential components and group these in some way that helps students understand how the course is structured. A course can be organized in a number of different ways including theoretical domains to more practical or applied positions; simple, familiar concepts to more complex, less familiar ideas; major themes to more specific themes or issues; or by related themes or in chronological order. Different subjects lend themselves to different strategies for organizing content and these need to be addressed specifically within the context of the various disciplines and their associated cultures.

Organize the course systematically

Consider how the content will be covered in the semester. Draw up an overall plan of when various parts of the course will be covered and how the course is organized including times/dates for class contact, assignment due dates, examinations, field work, collaborative project work etc to be undertaken. Remember to schedule in public holidays and class-free-from-contact times. Build in enough time for regular review and reflection and time to integrate the various components in the final weeks leading up to the examinations. Allow time for out-of-class activities such as groupwork, reading and research.

Select set texts in line with course objectives

Students are often expected to read a great deal and to cover too much ground (MacDonald-Ross and Scott, 1995) and this can lead to a superficial approach to studying (Salijo, 1982). It is, therefore, important to select texts and readings for students to work through very carefully. Consider what students will gain from the text. For example, will the text reinforce the course content, elaborate or extend class activities, or provide contrast to class activities etc? How does the text relate to the overall aims of the course, how should students use the texts and readings and what should they do with the information once they have read it?

Also consider the suitability of the selected text in terms of user-friendliness and readability (Hartley, 1994; Rowntree, 1990). Hemmings and Battersby (1989) and Wright (1987) provide useful guidelines for selecting textbooks and readings. Finally, how you present prescribed reading influences student behaviour. Research carried out in our institution across a number of disciplines has shown that how and indeed, whether, students read set texts is influenced by the emphasis the instructor places on the importance of reading *per se* for learning and on the perceived value of particular reading for mastering the course content (Kirkpatrick and Mulligan, 1996).

Instructional strategies and activities

Encourage active student involvement in learning

Select learning activities which require students to engage with the content (Wang and Palincsar, 1989). Activities such as paired problem-solving, 'jigsaw', reciprocal teaching, question generation and role-play can be used as part of regular class activities to encourage student participation in learning (Meyers and Jones, 1993). (Details of some of these activities which are dependent on collaborative work are outlined in the next chapter.) Allow time in class for short self-marked quizzes, buzz groups and pauses for reflection. When setting reading assignments, provide specific questions to guide student reading.

Encourage students to work cooperatively

Help students to learn with and from one another by encouraging cooperative learning as an integral part of your course (Bossert, 1988). Set group learning tasks and provide opportunities for students to work together on activities outside class time. Discuss with students how to maximize group learning and overcome common problems in working with others. Encourage students to work in informal study groups or set up a 'study buddy' or a student mentoring system. Make explicit the connection between working effectively in groups and the skills needed to be a successful team member in future professional life.

Structure class times carefully to maximize learning

Students learn most in classes in which they are actively involved. Traditional lectures are least likely to provide opportunities for active student involvement (Gibbs, 1992) so consider dispensing with the traditional one-way delivery lecture and use the lecture time for small-groupwork, self-instruction perhaps using self-paced or computer-based material, or for working in pairs on a specific topic or on problems or case studies using resources such as textbooks, journals, audio-visual material and other forms of information technology.

Increase feedback but reduce formal assessment

An effective teaching programme requires two-way communication between students and instructors, therefore, provide opportunities for regular feedback about learning and teaching throughout the semester. The Five Minute Exam or Half Sheet Response are both quick and easy ways to monitor progress, even in large classes. These and other strategies for assessing student learning are described in Angelo and Cross (1993). Encourage students to seek feedback from a variety of sources including peers and provide opportunities for students to develop skill and confidence in self-assessment as part of regular class activities. Help students distinguish between formative and summative assessment.

Emphasize the importance of learning to learn and lifelong learning

Build into your classes explicit instruction and opportunity for practice with feedback in strategies such as strategic reading, effective writing and study strategies necessary for successful learning of your subject. Include also 'generic' strategies such as goal-setting, time and self-management. Discuss how 'experts' in your field think and learn. Make transparent and model the strategies you use for developing understanding and skill in your subject. Provide opportunities during class for students to talk about how they learn and the strategies that work for them. Emphasize the 'how to' and not just the 'what' of the subject.

Conclusions

The suggestions we have made for helping students become effective learners by 'unstuffing' the curriculum are, for the most part, neither very radical nor necessarily expensive to implement. They do, however, require a systematic approach to course design and planning and thoughtful application of what we know about learning and instruction to foster self-directed learning and encourage lifelong learning. Most importantly, they depend on a genuine interest in, and commitment to, teaching and a concern and respect for students.

The challenge for instructors is to reflect on their current practices and to have the courage and will to change those which may actively prevent their students from becoming effective lifelong learners. In order to do so, they themselves need to develop the skills and attributes of lifelong learners. Universities for their part should ensure that there is appropriate recognition and reward given for learning and teaching which emphasize the development of learning to learn, the core skills needed for lifelong learning. Only then will universities truly embody and reflect the ideals of a learning society.

Chapter 17

Promoting core skills through cooperative learning[1]

James L Cooper, Pamela Robinson and Yvette Miyazaki

Introduction

This chapter will not explicitly present the history of interest in core skills and lifelong learning; nor will we try to give a definitive discussion of these areas. We acknowledge that there is much debate concerning the formal properties of core skills and their relationships to lifelong learning (Longworth and Davies, 1996) and we leave the tasks of explanation and historical background to other chapter authors who are more qualified than us.

We believe that core skills (cognitive, affective and other skills which help individuals develop their fullest potential) are important. In this chapter we identify what we believe is a powerful pedagogy which can be used to teach a variety of core skills in a relatively cost-effective manner. The technique is called cooperative learning. After discussing this area, we outline eight areas of core skill development identified by major international bodies as important in the context of cooperative learning, and consider research evidence in relation to each. Finally, we briefly describe 4 of the more than 100 cooperative learning techniques which have been identified by researchers and practitioners.

Cooperative learning: definition and characteristics

Cooperative learning is a structured, systematic instructional strategy in which small groups work together to produce a common product (Cooper *et al*, 1990). The technique differs from many forms of small-group instruction in two ways. First, cooperative learning stresses explicit structures to promote *positive interdependence* among group members. Such structures include:

- requiring students to teach one another discrete portions of the assignment;
- rewarding all group members who achieve at a pre-stated standard (eg, if all achieve 90 per cent or higher on a task, all members receive a small grade bonus);
- assigning different roles for each team member (eg, team leader, recorder, resource provider).

Second, most cooperative learning adherents also believe that cooperative activities must build in structures to discourage the 'social loafing' that often occurs in many forms of small-group learning, when team members realize that they can get by without significant effort because their harder working team mates will do more than their fair share of the task. This 'loafing' is often associated with small-group techniques in which instructors offer undifferentiated team grading, so that all members receive the same grade, regardless of differing levels of commitment and productivity. To combat this social loafing phenomenon, many cooperative learning adherents require that course grading be totally, or largely, based on *individual accountability* – that is, although there may be some reward for group performance, most course grading is based on individual testing and assessments of each individual's contributions to group projects and products.

Cooperative learning tends to be more teacher-centred than other forms of small-group instruction. Debate continues among small-group researchers regarding the relative efficacy of the more structured, teacher-centred approaches to instruction and the more constructivist, student-centred techniques often identified as collaborative learning (Matthews *et al*, 1995). Readers interested in more detailed discussions of cooperative learning research and practice may wish to examine the Abrami *et al* (1993) and Cooper *et al* (1990) workbooks, and the Robinson and Cooper bibliography (1995).

Core skills fostered by cooperative learning

As suggested above, there has been a considerable amount of research in the area of cooperative learning, and in this section we offer a research-based assessment of how the technique has impacted on eight core skills areas identified by such groups as the Association of Creative Education Foundation, UNESCO, the European Initiative on Lifelong Learning and the World

Initiative on Lifelong Learning. These skills areas range widely, from those which relate to the development of a caring and community-based society, with tolerance of difference, to the more traditional academic skills such as 'critical thinking' and writing, or oral presentation. Overall, they provide a comprehensive rational for undertaking groupwork in higher education, both in terms of living in a democratic society and of cognitive growth.

1. Citizenship

The late Ernest Boyer made a strong case for cooperation in his 1987 book *College: The undergraduate experience in America*. Boyer asserted:

> If democracy is to be well served, cooperation is essential... and the goal of community is essentially related to the academic programs, and, most especially, to procedures in the classroom. We urge, therefore, that students be asked to participate in collaborative projects, that they work together occasionally on group assignments... and that special effort be made to create conditions that underscore the point that cooperation is as essential as competition in the classroom.

2. Liberal education

In 1993, Alexander Astin, arguably the most influential American thinker in research on higher education, published his book, *What Matters in College: Four critical years revisited*. In an exhaustive analysis of hundreds of student and institutional variables which might promote such goals of liberal education as commitment to helping others, interest in cultural events, appreciation of diversity, problem-solving and leadership development, he found that: (1) curricular issues were not specifically related to most outcomes; and (2) the best predictors of positive outcomes were student-student and student-faculty interactions.

Astin has spent considerable time since this study specifically promoting the case for cooperative learning in all levels of education, but particularly focusing on higher education.

3. Sense of community

As we examine the world in which we live, it is difficult to feel encouraged about the state of the social fabric. Whether it is racial issues in the USA, religious and social issues in Northern Ireland and the former Yugoslavia, tribal conflict in Africa, nationalism in the former Soviet Union... it is clear that we have a long way to go in developing a sense of community and shared concern for others. Researchers at the University of Minnesota, Concordia University (Montreal) and the University of Tel Aviv have published research syntheses which document the efficacy of cooperative learning in fostering such affective outcomes as pro-social behaviour, altruism, social support for others, coping with stress and general psychological health. A key element of cooperative learning is the insistence on building structures designed to foster positive interdependence, the notion that we are our brothers' keepers. Our experience, and that of hundreds of colleagues, is that students exposed to well-designed cooperative learning teams develop friendships with people who they would never have the opportunity to meet in other college classes, and that these friendships continue long after classes end.

4. Appreciation of diversity
Related to developing a sense of community is the issue of tolerance of, and even appreciation of diversity. Our colleague, Rachel Hertz-Lazarowitz, wrote movingly about teaching a class using cooperative learning at the University of Haifa in Israel (Hertz-Lazarowitz, 1995). Half of her students were Arabs and half were Jews. These students began the class highly distrustful of one another. One of the problems that kept students at a distance was the simple difficulty of Jewish students remembering Arab names, and vice versa. As part of the team-building activities used in most cooperative learning activities, students in Dr Hertz-Lazarowitz's class shared their personal stories of growing up on the Left Bank. Students then worked together in mixed Jewish/Arab teams in a group investigation cooperative technique (see below), researching such questions as ethnic identities, the history of Arab/Jewish conflict and the Intifada in Palestine. She reported that students increased their tolerance for each other's differences.

One key to effectively developing appreciation of ethnic, gender and other diversity appears to be working together *as equals* on a common task. Cooperative learning attempts to build in structures to ensure that all group members can contribute something to the ultimate group product or outcome. For example, many instructors form groups so that each team member brings something to the group that is needed to successfully complete the group's work. One member may be a good writer; another may be strong in mathematics or computers. If people are placed together in positions of differing levels of power (such as the unsuccessful attempt to bus students in American schools), the research suggests that such groups may actually exacerbate tensions between diverse groups. The single most replicated finding in the literature of cooperative learning (Johnson and Johnson, 1989) is that it improves racial/ethnic relations. Recent work at the college level suggests that it can have this same effect in fostering positive gender relations. Abrami *et al* (1993) also report that cooperative learning can positively influence attitudes of 'regular' students towards those with handicaps.

5. Critical thinking

Debate continues regarding the definition of critical or higher-order thinking. Some argue it is discipline-specific (McPeck, 1981); others claim that it is a relative generic skill which may be applied across many settings (Kurfiss, 1988). There is also debate whether it is deductive, or inductive. Whatever the definition, there appears to be wide agreement concerning factors which contribute to its development, factors which are incorporated in cooperative learning structures. Cooperative learning requires students to actively engage with academic content and to manipulate and elaborate on conceptual material in a social setting. Students are challenged by peers to develop cognitive processes such as problem clarification and justification, and evaluation of arguments and positions. Diverse critical-thinking theorists and researchers in America (such as Kurfiss, Paul, Halpern and Palincsar) all agree that cooperative, small-group instruction is a powerful tool in fostering critical thinking. Researchers and theorists associated with the cognitive development theories of Piaget, Perry, Belenky and Vygotsky also call for more cooperative, small-group instruction in primary, secondary and tertiary education.

6. Writing skills

Kenneth Bruffee (1978) has written very eloquently about the impact of cooperative and collaborative learning in fostering writing skills. He argues that small-groupwork helps students write for an authentic community of peers who speak the same language. For Bruffee (1983), writing 'is not an inherently private act but is a displaced social act [so collaboration with peers] is not merely a helpful pedagogical technique incidental to writing. It becomes essential to writing'. Nystrand (1986) found that students working in groups evidenced greater gains in essay-writing and made higher-quality revisions in their writing by the end of the term than did students working alone.

7. Oral communication skills

Public speaking is among the highest reported fears of both adolescents and adults (surpassing that of death and cancer) (Cuseo, 1996). Many students, particularly women and members of minority groups, are often the least likely to contribute to class discussions. Cooperative learning provides a safe environment for the voices of these groups to be heard. Successful practice in small groups can lead to more risk-taking in whole-class work, whether it involves volunteering an answer in class or making an oral presentation. The research on public speaking lists practice in small groups with feedback from the group as one technique of decreasing apprehension and increasing performance skills of students in larger-group settings (Neer, 1987).

8. Numeracy and scientific knowledge
A recent report of science and mathematics literacy by the National Assessment of Educational Programmes places 13-year-olds in the USA, Ireland and Scotland in the bottom third of 15 countries listed. National reports in many countries point to the lack of skilled workers having adequate science and technology knowledge to prepare business and industry for the technology-based society of the future. In a recent meta-analysis of college-level research on science, mathematics, engineering and technology performed at the University of Wisconsin-Madison, cooperative learning was reported to have 'robust' impacts on general academic achievement, liking for the subject matter and increased course and programme retention. This meta-analysis mirrored at least three meta-analyses conducted in the 1980s and 1990s by researchers at Johns Hopkins, the University of Minnesota and Concordia University (Montreal). This indicated that cooperative learning classes had powerful impacts on a number of achievement and attitudinal measures at the primary, secondary and tertiary levels. However, the Wisconsin study was the first to specifically focus on science and mathematics at the college level.

Further work indicates that cooperative learning and other forms of small-group instruction may have particularly powerful impacts on women and minorities in fields historically dominated by white males (including engineering, mathematics and science). Based on this and other research, the National Research Council's Committee on the Mathematical Sciences in the Year 2000 called for revitalization of mathematical science education, re-examination of the traditional lecture forms of instruction, and getting students more actively involved in the learning process (Steen, 1992). The American Medical Association committee on preparing physicians also calls for 'reduction in lecturing' and 'replacement of lecturing by small-group instruction' (Project Panel on the General Professional Education of the Physician and College Preparation for Medicine, 1984).

Types of cooperative learning

There are over 100 specific cooperative learning techniques or structures (Kagan, 1994). The variety of techniques can range from very quick, informal techniques to quite elaborate term- and year-long formal structures, and from teacher- to student-centred procedures. We offer a sampling of these procedures, along with recommendations concerning when each might be most appropriate.

1. Think-pair-share
This is a very easy procedure to embed in almost any class, ranging from large

lecture, to laboratory, to discussion sections. After some period of directed teaching or discussion, the instructor asks students to individually reflect on an issue, question or problem. After a minute or two of reflection, students are asked to share the results of their thinking with another person sitting nearby. Finally, pairs of students share the results of their paired discussion with the entire class. This technique has tremendous flexibility in that it can be used in every discipline and can call for relatively low-level, knowledge-based responses as well as higher-order thinking. It can be used in lecture halls of several hundred with fixed, auditorium seating. It is a relatively low-risk exercise that does not require elaborate planning and organization. When students move 'off task' during a lecture, perhaps after significant teacher-directed presentation of dense content, a think-pair-share activity can bring up the energy level of the class.

2. Scripted cooperation

This technique can also be used in many contexts, but is particularly useful in lecture classes containing complex content. About every 20 minutes, the lecturer stops and students pair up. One student takes the role of the summarizer, identifying key points in the presentation. The other student takes the role of the checker, ensuring that the content described is correct. Both partners then elaborate on the information, personalizing it and perhaps thinking of mnemonic devices to help the pair retain the information. A useful addition to this procedure is the use of concept maps, in which the teacher shows transparency overheads or provides hand-outs that identify the major points and sub-points for instruction. This has the effect of providing an overall organizational structure for the students, allowing them to focus on understanding content without simultaneously attempting to assess how concepts fit into the larger course organization. As students become more skilled, more and more of the map is completed by them rather than by the instructor.

3. Constructive controversy

Also known as 'structured controversy', this technique is more student-centred than the previous two structures. In 'constructive controversy', two pairs of students within a team of four take positions relating to a problem, an ethical issue or a controversial topic. The pairs generate information in support of their positions. At times they generate this information as part of a collaborative homework assignment. If time is short, the instructor simply summarizes the information for the pairs. After the information generation phase, the pairs discuss the two differing positions they have been assigned. The pairs then switch positions and argue for the opposite of what they were just defending. The point is not to win the debate but to adduce as much information on both sides and to attempt to fully comprehend the complexity of issues of importance.

4. Group investigation

This technique is the most student-centred of the approaches described in this chapter. Students initially discuss potential issues within a given course and settle on a relatively specific topic. Then teams of four plan and follow through their investigations of the issues using a variety of sources, which might include library researches, interviews and experiments. After the investigations, teams make presentations to the total class. The presentations may be exhibits, skits or plays, tapes or slide presentations, or experiments. The teacher and other students give feedback to the teams regarding the quality of the presentations.

Discussion

As noted above, there are a large number of cooperative learning structures, many having solid research bases. Several of the structures may be used within one course or on a single project. As Johnson and Johnson (1989) note, cooperative learning is one of the best-researched instructional procedures in education, with over 800 studies conducted on the impact of the technique on a large number of outcome measures. However the research on cooperative learning in higher education is relatively recent in comparison to that in primary and secondary education (Robinson and Cooper, 1995) and there remains much to be done in documenting its impact.

As Dunne (1992) notes, although there appears to be a lack of clarity regarding the details concerning a formal definition of core skills, there is great interest in critically assessing what skills we teach our students and the extent to which skills truly prepare students to function in a learning society. An influential article in North America has suggested that higher education needs to turn from a concern with teaching to a concern with learning (Matthews *et al*, 1995): that is, as instructors we need to focus on the *skills* we are teaching our students. In addition, we need to make sure that those skills are particularly important (core) skills, such as critical thinking, appreciation of diversity, teamwork and other issues mentioned previously in this article and by other authors in this study. If there is not sufficient documentation of a positive impact on students by a teaching technique, then we must question using such a method. Cooperative learning has a significant empirical base of a positive impact. Further, it is consistent with both empirical and theoretical work regarding powerful pedagogies.

No longer can we focus largely on a canon of relatively unrelated facts and details. We need to emphasize core skills which will prepare students for a learning society. Based on the hundreds of studies conducted on cooperative learning in the USA, Canada, Israel, Australia, the Pacific Rim and other countries, we believe that carefully structured use of cooperative learning can be one cost-effective method of preparing students for the next millennium. Cooperative learning can not only increase cognitive skills, but can also foster affective skills commonly associated with the family, the minister and the community, including teamwork, altruism, self-esteem and concern for others.

Notes

1. Much of our discussion of core skills and cooperative learning was influenced by the work of Dr Joseph Cuseo, Marymount College, Rancho Palos Verdes, California.

Chapter 18

Assessing skills in Scottish higher education

Dai Hounsell and Mary McCulloch

Introduction

If we wish to discover the truth about an educational system, Derek Rowntree has famously observed, then we must 'look into' its assessment procedures, for 'the spirit and style of student assessment defines the *de facto* curriculum' (Rowntree, 1987). Yet any such approximation of the 'truth', even if it were to be attainable, might have to proceed from the assumption that teaching, learning and assessment practices are essentially stable and static –an assumption that seems especially questionable in the late 1990s. Indeed, in many countries of the world, higher education in the present decade has been characterized by flux rather than stasis, by pressures to review and rethink traditional curriculum and teaching practices. What might, therefore, be most appropriate in such a period would be systematically to 'look into' the nature, scope and scale of change in practices which were being introduced (which might, in turn, throw light on shifts in the 'spirit and style' of student assessment as well as on the new learning society which is emerging).

Such an inquiry ought to be of value in clarifying an immensely important but much neglected relationship: that between pedagogical 'theory' and exhortation as embodied in the current literature on the one hand, and everyday pedagogical practice on the other. For it seems to be a little noticed phenomenon that what might reasonably be referred to as the 'literature' of teaching and learning in higher education appears also to have changed in character. While this literature (like the literature of education more generally) has always been a distinctive and sometimes uneasy blend of reports of empirical research, reflections on experience and documented accounts of developments and innovations in practice, the relative proportion of the last of these three seems to have grown very considerably over the last decade. And while this literature commonly includes abundant illustrations of how a given idea (eg, transferable skills, experiential learning, resource-based learning) has been put into practice within particular course and institutional settings, such illustrations do not amount to a 'representative' picture of changing practice generally in higher education. They are, rather (and necessarily), the products of a selective and opportunistic focus on known examples. Although they provide illustrations of how an idea has been and might be implemented, they give us little sense of how widespread or pervasive changed practice of that kind might actually be, across disciplines, across institutions, or even across systems of higher education.

A recent study in Scotland, however, helps to bridge that gap, since it sought to identify and document changing assessment practices across a disciplinary and institutional spectrum rather than in selective cases. This chapter sketches in the background to the study, reviews the findings which have emerged on the assessment of skills and discusses some of the implications arising from these changing practices.

Surveying changing practices

The ASSHE (Assessment Strategies in Scottish Higher Education) project was set up in August 1994 with three interrelated aims:

1. to identify the diversity of ways in which assessment practices had been changing in recent years in all the Scottish higher education institutions;
2. to document and analyse the changing practices identified;
3. to disseminate the findings to everyone with an interest in or a responsibility for student performance and achievement within Scotland and more widely.

The two-year project was undertaken by a joint University of Edinburgh/ Napier University team, working under the auspices of the Committee of Scottish Higher Education Principals, and with the financial support of the Scottish Higher Education Funding Council. As part of the project's dissemination programme, a series of newsletters was distributed, a selective inventory of changing practices was published (Hounsell et al, 1996), a national conference was mounted alongside a variety of conference and workshop presentations, and the project's database has been made available electronically, in down-loadable form, via the Internet.

The project sought to survey changing assessment practices in the 21 universities and colleges funded by the SHEFC (Scottish Higher Education Funding Council), together with the Open University in Scotland. The survey, therefore, covered a wide range of institutions. These broadly mirror in scope and diversity those of the United Kingdom as a whole, including large, long-established metropolitan universities, the 'new' (ie post-1992) universities, and typically smaller monotechnics specializing in initial and in-service teacher education, art and design, or music and drama. In 1994/95, 114,431 full-time and full-time equivalent students were enrolled in the SHEFC-funded institutions in Scotland. The corresponding figures for 1995/96 are 116,331 (SHEFC, 1996a, 1996b). Enrolments at individual institutions in 1995/96 ranged from 430 to 14,974.

In surveying staff, the approach adopted varied from one institution to another, according to local circumstances and preferences, but the common objective was that of trying to ensure that all relevant staff were circulated with information describing the aims of the project and had an opportunity to participate. Institutions were surveyed in four phases over the period March 1995 to July 1996.

By the conclusion of the survey phase of the project in summer 1996, a total of 311 completed pro formas had been returned for inclusion in the database, while a further 460 members of staff had formally registered interest in being kept abreast of the project's findings. Gauging the nature of this response is extremely difficult, since there is no way of determining precisely how many relevant assessment initiatives might potentially have been identified across the full span of the Scottish higher education system. It is, therefore, not possible to calculate a meaningful response rate. In addition, such a survey must rely predominantly on self-reporting, with the inevitable hazards that carries with it, but also on respondents' own judgements that the initiative they are reporting represents a significant change in their assessement practices. Such judgements are inevitably fraught with difficulties, since what is deemed 'innovative' in one department or subject area may be considered 'traditional' in another, and vice versa. Nonetheless, a database of this kind, even if not necessarily 'complete' in a definitive sense, does provide worthwhile data on the scope and scale of changing practices. They have strong ecological validity (Parlett and Hamilton, 1977) since they are contextually anchored in specific and named course settings. At the same time, it is possible to assess the extent to which the initiatives documented are representative, using a number of broad measures:

- The completed pro formas were drawn from across all 22 institutions surveyed, and ranged from one pro forma from one of the smaller institutions to 70 from one of the largest.

- Collectively, the overall subject spread of the completed pro formas (Figure 18.1) broadly mirrors that for the higher education system in Scotland as a whole, where student enrolment by subject area is taken as the yardstick for the latter.
- Similarly (and again using student enrolment figures), an analysis of the distribution of pro formas has shown no marked bias in relation either to the 'old' (pre-1992) or to the 'new' universities, or to the colleges and institutes of higher education.

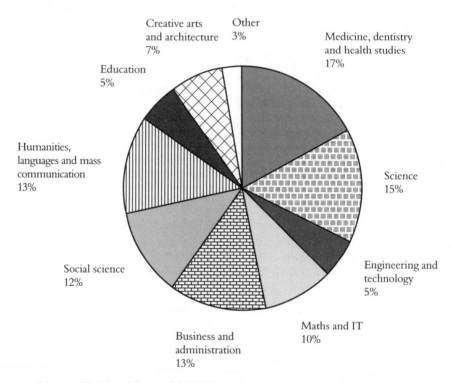

Figure 18.1 *Breakdown of ASSHE database entries by subject area (n = 311)*

The assessment of skills

The 311 entries in the database cover a very wide spectrum of changing assessment practices. The most direct way of pinpointing initiatives relevant to this chapter is, therefore, to extract from the ASSHE database all those which make explicit reference to the assessment of one or more skills in some way or other. The outcome is shown in Figure 18.2, which clusters the skills identified into six broad groupings. The largest of these groupings is communication and presentation skills – not surprisingly, perhaps, given the centrality of these skills in academic and workplace settings as well as in everyday life. However it is also apparent that, within this cluster, writing skills (that mainstay of conventional academic practice) feature much less prominently than oral, presentation and other communication skills. Similarly, although a traditional academic concern with higher-order skills is also evident, problem-solving is much more strongly represented than the analytical and critical thinking skills which have historically been to the fore in debates about the goals of higher education. And while a significant interest in interactive and interpersonal skills could hardly be considered to be a novel development in a higher education system which has long prized the pedagogical benefits of seminars and tutorials, these findings may well indicate more deliberative attempts to foster these skills, rather than relying on them being picked up incidentally.

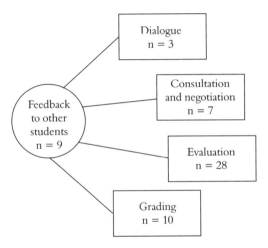

Figure 18.2 *Varieties of student involvement in assessment*

A second approach (and one that is less reliant simply on the skills selected for description) proceeds from a content analysis of the types and forms of assignment and assessment recorded. This complementary vantage point throws fascinating additional light both on communication skills and on the interactive and personal skills associated with group- and teamwork.

Assessing group and communication skills

Overall, group- and team-based assignments were represented in a little over one-quarter of the initiatives documented in the ASSHE database, and can be categorized in terms of three modes of communication involved:

1. There are 35 initiatives concerned with written assignments of a variety of kinds, including group reports (27 initiatives), group essays and collaborative book reviews.
2. There are 30 initiatives featuring oral assignments: group presentations (22 initiatives), paired presentations, student conferences, group debates and videotaped meetings.
3. A third cluster of 52 initiatives comprises assignments in a mixed mode (ie, combination of written and oral presentations, sometimes with a visual element as well), and includes group business plans or scheme proposals, team portfolios, group posters, displays and exhibitions, and – 39 of the initiatives – group projects.

These findings, then, underscore the growing pervasiveness of group- and team-based assignments in higher education. It should nonetheless be recognized that the promotion of a particular key transferable skill has not been the sole stimulus. An important additional contributory factor has been the need to recast teaching–learning practices in the face of fast-rising class sizes coupled with a significant decline in the unit of resource (Gibbs and Jenkins, 1992; Hounsell, 1994). Group- or team-based assignments are increasingly seen as offering a less labour-intensive approach to teaching and assessment. Nevertheless, the consequences have been not only a shift away from the traditional archetype of the 'lone scholar', but also the alliance of groupwork to a much more varied array of types and forms of assignment. In combination, these would seem to offer rich possibilities for strengthening and enlarging the skill repertoires of students.

Furthermore, there is remarkable diversification in the nature of assessed coursework assignments – even more strongly in evidence in individual than in group-based work. Assignments do not simply stretch students' communication skills in the direction of familiarity with a much wider variety of forms than the hitherto ubiquitous essay (in the humanities or social sciences) and the practical or laboratory report (in engineering and the natural and physical sciences). They also nurture student expertise in addressing a range of intended audiences which extends considerably beyond the tutor as examiner (Hounsell, 1998). Thus students, in initiatives documented in the ASSHE database, would be asked, for instance, to prepare a 'crisp' conference presentation to other students and staff not directly involved in a particular course (and, therefore, not well briefed on the topic concerned); to prepare a consultancy report tailored to the needs and circumstances of a particular client or user group; or to display the results of a community-based project in a form accessible to the public at large. A further benefit applies exclusively to group and team assignments, where experience of joint or collaborative authorship – whether as writers, designers, speakers or producers – can help students to develop hitherto fallow skills in revising and formulating plans or drafts in response to the thoughts and reactions of one's peers.

Student involvement in assessment

Another remarkable finding brings into sharp focus a set of skills which was seldom to be found in the typologies of personal transferable skills which came to prominence with the Enterprise in Higher Education Initiative (Denicolo et al, 1992). It comprises the skills associated with what has usually been called *student self-* and *peer-assessment* (Boud, 1986, 1995), but is perhaps rather more aptly described as *varieties of student involvement in assessment.* Within the ASSHE database, and across a wide spectrum of disciplines and fields of study, over one-quarter of the 311 initiatives documented draw students into the assessment of their own work, or that of their fellow students, in some way or other.

Figure 18.3, which stems from an analysis of a subset of 49 initiatives (Hounsell, 1997), encapsulates the main forms of involvement. In some instances, students may play a part in dialogue about how a given assignment is to be evaluated (with the aim of enhancing their understanding of assessment criteria and their application), or be involved in consultation and negotiation over the particular criteria to be adopted and their relative weighting. Involvement of these kinds is essentially formative in purpose, and may or may not lead to a substantive student role in applying the criteria concerned. In other instances, students are invited to appraise the quality of their own work or that of other students (but often in the form of evaluative comments which are not specifically linked to a particular mark or grade), or to go further and both propose and justify a provisional particular mark or grade which the tutor is then at liberty to endorse or amend as he or she sees fit. Alternatively or simultaneously, students may be invited to share their perceptions and comments with one another – an activity which opens up opportunities not only for practice in self- and peer-appraisal, but also in the equally exacting interpersonal skill of drawing on their evaluative judgements to give and receive feedback constructively (Jaques, 1991).

Changing practices and their implications

Self-evidently, one contemporary 'truth' of the higher education system which the ASSHE findings help to disclose is a heightened concern not only to assess knowledge and understanding but also to evaluate the attainment of skills and competencies, particularly communication and presentation skills

Communication and presentation skills (58)

Drafting
Oral/communication
Presentation
Writing
Communication

Interactive and interpersonal skills (22)

Group
Leading discusions

Practice-related skills (25)

Clinical
Entrepreneurial
Practitioner
Technician
Legal
Orchestral conducting

Higher-order cognitive skills (34)

Analytical
Critical thinking
Data analytic
Problem-solving
Study
Synthesizing

Information handling skills (31)

Data handling
Information
Research
Mathematical

Personal development and personal transferable skills (6)

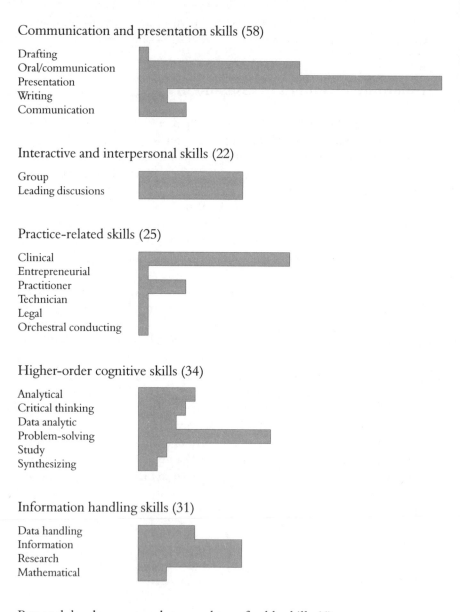

Figure 18.3 *Skills identified in the ASSHE database (n = 176)*

and the interpersonal and interactive skills associated with group- and team-work. At the same time, they help to bring into the limelight – notably in relation to student involvement in assessment – skills which have gone relatively unacknowledged hitherto. These can nonetheless now be recognized as significant personal, transferable skills relevant to a variety of social and workplace settings beyond graduation.

However we also need to remind ourselves that the 'truth' of an educational system, as Rowntree (1987) has argued, is to be found not only in practices and procedures but also in the values which underpin these. In the context of the assessment initiatives explored in this chapter, issues of pedagogy arise which are as much ethical as strategic and practical. The following three examples may help to illustrate the dilemmas raised.

First, there is the growing practice of assessing the contributions of individual students in tutorial or seminar discussions, as a facet of group and communication skills. In the past, an unspoken element in what might be called the *study contract* was that it was acceptable to be a thoughtful listener, an occasional rather than frequent contributor to tutorial discussions. However a shift towards evaluating individual participants on the basis of their inputs generates pressure on each of them to 'perform' overtly by contributing actively and often. Are we convinced that the pedagogical consequences of a pressure to perform are wholly desirable? And if so, should we take more public steps to make it clear to incoming students that the terms of the study contract have changed?

A second example also concerns group and communication skills, but in settings where students are engaged in collaborative projects which result in a mark or grade to the group or team as a whole. The dilemmas arise in the treatment of one or more individuals in a group who fail to pull their weight or simply find it almost impossible to get on with other group members. Should a high-achieving and strongly motivated student have the option of parachuting out of a dysfunctional or underperforming group, to preserve his or her mark average? Or should a group as a whole have discretion to safeguard a potentially good mark by expelling members who are contributing little or are a source of interpersonal conflicts? Or should the view simply be taken that these are commonplace difficulties in group- and teamwork and ones that students have to learn to put up with, and should try to resolve as best they can?

A third example relates to the advent of the oral presentation, which entails assessing a 'product' that is ostensibly much more ephemeral than the traditional written assignment or examination script. It cannot be stored away for future reference (except perhaps via the costly and cumbersome option of video), nor be subsequently referred to a third party (a further internal marker, say, or an external examiner) for arbitration and, therefore, does not offer the conventional avenues to accountability. Should additional safe-guards, therefore, be built in for accountability's sake – for example, by also requiring an accompanying written submission – or should it be acknowl-edged that the value of bringing oral skills into the assessment fold outweighs concerns about accountability?

Finally, a further and equally important consequence of initiatives to assess skills has been to help disclose certain essentially tacit features of long-established practices which had been taken for granted and which thus had not previously called for specific justification in themselves. This would include: assessing students solely in individual terms, requiring assessed work to be almost exclusively in written form, and confining the audience for completed assignments to the closed circle of the teacher and examiner. In-verting norms in this way not only throws down a gauntlet to more tradition-ally minded colleagues who may prove unwilling to countenance a break with convention. It also necessitates a more thorough-going reconsideration of what counts as 'good practice' in assessment in higher education, and what might be deemed to sustain or undermine 'high standards' (Hounsell, 1997). In the past, discussions about the nature of good assessment practice have mostly been conducted in a localized way, within departments or schools, and within institutions. In the learning society of the future, it may be argued, these are issues which need to be addressed system-wide.

Chapter 19

Teams in Law on trial

Sue Prince

Introduction

The traditional perspective of a law degree taught at the University of Exeter
has changed over the last few years because of the integration of core skills
into the curriculum. Following a major review of educational practice during
1994, the Department of Law redesigned some of the courses that had previously been taught through traditional lectures and tutorials and began to rely
on a variety of different educational methods. The purpose of this was to
enhance students' ability to learn and understand the techniques and skills
necessary for a foundational study of the law.

Specific legal research, such as the *First Report on Legal Education and
Training* (ACLEC, 1996), highlights the erosion of a distinction between the
'academic' and 'vocational' stages of legal education and asserts that legal education should be a liberal discipline which prepares students for a variety of
different high-level careers. Analogous to this idea, the key aims of the review
were, firstly, to ensure that general transferable skills, such as communication
skills, problem-solving skills and information technology skills, were explicitly integrated into the teaching and learning of particular core subjects; and
secondly, to encourage students to become more independent and autonomous as learners. The intention was that this should enable students to present their ideas more effectively, at the same time as giving staff more time to
focus on research interests. This chapter explores how these skills were initially integrated into the first-year law degree and how the themes and objectives were developed and refined over time.

Background

The University of Exeter is keen to ensure that students learn general transferable skills within their own departments and has stated this in a recent strategy document (University of Exeter, 1995). This identifies that students should enhance the following skills while at university: self-management, learning, communication, teamwork, problem-solving and data handling. Within the Department of Law, many of these skills were developed previously, albeit implicitly, through tutorial work.

Following the review, first-year law courses continued to be structured around lectures but rather than being supported by tutorials, a new system of workshops was introduced which encouraged students to work together in learning groups. These groups concentrated on developing both interpersonal and legal skills through the study and analysis of the content of the law. Workshops encouraged students to work together in the same focused small groups across each core law subject. The word 'group' is used descriptively here because, although it is recognized that groups and teams are different entities, it is difficult to say exactly when any group of individuals working together becomes a team. Some do so early on in their studies; other groups never become integrated enough to become teams, but members may still perform successfully in their individual studies.

The method of assessment of the courses was also altered in order to encourage the development of legal writing skills. The importance of stressing this variety in skill development was to encourage students to become more discursive and to develop a deeper level of learning at the beginning of the law degree, so that this could be built on and cultivated throughout the remaining years of study. Although the emphasis here appears to be group rather than person-specific, the aim of the changes was to help individual students to develop a critical and informed mind and an awareness of others' concerns and interests – as well as making the learning process more enjoyable overall. Importance was, therefore, placed on encouraging students to work in groups in order to develop other interpersonal skills, alongside becoming better at working in groups or on a specified workshop task. For example, groupwork improves communication skills, or, at the very least, focuses the student's mind on their own or others' ability to communicate, and on the barriers that may be put in place during communication.

Stage 1: evaluation of the initial experiment

The initial changes to the law programme were deemed a cautious success. The students worked together on workshop projects and began to develop their presentation, report writing and other analytical and interpersonal skills. Management savings, in the more efficient use of staff time, were created by encouraging students to work together. In comparison to tutorials, where the emphasis had been very much on the role of tutor as teacher, workshops encouraged the tutor to 'facilitate' learning rather than dictate. Hours spent on small-group teaching in first-year law subjects had been reduced from approximately 1,500 hours per academic year to approximately 300 hours with little noticeable effect on learning, and with the added advantage of 'freeing-up' staff time.

The students generally responded positively to the changes and stated that continual exposure to these skills had made them more confident and willing to take on more complex tasks in the future. However, one difficulty was the large number of students in each group. In order to make learning groups an efficient method of teaching, bearing in mind the low staffing numbers, it was necessary to have a minimum of 10 students in each group. This was appreciated and taken into account when creating workshop assignments, for which students were allocated tasks to prepare in smaller subgroups. However, the problems of communication within the larger group were not really addressed or overcome. Stress was placed on the content of the law and the practice of skills. However the more ambitious aim of using the group context for improving students as learners was not included as part of the experience. Evidently, there was a gap in the structure of the workshop programme. The obvious solution to filling the gap, by use of dedicated staff time and support, went against the principle of autonomous learning and student responsibility which was inherent to the changes. It was, therefore, necessary to look outside the law department for a solution.

Stage 2: how to give the workshop groups an identity

The involvement of employers and industry in the development of skills in undergraduate students is a welcome initiative and keenly supported by the Dearing Report (1997). BP (British Petroleum), for example, appreciate the benefits of teamwork within their own working environment and are enthusiastic to develop similar skills in undergraduates through an initiative called 'BP Team Development in Universities'. Exeter University became part of this project in 1996 when a group of academics were invited to attend a BP training course. The aim of this course was to provide university teachers with the experience of working as team development tutors who could then introduce aspects of team development into their own departments. The programme reflected a similar course run for undergraduate students, and used a series of outdoor problem-solving activities combined with reviews.

These reviews focused on an understanding of how working with others could enhance the learning process. As a consequence of attending this course, it was decided that a similar course for undergraduates should be run in the law department, combined with follow-on exercises, in which it was hoped that skills learnt on the course would be transferred into law workshops. Huge timetabling and room allocation difficulties were overcome. The BP-appointed trainers modified their normal programme (which was devised originally for 32 students over a two-day period) to cope with between 50 and 60 students a day over three consecutive days (a total of 160 students). Understandably, the BP trainers were hesitant as to whether this shorter course would have any benefit at all.

The training course had three explicit aims:

1. to emphasize the benefits of effective teamwork;
2. to give students a framework and process for purposefully tackling group projects;
3. and most importantly, to help build an identity for each team.

It was first piloted in October 1996. The objective was that all first-year law students should take part – in their prearranged workshop groups – prior to working together on the specific legal tasks which made up their core law curriculum. The main objective for running the course at this time was to introduce new students to the process of working together as a team before they had formed rigid preconceptions of what the learning of law should include. This introduction could then serve as the basis of a structure which they could apply to academic legal education.

Law students, arriving at university and expecting to engage in complex legal argument, were first introduced to a series of exercises involving equipment such as planks, plastic tubing and pieces of rope, in a rainy outdoor environment. This was far removed from their expectations, but it lifted the pressure of those early introductions to law and, during the reviews of the activities, they learnt about each other and discussed their own expectations and concerns. The feedback from evaluation sheets and discussions with students who had participated in the programme was overwhelmingly positive. Sixty per cent of students wrote that the course was an excellent, valuable, worthwhile, useful, interesting or thought-provoking experience. All other students also offered positive statements; about one-third spontaneously wrote that it exceeded their expectations. The emphasis of the course was facilitative rather than instructive: focusing on students' analysing their performance for themselves, on taking their own decisions as to how to work most effectively together and on respecting that people learn and work in different ways. Tutors guided the students' reflection and self-evaluation during the review process following each activity.

One of the main areas commented on by students was that the course offered a chance to get to know their workshop team and helped them to build 'a good working relationship'. There was evidence that this process allayed concerns, allowed 'getting over nerves' and 'developing confidence'. It was praised for helping students understand the benefits of teamwork. One student commented on how she 'realized you get more out of everything' by working as a team; another said that 'our problem-solving skills improved even in the course of a day. We all had individual approaches and ideas – but by the end of the course we all worked together'.

In order to encourage students to transfer the skills gained from the BP programme, each workshop group was allocated one of five tasks to be undertaken as a group, requiring research and analysis of a general legal theme. Presentations on these topics were then given in front of other workshop groups and a law tutor. They were not assessed but there was, nonetheless, full attendance by students. Tutors commented on the enthusiasm, the quantity and quality of work and the creative style of presentations. There was evidence of making use of individual strengths and weaknesses, of dividing the task into manageable units and of undertaking peer tutoring where appropriate. The students appeared to have confidently taken the lessons learnt from the BP course and applied them to the law, using fairly sophisticated management techniques.

There was, therefore, optimism in the law department that the skills learnt would be transferred to the workshops and that first-year students would continue to build on the techniques they had discovered so enthusiastically at the beginning of term. This was not the feeling of tutors at the end of the academic year. Presentations were, as they had been in the past, generally stultified, uncreative and conservative. The groups seemed keen to break down the tasks they were given into manageable sections to work on in pairs or as individuals, but then only concentrated on the selected tasks. This meant that their knowledge of content was focused upon a very narrow legal area. They were also unenthusiastic to learn from others in their groups or engage in discussion. It appeared that the interest and enthusiasm generated by the 'BP Day' soon dissipated in the less exciting and more formally assessed atmosphere of legal studies. The notion of transferability appeared to be absent, even though tutors had tried to make it explicit that there was a link between the outdoor team activities and the legal workshops. The next task, therefore, was to maintain the momentum created by the one-day training course.

Stage 3: how to maintain a sense of cohesiveness within the groups

The project was now entering its third year, and a university teaching development grant was obtained in order to introduce changes which would further consolidate and integrate the system already in place. The focus of the project was now strategically to shift the emphasis on first-year teaching within the department to actively encourage students to take more responsibility for their own learning. It was felt that the pitfall of the project so far was the lack of assessment of any groupwork, which would automatically shift the emphasis towards the importance of skills development. Workshop performance was assessed on a very general formative basis but this did not contribute towards any summative assessment, unless there was a particular question as to a student's abilities, for example, in relation to borderline performance in an examination. It was decided that in one introductory legal subject there would be no workshops and, therefore, no ongoing relationship with a tutor. Students would be expected to work on a particular legal assignment with only the minimum of teaching support. Indeed, they were to be actively discouraged from seeking support outside their group. The assignment would count for 10 per cent of the marks for that subject, and marks were awarded jointly, concomitant on both legal content and management of communication within the group. The assignment was given out during the 'BP Day' at the beginning of the first term and the groups were asked to complete a 'groupwork organizational plan' which, it was hoped, would highlight any problems which might arise.

Sixteen groups undertook the assignment, which ran concurrently with workshops and lectures in other subjects. At the end of the first term, midway through the period allocated for completion, they met with a tutor for a half-hour prearranged meeting to discuss their progress and their timetable for final submission. Discussions suggested that, even though some of the students were finding working in groups hard, many commented positively both on the nature of the assignment and how the BP Team Development Programme had given them a starting point for their working relationship. They admitted difficulties, such as some group members not pulling their weight or some individuals adopting an apathetic or minimalist approach which upset others who were more diligent. Asked to reflect on working together as a team, groups commented honestly on the difficulties of arranging meetings, the obstruction of dominant personalities in group meetings, the waning of initial enthusiasm and the pressure of other commitments on particular group members. It was evident that students were beginning to use reflective language which they had been encouraged to develop on the BP Programme, were transferring some of their learning into a legal context and were starting to work together to rationalize experience sharing: '[we] found a natural level where everyone could work effectively with each other'; 'the group still managed to remain friends'. However, informal conversations with students, which were supported by the findings of an independent interviewer, led to the conclusion that, although the assessed project lent a focus to students learning to work together as a group, there was a long way to go before they fully appreciated the benefits of what they were doing. It was only at the completion of the project that most groups could see these benefits: 'eventually we managed to pull together well'. Inevitably, even with the inclusion of the groupwork project, it appeared there was still a huge gap between individual and team.

This again points to possibilities for development in the future. The inclusion of team 'mentors' – students who have undertaken to further develop their team skills and could, therefore, coach individual groups through difficulties would, potentially, help to fill this gap. This type of group support or coaching cannot necessarily be given by a tutor who may be seen as too judgemental; also, when the project is being assessed, there may be a conflict at any point between the roles of facilitator and of assessor. It is also an undesirable route because of the objective of making the most efficient use of staff time. For a student mentor, however, there is the opportunity for formal development and progression through understanding and insight developed when supporting individual groups. The mentors would be asked to write reflectively about their experience, for which they would receive a certificate, giving them the incentive for progression, and thereby stretching still further the group/ individual learning experience.

Conclusion

In the traditional environment of the law department at Exeter, the emphasis has always been very much on learning as an individual activity. There has been much resistance towards considering the social and cognitive benefits of including learning groups within the curriculum, beyond their being a vehicle for disciplinary learning. However, the educational climate is changing. Although they do not exert a direct control over the content of core subjects, the Law Society and Bar Council are currently discussing the production of a 'joint statement' on the obligatory provisions of qualifying law degrees and have recognized the need for analytical and problem-solving skills to be included. A recent project (Bell and Johnstone, 1998), funded by the Department for Education and Employment, determined that general transferable skills are 'not an optional extra matter to be studied, but specific attention needs to be given to them so that students are able to recognize the skills they are developing and to articulate their achievements. The ability to transfer such skills to new contexts is a distinctive attribute'. There is pressure, therefore, for the newly formed school of law at Exeter to reconsider and evaluate its teaching.

From the experience of trialing groupwork and team skills, it can be seen that this is not something which happens overnight, but is instead a long-term project which requires constant evaluation. The issues raised by each new development lead to answers that inevitably raise greater and more compelling questions. The commitment to finding answers to these questions needs to be undertaken. This is because team-building is at the centre of the development of other core skills which helps students prepare for a professional future. On this degree programme, although students continue, as in the past, to learn about the content of the law, they are also beginning to think about and reflect on the process of learning itself. This is the kind of skill which should prepare them to make the most of any learning situation in the future and enable them to be continuing members of a 'learning' as well as a 'learned' society.

Chapter 20

Self-evaluation as a tool for developing lifelong learners: a South African perspective

Lee Sutherland

Introduction

South Africa has recently emerged from an oppressive political and educational system, and many students who were educationally disadvantaged by the previous political system are now entering the field of higher education. Academic Support Programmes were introduced in South Africa in order to meet the needs of these students. However, the concept of Academic Support has evolved into one of Academic Development, where it is acknowledged that institutions of higher learning need to adapt to the new profile of our student populations. One of the results of the changes taking place is that the specific focus of education has now been overtly stated as being 'to produce lifelong learners'. South African educators now acknowledge the need to become a learning society, and the ability to understand how one learns most effectively is central to this.

This chapter describes a first-year course in Historical Studies at the University of Zululand. Many students come to this university from educationally disadvantaged backgrounds, where passive rote learning has resulted in a surface approach to learning. For most, English is a second, if not third, language, although it is the language of learning at the university. In this course, students are taken through a writing programme that runs in tandem with the academic content, and that aims to promote greater meta-cognitive awareness with a view to developing students' capacity to learn more efficiently.

Students are thus encouraged to reach an understanding of how they learn. This small-scale study attempts to gain entry into the meta-cognitive world of the students through their self-evaluations which were part of the writing programme.

Theoretical framework

If tertiary institutions in South Africa hope to produce lifelong learners in a learning society, students need to acquire the ability to assess the value of their own work. Self-assessment can then become a vehicle for self-directed learning. Such thinking on assessment is in line with the emergent paradigm of assessment which Broadfoot (1993, cited in Klenowski, 1995) describes as one in which '*it is learning* itself, rather than simply the measurement of that learning, which is its central purpose'. In keeping with international trends, higher education in South Africa is starting to recognize that 'one of the main goals of professional higher education is to help students develop into "reflective practitioners" who are able to reflect critically over their own professional practice' (Kwan and Leung, 1996).

The notion of reflecting on one's experiences and practices with a view to improving them is a well-documented one (Schön, 1987). The reflection referred to here is characterized by Boud *et al* (1985) as one pursued with intent, rather than undirected, indulgent day-dreaming. It is also one in which the affective component has a role to play: positive feelings and emotions can greatly enhance the learning process.

Up to now, many of the assessment practices have been grounded in a traditional paradigm of educational theory and have rewarded rote learning and the regurgitation of facts. As assessment is a perspective of the curriculum, assessment practices will also change: Orsmond *et al* (1996) point out that traditional assessment practices have limited scope for developing student responsibility and autonomy. Further, it is argued that 'it is becoming apparent that in order for students to become more self-reliant with regard to their academic development, changes in staff assessment practices will have to be made in that some power will have to be handed over to students'.

Boud *et al* (1985) have developed a model of reflection that is symbiotic with self-assessment. They argue that 'reflection in the context of learning is a generic term for those intellectual and affective activities in which individuals engage to explore their experiences in order to lead to new understandings and appreciations'. Furthermore, if greater numbers of teachers and learners understand this reflective aspect of learning, the more effective learning can be. Various researchers have emphasized both the role that self-evaluation plays in learning and the educational merits of using self-assessment as part of the learning process. As Boud (1989) points out, it is now well accepted that the ability to assess one's own work is an important element of learning. Brown and Dove (1991, cited in Kwan and Leung 1996) suggest that self- and peer-assessment, if handled successfully can (among other things):

- foster students' feelings of ownership for their learning;
- encourage their active participation in learning;
- make assessment a shared activity rather than a lone one;
- lead to more effective and directed learning;
- signal to students that their experiences are valued and their judgement respected;
- produce a community of learning in which students feel they have influence and involvement.

The use of student-derived marks for formal grading purposes is a controversial one and is not a matter for debate in this chapter. It is raised as an issue elsewhere in this book, and can be pursued, for example, in Kwan and Leung (1996). In this study, student self-evaluations were conducted for formative assessment, that is, as a learning tool, rather than as a grading process (summative assessment).

The writing respondent programme

Students participate in a WRP (Writing Respondent Programme) which is integrated into the course material of the first-year History course. The programme is premised on the well-researched notion that writing can be used as a tool for learning. In other words, students are encouraged to write to learn, rather than to learn to write. In addition, it is based on the assumption that students learn by being actively engaged in the learning process. A process-oriented approach to writing is adopted by the close integration of the writing task with the course content (see Boughey, 1994, for a more detailed theoretical explanation of this approach).

Students are required to write a reply to a question at various intervals during the course. They are subsequently provided with a response to their work in which the writing respondent engages the student in a written dialogue. This takes the form of questioning and challenging the student in areas where, for example, there is vagueness or conclusions are unsubstantiated. At the end of six such writing sessions, students submit a portfolio of writing for which they receive marks. The students are also asked to submit a self-evaluation sheet, consisting largely of open-ended headings and questions, without which their portfolios are considered incomplete. This sheet requires that students reflect on their strengths and weaknesses, both in their understanding of the academic content and in their writing skills. It is also intended that it will encourage students to be more self-critical, as well as providing them with the opportunity to express their self-development. A broader aim of the study is to assess the extent to which the self-evaluative exercise had developed students' meta-cognitive awareness.

Self-evaluation

The data obtained from the self-evaluation sheet suggests that the students do not start off with sophisticated and reliable judgements about their own work. As Gibbs (1995) observed in a similar study, they need practice and training in order to develop this judgement. They also need to be convinced of the value and validity of the self-assessment process. In addition, research shows that students who come to the University of Zululand have very little understanding of what will be expected of them in higher education. They demonstrate a lack of insight into their own work and a poor understanding of the 'standards' which staff thought were being applied.

The 'inability' to judge their own worth effectively is often particularly characteristic of second language learners, who prefer to measure their worth through the reflections of others. This is illustrated by the following kind of comment: 'I did not see any improvement because no marks were allocated'. This dissatisfaction is compounded by the notion that, as Boud (1989) points out, students do not have a well-defined sense of the criteria which should be used to judge their work, and that they may find it difficult to interpret criteria with which they have been provided. What emerges is a picture similar to the one painted by Main (1988) when he says that students 'seem to be unable to predict confidently the consequences of different study methods or learning styles. It is as if they believe that success or failure is determined by external agents – using inscrutable criteria'.

Many students revealed that the portfolio and its self-evaluation had been cathartic in gaining a perspective on self-value. The following comments support this notion:

- 'If I compare assignment one to other assignment I felt that my performance was better'.
- 'I thought I understood what I were asked but I was surprised to see a lot of questions being asked'.
- 'Piece three, I am not happy with it because I failed to express precisely what I want to say'.
- 'For the first time I was able to stick on the point of argument, but now I

can understand the topic clearly and follow it in context'.
- 'I didn't do well in assignment four because I was not able to focus directly on the topic'.

However, there remained a group of students who demonstrated an inability to measure the worth of their work. For example, in response to the question: 'What does your portfolio show that you can do?', some students suggested that they could only measure or judge this through the reflections of others:

- 'My portfolio doesn't show how I can do because there is no mark and indicates how marks I obtained, but there is a lot of questions'.
- 'I do not see any improvement because no marks were allocated'.
- 'I selected this piece (one) because I performed very well in my first test'.

Approaches to learning

A variety of different frameworks have been developed in order to investigate approaches to learning. The most recurrent of these (Entwistle, 1987) is one that makes the distinction between deep learning, where the learner attempts to understand and interact vigorously with the content, and surface learning, where there is a reliance on memorization and an uncritical, passive acceptance of the content. In addition to these two broad categories are the non-academic approach to learning (where the motivation for improvement is extrinsic rather than intrinsic) and the strategic approach (where the learner manipulates the learning environment in order to achieve success).

In addition, Entwistle and Ramsden (1983) describe the deep approach as being characterized by, among other things, an integration of formal learning with personal experience and as one associated with a reflective approach. Alternately, the surface approach is characterized by an attitude of unreflectiveness. Boud *et al* (1985), however, state that these approaches are not consistent in any one student, but depend on the specific circumstances and intentions. The study bore testimony to this.

Main (1988) sums up the thinking of Gibbs with regard to the relationship between study habits and academic success and states that there is little evidence to suggest a clear relation between the two. This is of great significance to the University of Zululand, in that there is an ever-increasing demand for programmes on study methods which give advice in the generalized way that Gibbs and others argue against. Students' responses were, however, revealing with regard to the underlying assumptions that they make about learning and the approaches they take to learning. In response to the question: 'Which pieces of writing are you unhappy with and why?', one student said: 'All of them because I do not exactly know what was required from me to do. To me, this assignment shows no improvement. Instead I'm extremely offended because the test book said Free Burghers. It does not go into detail explaining to me who they are, as you ask in my assignment, so really I'm sad'.

This kind of response is fairly typical of both the cognitive and affective components of our students' learning experience. Many students want to be told precisely what to do in essays and other work. This would suggest that many students assume what Entwistle (1988) refers to as a 'reproducing orientation' to learning. In keeping with this orientation to learning, the student above is typical of many who tend to read very little beyond what is required for completing assignments.

Some of this sample revealed a notion of an entirely teacher-directed education, wherein students are simply passive recipients of information. These students prefer not to be challenged in any kind of way. The following comments are revealing of this approach to learning:

- 'I would like to see mistakes being corrected not be asked questions to something which I've never understood, for example DEIC (Dutch East India Company). How can I explain what it was'.
- 'The one who marked my assignment I will be happy if he/she can make corrections in my assignment not ask questions to what I wrote'.
- 'I would like to be asked a question and the marker should tell me what am I supposed to do if I correct my mistake because it seems as if I make one and the same fault'.

Meta-cognitive awareness

Although students are universally reluctant to take part in activities which are not awarded formal marks that will influence their success in a particular course (Boud, 1989), this study suggests that students had achieved greater meta-cognitive awareness. For example, in response to the question: 'In what ways have you improved?', one student said: 'I understood the question clearly and I feel I provided enough information. I had enough time to prepare for it, redrafting it. I tried with effort to correct the mistakes of past assignments'. This suggests that the student is reflecting on a process that would prove to be academically successful.

There is further evidence of such student awareness:

- 'It shows me that I must write the assignment with my own understanding'.
- 'I have just took the text and read through out the relevant topics and close it up and bring about my own understanding'.

- 'It (my portfolio) showed that I must read with understanding and ask myself questions while I'm reading'.

Some of the specific areas in which students achieved greater meta-cognitive awareness are highlighted below.

What 'good writing' means

Some students showed an awareness of reading as an intelligent reader, of engaging with the content and of attaching personal meaning to reality, which is essentially a constructivist view of learning. These responses also reveal an approach to learning which Entwistle (1988) refers to as 'meaning orientation' (essentially associated with a deep approach to learning) where students look for personal meaning and have academic motivation. The Writing Respondent Programme allowed students to find the 'voice' of which Cleary (1991) talks, rather than aping an academic style without understanding it. These are some of the comments that students made about the writing that they were required to do:

- 'If people can be given freedom to write whatever they like as long as it is relevant to the question and it is true. Not to be asked where did you get this'.
- 'I selected this piece because I revealed all the information that was needed and I didn't relay (*sic*) on a book only but I wrote with my own ideas'.

Moving away from plagiarism

Many students saw the need to move away from plagiarism in an attempt to develop both their skills as a writer and their own 'voice': 'I selected this piece because I write my assignment with my own words, even the marker appreciate it'. Angelil-Carter (1995) argues, however, that at first-year level plagiarism in student writing is rarely intentional, but a far more complex problem. As a lengthy discussion of plagiarism is beyond the scope of this chapter, it must suffice to say that many researchers, Angelil-Carter included, feel that imitation is an important part of the learning process and should not be 'criminalized'.

Awareness of discourse

One student demonstrated a rudimentary sense of awareness of the discourse of the discipline. In response to the question: 'Which pieces are you unhappy with and why?', the response was: 'Piece number 1. I did not write in any form that was expected to me as a history student'.

Awareness of audience

Cleary (1991) reports that second language learners often have less sense of 'appropriate' purpose and audience. While this was evident in some responses, the WRP proved to be successful in creating an awareness of audience within other students without deliberate or overt attempts to do so. The following comments provide evidence of this: 'It also show that I must explain and elaborate some words or terms. It also show that I must write as if one who is marking don't know the story'. However, an inappropriate awareness of audience could be detrimental if students develop what Cleary calls a 'please-the-teacher mentality'. Furthermore, she sees this as part of the submission/dominance power structure set up in classrooms. Such a mentality may be associated with the strategic learning approach that Entwistle (1987) and others talk about. In this research, there was a strong inclination on the part of some students to find out 'what the teacher/lecturer wants'. A number of students made comments on this: 'I would like the lecturer to tell me the way he/she like me to answer the question and show me the corrections'.

Contextualization

Students also came to realize the need to contextualize their writing for the reader: 'It (the portfolio) shows that I must answer the question accurately and avoid to write things that may lead the marker to ask why, when, what'.

Affective component

Boud et al (1985) argue that the reflective process is a complex one in which feelings and cognition are closely interrelated and interactive. Furthermore, negative feelings can form a barrier to learning, distort perceptions and lead to false interpretations. Positive feelings, on the other hand, can greatly enhance the learning process. The self-evaluation exercise in this research showed the importance of the affective component to the writing process of which Cleary (1991) and Boud et al (1985) speak. In answer to the question: 'What does your portfolio show that you can do?', one student simply said: 'I can write an assignment'. Another student put this point more directly: 'I would like to see positive comments in my work. I want to feel happy when I read my own writing knowing that what I have written makes sound sense'. Cleary (1991) also argues that when students see grading as a form of criticism or praise, as a mirror by which to view themselves or as a means of comparing themselves to peers, it had more effect on their writing confidence than on the development of writing ability.

Conclusions

This study corroborates the suggestions of Gibbs about six ways in which to facilitate students' learning development (1981, cited in Main 1988):

1. Take a student-centred approach.
2. Give responsibility to the student for his or her own learning.
3. Make changes of methods and approaches a safe activity.
4. Emphasize the students' purpose not technique.
5. Emphasize the reconceptualization of study tasks.
6. Emphasize the student's awareness of his or her own learning.

Students demonstrated that they had gained heightened awareness in the following areas:

- How writing can be used as a tool for learning.
- What 'good writing' means.
- The need to engage with the text and attach personal meaning.
- Awareness of audience in writing.
- The need to adopt a deep approach to learning.

As other research has shown, this awareness was not consistent in all ways of any one student's approach to learning.

While many showed traits and problems that have come to be known as being synonymous with English as Second Language learners, many others found the Writing Respondent Programme and the self-evaluative exercises empowering. The programme enabled them to find their own 'voice'. This chapter may appear to be judgemental of the students' abilities, but it must be emphasized that, for a number of students, the opportunity to critique their own work was both a new and cathartic experience. Given the educational background from which they come to the university, much needs to be done to foster their self-development. Students need to be convinced of the need to take control of their own learning (Boud *et al*, 1985). The findings from this study coincide with Boud's (1989) thinking when he says that 'there needs to be a greater emphasis on the relationship between learning and self-assessment'. Teachers need to find ways of incorporating some forms of reflection into their courses (Boud *et al*, 1985).

Educators in South Africa must heed the call to assist their students in becoming self-directed learners, in order to partake fully in the global view of establishing a learning society. The mission statement of our University in particular states that one of our teaching goals is to equip students with 'relevant skills, knowledge and techniques'. However, what these should be remains in the minds of the writers of the statement. Institutions of higher education in South Africa need to be more explicit to their stakeholders about the kinds of 'core' or generic skills with which we should be equipping our students in order for them to play a meaningful role in a learning society.

Chapter 21

Professional studies and career development: attitudes to learning in Fine Art

Heather MacLennan

The provision of a range of learning experiences appropriate to the needs of Fine Art graduates in the world of work is now a priority. In a changing society, the individual must be ready to respond to new opportunities. Graduates need core skills that enable them to manage their own careers, have confidence, communicate and deal with people. Many entrants to a Fine Art course are not necessarily career-oriented in the conventional sense of the term, although they do have a sense of vocation. Rather, they obtain a philosophy and experience that will provide them with a lifelong outlook in which art has a very special value.

An increasing proportion of mature undergraduates in Fine Art come from well-established careers, for example, nursing, state employment (civil service, fire service), the public sector (British Telecom), the armed services and the world of business. It was anticipated that students coming to higher education from previous careers would have different expectations of a compulsory assessed professional studies programme than the segment of the student population aged 19 – entering higher education directly from sixth form or an art foundation course.

A case study was established to discover more about students' perceptions of art education, independent learning and their careers as graduates (MacLennan, 1998). The project was inspired by a philosophy which seeks to defend a liberal arts education and yet is supportive of the provision of useful experience for the world of work, whatever this may entail.

The investigation focused on the learning experience of students and their self-reflection, a central theme being to test whether subject-based studies can successfully incorporate generic skills experience (Walker, 1994). To support this, work experience programmes focusing on enterprise and the use of initiative have been carefully integrated with the more esoteric aspects of the Fine Art curriculum.

Research into the delivery of professional studies work projects

The aim of the research was to enable staff and students to become better focused in the management of the learning process, through an overall understanding of the educative experience and its effect on the individual. Motivation and anxiety are key features of any analysis of students' problems encountered in the delivery of the curriculum. This is especially so in work schemes where participants are expected to initiate projects or respond to new situations. The Fine Art professional studies module incorporates an assessed project of this kind undertaken as part of the normal academic curriculum but outside the usual college environment. Projects are normally of a few weeks duration and include working with local art gallery and museum staff providing short programmes for the under-fives; print workshops; painting commissioned murals; artist residencies in schools; coordinating visual arts displays for department stores and businesses; helping to plan and run a local arts festival with open air exhibits; and organizing group exhibitions. Support and advice is provided and plans are sanctioned by the college, using learning contracts. This is a different type of provision from that which caters exclusively for professional qualifications in industry. The latter, while introducing undergraduates to a real workforce, does not necessarily offer initiative tests or challenges useful to future art and design graduates.

Some students were known to have an ambivalent attitude towards professional studies, viewing this part of the curriculum as significantly different from, and even unrelated to, their main aesthetic study – whether in sculpture, painting, printmaking or mixed media (MacLennan, 1997). The perceived conflict led to tensions which affected students' normally positive outlook and also raised a question about the nature and purpose of esoteric study in relation to other demands, for instance, the need for the curriculum to more directly address graduate outcomes (Dearing Report, 1997; AGR (Association of Graduate Recruiters), 1995). While there was a view among students that professional studies was necessary, some were deeply anxious that their performance in this area should not affect the assessment of the degree, which they liked to think principally reflected their achievement in the studio, since this was their prime aim in entering higher education.

Students in previous studies had shown very poor ideas of skills development and awareness, were vague about graduate outcomes, confused over non-traditional modes of assessment, and needed much encouragement. Coming from a wide range of backgrounds with different life experiences, skills and abilities, they demonstrated that they had much to offer, and evidently had a good deal to gain, from a well-managed professional studies programme. They were in need of a more focused attitude towards themselves and their potential careers. Their future survival depends on skills of self-employment and self-promotion; they will need to be able to undertake available employment whether skilled, unskilled or of a part-time nature in order to sustain their 'other life' as artists and designers, as well as using art and design skills in an adaptive way to support their studio practice or as their principal means of earning a living.

The research team set out to obtain an idea of the consensus within the cohort on a number of issues related to professional studies, through a questionnaire and by means of focus group interviews held before and after the running of the projects. The analysis of the findings was structured to gather any significant differentiation according to age, previous experience and gender in student attitudes to skills acquisition and their own abilities.

Questions throughout were directed at understanding student views about:

- the Fine Art degree;
- their previous educational experience;
- postgraduate aims;
- the inclusion of professional studies in the degree, the value of this and whether it should be compulsory;
- their changing understanding of what is involved in professional studies, their perceptions of core skills and attitudes to learning.

According to questionnaire findings, 92 per cent of students said they were satisfied with their degree, a result that matches interview evidence. Professional studies was thought to be important and useful for postgraduate careers, although postgraduate ambitions seemed vague and unformed. About half the group (male and female) aspired to artistic or creative work after graduation, rather than jobs related to art such as administration or teaching; 20 per cent identified with jobs in applied art or arts administration (all women); and a quarter elected for teaching jobs (mostly women). Just 8 per cent showed interest in jobs not related directly to art (male and female). Students were most highly motivated by the aesthetic and self-developmental thrust of the main subject, Fine Art, seeing this as a fundamental and positive, if esoteric, experience. Professional studies was not seen to be directly related to the content of the main study, and was even considered unrelated.

The following extracts from the questionnaire have been selected to illustrate the different perspectives found within the student group. While several seem to take a pragmatic view, their aspirations are nevertheless idealistic.

A 19-year-old male student defined education as an opportunity, 'to learn and acquire new skills which will help my progress within the art world… to bring my attitude and experience to a professional level'. On graduating, he wanted 'a job which involves creativity, personal organization. Something like an interior designer'. When asked what he thought about professional studies he said, 'The point is to get us ready for a real life situation, a view of how the world of art functions. To taste professional requirements'. When asked about the relevance of professional studies to the main subject, Fine Art, he replied: 'It links with the important process we have lost, communication, organization, the professional ability to fulfil a brief on time, the confidence to take on a task and motivate yourself and ideas'.

A 40-year-old female student defined education as an 'opportunity to provide intelligent challenging information'. She chose the Fine Art degree 'to position myself in an environment which interests me' and sought a job in gallery administration. She said that professional studies served 'to introduce students to a world outside college', and she eagerly looked forward to opportunities to operate in the business world, gain experience in a new area, and acquire practical experience with computers and galleries.

A 23-year-old female student saw professional studies as a separate entity from aesthetic studies and was critical of a conflict with time spent in the studio. She defined education as: 'The learning of skills to be taken through to a professional life as well as important personal skills [leading to] creative-based careers' and eventually wanted to work in film or television and to do a postgraduate course in this area. She felt no personal need for professional studies.

Another female student (age 21) defined education as: 'Learning and being taught about skills (practical, theoretical) and subjects which give us a wide knowledge of useful information and skills for helping us to integrate and work in society'. She chose Fine Art 'because I felt it was my strongest subject area which I wanted to continue, to express myself and my views to a wider audience than just for myself'. She envisaged a future job as: 'something which includes creativity and challenge – something which includes aesthetic judgement and interaction with like-minded people'. She saw professional studies as useful in 'helping confidence, to speak out, being professional'.

Overall, the results confirmed that students are unclear about the reality of graduate destinations and are not fully cognizant of the many career opportunities that exist in areas related to the arts, business and self-enterprise.

Student perceptions on the value of core skill acquisition

Before undertaking a work project

Students readily identified the following skills as useful outcomes from their anticipated projects, drawing from their recent experience of lectures given by Fine Art professionals, recent graduates and mentors:

- bargaining;
- diplomacy;
- making arrangements according to a schedule;
- being organized, managing people, resources, time;
- taking responsibility;
- using initiative;
- learning to be flexible, to adapt;
- being firm, making decisions;
- making contacts;
- meeting professionals;
- encountering difficulties;
- meeting deadlines.

Examples of typical responses from taped interviews held early on in the project demonstrate a familiarity with the language of skills. One response to the question, 'What kind of skills are being used in the project?' was, 'It depends on bargaining and being diplomatic. Trying to sort out exactly what was wanted for my project. Sorting out, arranging meeting times, things like that, which I wouldn't have done anyway, and I've now probably got more confidence for when I leave... to be able to go and present myself'.

In response to, 'What is the point of professional studies for Fine Art students?', students replied:

- 'It makes it more like an old apprenticeship. You don't get the job at the end, but you get the taste of work experience, like school, but it's heavier in the sense that you're running it and it's your responsibility'.
- 'When I finish my degree I've to be doing it myself, if I do it now while I'm still in college, it gives you a bit of protection I suppose against it all going wrong'.

Students were asked to complete a section in the questionnaire about their confidence in the area of core skills (on a scale of 1 to 6). While most responses placed them in the middle categories, there are some interesting and significant differences at the higher and lower ends of the scale. Women's perceptions of their abilities in skills areas seems lacking in confidence in relation to known performance abilities and, with the exception of team skills and being community-spirited, women mostly scored lower than the men. Responses to a variety of skill areas are outlined below.

Communication skills   Most of the group had a modest to good view of their abilities, but a larger proportion of women self-scored lower than the men. No men placed themselves in the lowest categories, whereas 18 per cent of women scored as 'poor'. Half of the men had greater confidence in their communication skills, compared with just under 30 per cent of women in the same higher categories.

Motivation   Men scored highly with 68 per cent indicating they regarded themselves as well motivated; by contrast women scored 41 per cent. Few men placed themselves in the poor category (13 per cent), in comparison with 59 per cent of women.

Creative skills   Men scored more highly: 63 per cent of men in categories 1 and 2, in comparison with 35 per cent of women.

Problem-solving   Men scored more highly: half of the men were in categories 1 and 2, in comparison with a quarter of women. Women had a poor view of their abilities (41 per cent of women), but only a quarter of men rated themselves in the low categories (5 and 6).

Community-spirited/team player   Women self-scored more highly than men in the community-spirited category, 42 per cent in 1 and 2, while men scored zero per cent; in the team player top category, men and women scored equally, but most men (three-quarters) thought less highly of their team skills.

High achiever   More men placed themselves in the higher category.

This small survey suggests there may be a difference in levels of confidence according to gender. This may indicate a need for more constructive support, targeted at particular core skills according to gender. However, students' subjective views need to be measured in relation to an objective assessment of their achievement. Many women students tend to perform well in modes of assessment constructed around written reports and, even when they perceive themselves to be less able, they do not necessarily under-perform in the academic curriculum. The findings are significant because of the role that self-confidence plays in motivation, and also because of the relationship of self-awareness to reflective learning. Anxiety levels vary according to each individual, but also seem to differ according to gender. While some women displayed a high degree of anxiety during the projects, some men appeared to be more relaxed, especially over issues of preparation. Age and previous experiences seem to be less influential than personality and gender when it comes to determining assertiveness and motivation in the individual.

After undertaking a work project

In the second stage interviews, held after most of the projects had been completed, questions were framed to discover:

- how the project had fared and what the students' experience had been;
- what the students' reflections were on the skills they had used;
- the students' view of the value of the project;
- their view of its compulsory nature;
- any reflections on former anxieties and whether their views had changed;
- their attitude to assessment and its process and views on whether the projects should be assessed.

Some students resented the stress that arose from initiating projects. In many cases it had been hard work, but all had been determined to see their project through and had not given up. They had a critical view of the relative value of different types of project and felt, on reflection, that projects had to be selected carefully. They seemed critically aware of the educative process, and were assertive and confident in putting their views across in interview. They spoke with greater clarity than in the first interview and were able to talk more coherently about outcomes. They spoke positively about core skills gained as a consequence of professional studies, and showed awareness of self-improvement in spite of some difficult experiences.

They stated that they had:

- gained social confidence, using communication skills and social skills;
- used their initiative;
- seen a project through;
- solved health and safety problems and tackled resourcing;
- dealt with problems of timing;
- got on with management;
- shown the ability to be flexible and to adapt ideas.

Examples of typical responses from taped interviews held after the completion of work projects give evidence of such features. When asked if, in principle, they thought it a good idea to do work outside the college as part of a degree, one student stated: 'I think we should because art is all about getting people to see it and getting involved with people out there'. If the module had not been compulsory, they felt they would have wanted to do some kind of work outside college: 'It helps us really, at the end of the day. It gives you so much more experience once you leave the college. Once you leave, you can come back but it's not the same. You're not in that environment. If you do well with professional studies then you get contacts outside and you've also got the confidence to go up to other people and actually ask them things'.

Most students felt that professional studies should be available within the curriculum and the majority thought it should be compulsory in order to spur them into action. Indeed, a third of them completed the programme and placement only because it was compulsory, whereas 56 per cent said they would have done it anyway (both sexes equally). They felt the projects had value, and appreciated the opportunity to gain useful contacts. However, their experience of negotiated assessment varied. Students showed considerable anxiety about assessment and wanted further clarification. Outcomes in relation to skills and experience were set out in their learning contract. Projects were assessed by tutors through a combination of:

- evidence of work carried out;
- documentation of the project in a portfolio of evidence;
- a critical report written by the student;
- a diary or journal; and in some cases a report from a professional in the field.

Three-quarters of the student group approved of being assessed within such projects, but most (65 per cent) felt that assessment should not count towards their degree. More women (71 per cent) objected than men (56 per cent). They were, however, very keen to have feedback about their performance from experts in the field.

Nearly all the students demonstrated that they are capable of running successful enterprise projects, that when encouraged and challenged they can overcome reticence about their abilities, and hesitation about taking on challenges. The investigation suggests that a level of anxiety about new situations is inevitable, but this is not necessarily a bad thing. Students thought it a good idea to do such projects while a support system was available in order to gain experience for when they leave college. They thought that professional studies gave an appropriate focus on 'graduate skills' and perceived these as useful.

Conclusions

Research suggests that the present balance between professional studies (about 12 per cent) and main studies (about 88 per cent) is appropriate for Fine Art students, that is, it fits in with what is likely to motivate them. However, while cognizant of the value of generic skills and their particular need to develop them, they do not necessarily relate these skills to the main subject of their degree. They do not necessarily see core skills in the same context as others that they value, such as artistic invention and creativity, mastery over technique, handling of media, and being held in high regard for aesthetic achievement in the field of Fine Art.

Interestingly, this division does reflect a similar distance in the rhetoric about art encountered in much twentieth-century discourse stemming from the modernist period, where traditionally art is seen as a lone activity surrounded by a certain amount of mystique, and where the pragmatics of making and commerce are downplayed in accounts of art production. The more transcendental characteristics of artistic experience are emphasized. This is notwithstanding the impact of post-modern theories on contemporary forms of art, whereby publicity, promotion and recognition of the sales market have changed the appearance of art as it embraces the media and the values of the capitalist world. Art has always existed in the market-place, but much of its surrounding rhetoric continues to deny this. The Romantic ideal has not been relinquished, indeed its philosophy sustains both consumers and practitioners of art alike.

Students' ideas of the purpose of the Fine Art degree (seen to be esoteric and self-developmental in the area of aesthetics through their main study – art practice) do not easily match with their initial understanding of the real world of opportunities outside college. Professional studies is seen as supplying a necessary missing element, the practical application of art to the wider world. Student awareness increases through the practical experience of work projects where they are expected to specifically address skills as stated learning outcomes. Feedback focused critically on relative strengths and weaknesses is designed to enhance self-development.

Subject-based studies can successfully incorporate graduate skills through assessed projects undertaken in tandem with main studies as long as tensions within the curriculum are skilfully managed in terms of timing and delivery. Student worries about projects usually subside after the event. Other (unpublished) studies have shown that final-year students have much more positive feelings in retrospect, valuing their work experience immensely (Dunne and Fraser, 1998).

Overall, this study suggests that emphasis placed on generic skills and self-development is advantageous. Learning awareness in students can be readily developed in a programme which has transparent aims and objectives. This kind of reflective learning on a negotiated basis within the academic curriculum can be helpful to an individual's growth, and can lead to higher levels of self-management and improved career planning.

Professional studies' provision that is sensitive to students' needs and provides a balance with subject-based studies is likely to succeed best in motivating students and in producing reflective practitioners. A major advantage is that the world of work is fully integrated within the curriculum and students have the opportunity to reflect on their experience in the environment of higher education. However, government policy, which rates individual value according to labour or skill, needs to be carefully examined when anticipating a future society. Each individual needs to have a sense of their own worth in a system that may measure their contribution according to the job market and trade and industry figures. A flexibility of working practice may suit many and be a necessity for the future, but with this goes anxiety as the individual needs to be in a continual position to anticipate and self-promote.

The learning society has demands that transcend the provision of utilitarian skills programmes. Above all, it is important to remember that a learning society is one in which the needs of the society and those of the individual are both met. This diversity of needs within a population, as well as student expectations of university education, makes programme planning, particularly for skills and careers provision, a challenge to educators.

Chapter 22

Teaching architects

Simon Unwin

Introduction

This chapter presents the methodological background of a course called 'Analysing Architecture'. The course has grown out of, and was conceived as a supplement to, studio-based design teaching. Its aim is to help students deal with the demands placed on them in their design projects by offering them ways in which they can 'see' – that is, order into a developing conceptual framework of thematic categories – how other designers have dealt with similar demands. Students are helped to understand architectural design, and thereby be better equipped to do it, by analysing the work of others in a structured way. The course extracts some of the underlying conceptual themes (intellectual patterns and strategies) evident in works of architecture, providing the beginnings of a framework for categorizing the powers of architecture as a creative activity. It aims to help students acquire a repertoire of seminal ideas that may be explored and developed in design, as a way of developing a personal but well-informed approach to architectural design. Students are encouraged to be autodidacts, to continue this process of 'making sense' of architecture for themselves. The objective is to produce professional architects intellectually equipped to continue increasing their understanding of the workings and potential of their discipline throughout their careers... maybe as exemplars for a 'learning society'.

Core skills

Design is the core skill for architects. It is the skill which defines an 'architect'. Notwithstanding the title's legal protection (in the UK, and some other countries, use of the title 'architect' is restricted to those with the required professional examinations), one cannot really be considered an architect without skill in design.

Design is central to the human adventure. All of us are engaged in it at a low level some of the time: we may design the day ahead, a route to a distant destination, an evening meal, the layout of a room… In journalese, the person responsible for the intellectual structure of anything is its 'architect', whether it be a building, a piece of music, a political policy, a battle strategy, a business proposition, a television programme, an educational curriculum, the plot of a novel… The skill of design is innate – life is inconceivable without it – but for the person who wishes to become a professional designer (in whatever field) the challenge is how to develop this skill to a high degree, such that results will be acknowledged as 'good' (according to whatever criteria hold sway), and people will want the benefits (for example, they will pay for them). The challenge for the design teacher is to be the 'architect' of an educational framework within which this can happen.

Architectural design is what might be called an 'open-ended' skill. Not susceptible to generally recognized systematic procedures, it is frequently faced with new challenges which demand new propositions. As an open-ended skill, architecture can never be finally *achieved*… unlike the ability to type, to carve letters in stone, to play a musical instrument in a technically perfect way, or to conduct and record scientific experiments with discipline and rigour. It is constantly being reinvented. The activity of architectural design does involve similar 'closed' (or 'semi-closed') skills – such as the ability to draw in a way which can be understood by others, or to use computer-aided drafting, or to build neat models – but at its core lies the more fundamental skill of being able to tackle new (previously unencountered) challenges in new (original and imaginative) ways. To be involved in design – whether as a student, teacher or architect – is to deal not in ways of doing things which are laid down and certain, but in finding routes through forests of uncertainty. This is often an unnerving situation to be in; one where polemic assertion and whim can easily usurp reason and sensible judgement.

The 'Analysing Architecture' module

The aim of the 'Analysing Architecture' module is to help student architects begin to 'map' these 'forests of uncertainty', to gain a better understanding of the 'powers' available to them as architects, and how they might deploy them in their own designs. This is done by analysing works of architecture to discover underlying intellectual patterns and strategies. Some analyses are presented in lectures, but students are also asked to prepare their own, building up a personal notebook which they may use as a tool for reflection when faced with design challenges in the future.

The module runs through the autumn semester of year two and is attended by about 70 students. They will be working towards the first of three parts (which take seven years in total) of the RIBA (Royal Institute of British Architects) professional qualifications; that is, they intend becoming practising 'architects'. About 10 third-year Architectural Engineering students also attend. (Architectural Engineering students are encouraged to attend such courses as a way of supplementing the necessarily formulaic problem-solving emphasis of their own course, and to get a better understanding of the ways in which architects, with whom they will be collaborating in their professional lives, work.) Each module morning lasts four hours, and is composed of two or three short (30–45 minute) lectures with related exercises.

Architectural design education has been founded on the principle of 'learning by doing'; students in schools of architecture spend the majority of their time 'in studio', working on design projects which become more complex as the course progresses. The 'Analysing Architecture' module is conceived as a supplement to studio teaching but has the form of a 'taught course', based in the lecture theatre rather than the design studio. In the lecture theatre, significant insights by any participant can be shared by all, and points which may arise repeatedly in individual studio tutorials can be made just once to the cohort as a whole. This setting also allows group discussion and feedback, as well as presentations by students to their colleagues.

As module tutor, my role is to take a lead; I try to do so not as an unquestionable 'authority' but as a fellow student, albeit with some years more study behind me. Pedagogically, my contribution is to describe 'regions' of the 'map' of architectural design as I see them, partial (in both senses of the word) though it may be. This is presented through a series of lectures, building up during the course into (the beginnings of) a many-dimensioned, multi-layered, conceptual framework for understanding architecture.

There is no space here to describe the content of the lectures in detail. Their themes are contained in the book *Analysing Architecture* (Unwin, 1997). Briefly, they discuss the purposes, premises, conditions, concerns, elements, context, attitudes, aspirations, ideas, strategies... of architecture, more or less in that order. They begin with a discussion of the first four – the purposes, premises, conditions and concerns of architecture – followed by the presentation of an argument that 'Architecture' should be considered primarily as 'Identification of Place'. The concerns that occupy an architect's mind when designing are then categorized as: the *conceptual organization of space into places*; the physical activity of *building* as a means to that end (*tectonics*); the refinement of the *visual appearance* of the resultant built forms; and, the manipulation of related *symbolic* or *semantic meanings*. This forms the theoretical foundation of subsequent parts of the module. The next two lectures deal with: 'Basic Elements of Architecture' (*defined area of ground, platform, wall etc*), 'Modifying Elements' (*light, sound, smell, scale, time etc*), and their combined contribution to the identification of place. Other groups of lectures deal with: 'Primitive Place Types' (*fireplace, performance place, altar, bed etc*); attitudes to conditions and context – 'Using Things That Are There', 'Architecture as Making Frames', 'Temples and Cottages' and the many roles played by 'Geometry in Architecture' (*the geometry of being, social geometry, the geometry of making, ideal geometries etc*). Later lectures illustrate strategies for organizing space into places: 'Space and Structure', 'Parallel Walls', 'Stratification', 'Transition, Hierarchy, Heart'. The concluding lectures present some 'case studies' in which selected buildings are subjected to analysis using the conceptual framework built up during the preceding lectures.

Temperamentally, I am disinclined to present my 'map' as '*the* map' (though I suspect some less critically minded students take it as such), partly because I am hard to convince that my map is incontrovertibly 'right' – it is no more nor less than my 'best shot' (and under constant reassessment and revision) – but also because students, as initiate professionals (and, hopefully, 'lifelong learners' in a 'learning society'), should possess an abidingly critical attitude to their own knowledge, beliefs, aspirations, attitudes etc. Also, there is, in the culture of architecture, a sense in which no one may presume to tell others what to think or do. Architects jealously guard their intellectual independence. This is a (probably healthy) symptom of working with an 'open-ended' skill. (It has conditioned my own research and teaching, so I cannot complain if I encounter it in colleagues!)

The thematic lectures form the core of each module morning. Their content is influenced and informed by available theoretical texts on architecture, but derives mainly from analysing examples from personal explorations. These provide the basis of each lecture, with their underlying patterns and strategies illustrated in the same medium used generally for design – drawing – helping to imply a bridge between what the students 'see' and what they 'do' in their own work.

The purpose of the lectures is not only to offer a framework for understanding architecture. Another objective is to achieve a 'flip' in students' ways of thinking about architecture. To define it, a 'flip' occurs when one sees something one thinks one knows well, differently; rather like the well-known optical conundrum of the two faces and the vase – when one's perception 'flips' between seeing the vase, and then the two faces. A typical 'flip' occurs when students are asked to think of architecture, not so much as *the design of buildings*, but as *the identification of places* (with buildings as a means to an end rather than ends in themselves); or when they are asked to think about a 'room' – a concept they have lived with all their lives – as a 'frame' which mediates between its content and the world outside. Both are insights which can stimulate the imagination. All our lives are so inextricably entangled with architecture, that such 'flips' are essential ways of getting students to think afresh about things they may have taken for granted, and never consciously considered in the ways they need to as professional designers. 'Flips' can also provoke self-motivated study and reflection.

The exercises which the students are asked to do in response to each lecture help them construct that important bridge between what they 'see' in the work of others and what they 'do' in their own design. The exercises always involve drawing, with verbal annotation where necessary. Some consist of finding and analysing a work of architecture that illustrates the theme of the lecture; some ask students to explore the theme through a short design.

The students' responses to the exercises are collected at the end of each morning and the subsequent module morning begins with feedback on the previous week's exercises to the whole cohort, using between six and ten pieces of student work as a focus for discussion. Individual students are sometimes asked to explain their work to their peers. In this way the issues which emerge in the lectures are restated and reinforced through their re-presentation in the students' own work, and by general discussion. Often related issues, not covered in the lectures, are also aired. These feedback sessions can be the most interesting parts of the module mornings. (They are also when I learn most.)

The architecture notebook

As part of the module students are required to keep what is called an 'Architecture Notebook', which is considered an indispensable 'machine for learning' during the course, and suggested as a good practice to maintain in the future. Every designer must be an autodidact. The notebook is a loose-leaf file in which students keep their responses to the exercises set in the module mornings. They are also encouraged to fill their notebooks with their own explorations in analysing and designing works of architecture. (The notebook accounts for 50 per cent of the module assessment. The other half is by a two-hour examination at the end of the semester in which students analyse an example from a report in an architectural publication.)

The notebook is a forum for continued personal reflective study. It consists of a loose-leaf file full of tracing paper and graph paper, a form which allows certain useful activities: tracing plans from publications; drawing analytical diagrams; and developing sketch designs by overlay. The loose-leaf form also allows organization of material into thematic sections (maybe in supplementary 'archive' files), and easy removal for photocopying and scanning into essays and dissertations.

The notebook is also a 'commonplace book', containing an ever-growing collection of ideas which can be used as a quarry when faced with new design challenges. It is important to the success of the course that students see their notebooks as something they will continue to use creatively (not just refer back to) throughout their professional careers, as an adjunct to their memories and a stimulus to their imaginations. Intellectual habits like this, initiated in the environment of higher education, can make a significant contribution to continued personal and professional development.

The module in relation to architectural history

One of the issues which has had to be addressed in developing the course is its relation to orthodox architectural history teaching. In schools of architecture, discussion of the architecture of the past has tended to be the preserve of architectural history which, with its roots in the methodologies of art history, possesses its own (epistemological) paradigm. Though popular with students, architectural history *per se* is a discipline which is not geared to their creative needs as architects. Architectural historians cultivate a sense of detachment, whereas architects must be involved. There is a broad (and understandable) tendency in architectural history writing to deal with architecture as something 'out there' (like rocks in geology or plants in botany) rather than as an activity in which the mind itself (one's own mind) is engaged.

Development of the 'Analysing Architecture' module was provoked some years ago by personal dissatisfaction with (my own) architectural history teaching. Students were treating architectural history as an academic subject irrelevant to their own problems in generating design. I became increasingly aware that examples of architecture from the past contained many lessons that would help them understand better what they were doing when designing, but that to expose these lessons a paradigm other than that offered by architectural history would have to be evolved. I began extracting these lessons, analysing examples, and organizing lectures around the themes that began to emerge. In some lights this could be seen to be mildly subversive, challenging or ignoring the orthodoxies of an established academic subject. However orthodox architectural history was not providing students with something they needed to develop as creative people. Architectural history is useful for its exposition of the cultural context of architecture and its development through time, but students also need different sets of cognitive filters, tailored not so much to the historian's mindset focused on the truth about the past, but to that of the architect who needs strategies for dealing with present and future challenges.

In the module lectures, examples are taken from all periods of the past, from pre-history to recent times, and from many regions of the world, often with what historians might condemn as cavalier disregard for established classifications of style, movement, region etc. Conventional architectural historical terminology ('Classical', 'Gothic', 'Arts and Crafts') is occasionally used, but generally avoided as a way of ordering the material presented to students. The rationale for this approach is radical, and unconventional, but it is essential to the intention and aspirations of the module. When, for example, one is considering the relationships between spatial and structural organization in architecture, and the organizational power of a pair of parallel walls, it can be quite appropriate to put a Greek temple from the 5th century BC next to a Finnish church from the 1950s (Figures 22.1 and 22.2).

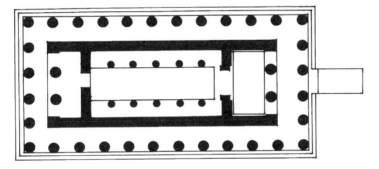

Figure 22.1 *Greek temple*

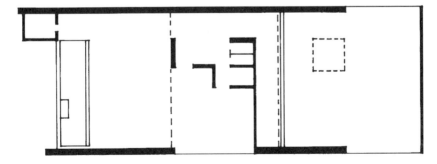

Figure 22.2 *Finnish church*

A characteristic of architectural historiography is that buildings are often explained as *products* of their time and culture. While this is a tenable theoretical standpoint for the historian, the implication for student architects – that their individual imaginations and will to act are impotent in the face of cultural forces – can cause confusion, self-doubt and insidious paralysis of the creative faculty for design. For student architects, in particular, ways need to be found of discussing works of architecture as products of the interaction of conscious, wilful, individual designing minds (like their own) with the conditions in which they found themselves (including the historical and cultural) and the challenges they faced. Architecture, after all, is quintessentially *not* a natural phenomenon.

The module in relation to the culture of architectural education

Somewhat in contradiction to the ethos of architectural history, there has also existed in the culture of architectural education an abiding belief that the open-ended skill of architectural design cannot be taught, it can only be learnt by practice (under the guidance, perhaps, of a 'master'). I think I would subscribe to that belief, too, but not that it precludes the promulgation of design-related knowledge. The problem can be compounded in the cases of students (and some teachers) who believe it is possible to 'design from within' – that each individual is in some way a fount of creativity who does not need to study the work of others and, indeed, would in some way adulterate their innate creativity if they did. The 'Analysing Architecture' module, acknowledging a debt to some enlightened theorists of the past (Lethaby, Rowe and Alexander among others), has shown that it is possible to build a knowledge base related to architectural design – similar perhaps to the relationship of music theory to musical composition, or grammar to language. Music theory does not provide a formula for composing music; grammar does not dictate what one writes; neither need the knowledge of architecture limit what one may design. All three can enhance the creative mind's appreciation of the possible.

Assessing the module's success

Objective measurement of the success of the module in achieving its aims is not easy. One has little more than subjective observation of student design work to go on. It appears that the course does help students produce design work with clearer and more consistent underlying intellectual structure than they would otherwise. However progress has been gradual and results confused by many other factors including changes in secondary education, and in the collateral teaching of colleagues. Departmentally organized student appraisal scores are generally high for this module, though responses to a separate questionnaire, which requires verbal rather than numerical responses, while being enthusiastic about the module and its content, sometimes expose significant misconceptions in students' minds about the module's purpose. Addressing these misconceptions is one of the ways in which the module is amended session by session, but another way of understanding some of them is that students have been conditioned, through a dozen and more years of formal education, to expect the process of learning to be primarily a matter of being *provided with* knowledge. This is a model to which the 'Analysing Architecture' course does not quite conform, for good and essential reasons. Although it may be said in part to *deal* in knowledge, its primary concern is not to *dispense* it but to place students in situations where they acquire it, assimilating it as 'their own'. Provoking students to take the initiative in this is not easy, but such initiative is surely an essential attribute of a 'learning society'.

Conclusions

One of the challenges in architectural education is that although the faculty for architecture may well be part of the innate intellectual make-up of the human mind, it is one which is generally ignored through the years of formal primary and secondary education when emphasis is placed on developing the faculties for language and number, and subsequently the acquisition of the established knowledge bases of academic subjects. Even so, when young people enter architectural education (often with little understanding of what is involved other than that it is something to do with 'designing buildings') they are expected to become expert in this neglected faculty within a few years. It is not surprising that it is often not until they reach their thirties or forties, after some 10 or 20 years more of experience, that architects find themselves proficient enough to produce works of architecture with confident fluency.

The best description I can offer for what it is like to learn to design is that it can be compared to learning language; not learning '*a foreign*' language, where one already possesses a native language that can be used as a point of reference, but learning language formatively, as a child learns its mother tongue. And just as language allows one to say things that have never been said before, so architecture allows one to design things that have never existed before. The general intellectual patterns and strategies of architecture, unlike those of many languages, have never been codified (*pace* the protagonists of that particular species of architecture called 'Classicism'), but these are the subject matter of the 'Analysing Architecture' module.

However romantically attractive the image may be, no designer is an island, and although each new project may present itself as being a completely new challenge, the likelihood is that it shares some aspect with other challenges that have been met before. A way to build up a reserve with which to face the challenges is to study the work of others (as a child acquires a vocabulary of words and a repertoire of patterns of speech from those around). Myth suggests that the genius creates *de novo*. We all aspire to genius, but examination of the notebooks of great architects shows them to have been autodidacts, always analysing the work of others and always collecting ideas they could use in their own. Our approach should be to connect into the struggles of other minds to deal with issues faced, understand the purposes they set out to achieve, and to learn from the strategies they adopted, use them, adapt them, reject those that did not succeed, prompt one's own mind to conjure up new or probably hybrid strategies, make new propositions etc and move on, but with an understanding of where others have been.

In the 'Analysing Architecture' module students are encouraged to acquire, and to some extent are put in a position where if they are to be successful they *must* acquire, a productive study method, one that will lead them into a continually renewed understanding of the variety of ways in which other architects have designed and, from that, develop ways in which they can do it themselves. The intention of the module is didactic, but it is also motivational, helping students, who in many cases do not quite understand what is expected of them, to gain courage and conviction for the adventure of architecture.

Chapter 23

Drawing together the threads

Elisabeth Dunne

In writing the conclusions to this book, the main purpose is to draw a substantial and connected argument from a collection of chapters written from very different perspectives, in different contexts and in different cultures. The purpose in inviting a range of authors was to build a coherent and developed set of perspectives in the context of higher education, but it remains a challenge to do this and to assess the implications.

Some of the recurring issues are summarized below and will be further discussed in the sections that follow:

- inadequate conceptualization of skills;
- resistance to change among university teachers, students etc;
- lack of effective management;
- absence of strategic planning, or lack of agreement, among educators, government departments, commerce and industry and funding agencies;
- lack of attention to a model of learning or teaching, and what it means to be a learner.

Rather than summarizing or commenting on each and every chapter, the discussion will draw on and develop the general trends of arguments. There are clearly different views and perspectives from within any one country, and there are obviously differences between nations, some of which have long been discussing the issues and some of which are just beginning to consider them. However, the issues discussed throughout the book have strong and pertinent messages that are worthy of thought whatever the particular context and situation of any country.

Reviewing core skills

In higher education

Pressure for a reconceptualization of higher education has an idea of core skills at the centre. Although there is a lack of clarity about how such skills are conceived, and about terminology, a perception of challenge to a traditional knowledge-based culture is not widely welcomed. There is widespread concern that such skills inevitably imply a narrow vision of competence especially as their enthusiasts tend to come from outside the traditional university sector. Hyland (1994) shares these concerns and notes that their influence derives from having the attributes of slogans: 'They fully satisfy the mother-hood-and-apple-pie test by advocating practices to which no one could possibly object, and they are so vague and nebulous that they can be made to include just about anything'. He argues that the pursuit of such skills 'is nothing more than a chimera hunt, a disastrous and costly exercise in futility'. However slogans are not easy to refute.

The most recent report: *Skills development in higher education* (Committee of Vice Chancellors and Principals in association with the Department for Education and Employment and the Higher Education Quality and Employability group, November 1998) shows how far the emphasis in the UK has gone. It seems that *all* skills learnt in university are now termed 'employability skills' and a starting point for categorization is suggested as: traditional intellectual skills; the 'new' core or key skills; personal attributes deemed to have marketable value; and knowledge about how organizations work and how people in them do their jobs. Skills seem not only to be skills, but knowledge and attributes also. There is potential here for interesting discussion on the relationship of skills to knowledge, and on the role of personal characteristics and motivational aspects within this, but this is not invited.

In employment

One of the significant features of contemporary debates about higher education is the range of contributors. Employers have been remarkably successful in influencing government policy on higher education. Dearing (1997) illustrates this in arguing for a growing interdependence between institutions, the economy, employers and the State. Employers' organizations have been powerful advocates for skill development in higher education. Survey evidence shows how 'obvious' it has become to demand that graduates have skills appropriate to employment. This is one of the recurring problems. It is proving difficult for the debate about higher education to be conducted analytically because of the 'evidence' that is influential but lacks focus. It remains unclear what employers mean by skills, the contexts in which they are thought to be necessary and the differential role of employers and higher education in the training and development of skills.

This raises the important question of the extent to which key skills are genuinely used by employers for selection of applicants. In many cases a high-level degree classification is considered a priority and sometimes students from particular universities are more likely to be favoured. Meagher (1998) has also suggested that during interviews employers focus on personal qualities rather than skills. This tendency is also apparent in the recruitment literature aimed at graduate applicants, where skill demands are far outweighed by the requirement for specific personal attributes such as enthusiasm and tenacity (Dunne, 1995).

Although the idea of skill development is popular it remains confused. Interviews with graduate employees (Dunne et al, 1997) illustrate how a seemingly common vocabulary for skills obscures a widely varied practice. The variety of tasks and contexts means that a seemingly straightforward skill receives such varied interpretations that they may be undeserving of being linked. The clearest example was 'communication skills', which included a wide range of verbal activities including chatting, using the telephone and dictaphone, as well as such higher-order skills as interviews with clients and colleagues, together with a variety of writing skills. This puts into doubt the whole question of the terminology of core or key skills. Further, employer concern may be more about graduates who 'have the expected knowledge and understanding... [but] display a serious inability to apply that knowledge effectively to real workplace situations' (National Skills Task Force, 1999). This could have a very different implication for the concept of core skills.

Newly employed graduates may have strong views on the skills that they had developed, or would have been useful to develop, in higher education. However, Dunne et al (1997) report how graduates had a variety of perceptions of their courses. Some thought that they had acquired skills at university, as part of their disciplinary studies, that were directly relevant to their work. Others thought that the subject matter was of secondary importance, and the value of a degree was training in 'being methodical', or being given the opportunity 'to learn more effectively and to get higher order mental skills'. One graduate demonstrated an interesting change in perception over the first year of employment – from believing the subject matter of his degree as being irrelevant, to understanding the usefulness of what it had offered. The notion of long-term maturation in learning (and the complex interplay of knowledge, theory and practical action) is one that may have been lost in the move towards performance skills and the requirement for 'instant' employability.

When in work, many graduates took an implicit 'situated' perspective of skill development in work – as preparation for specific skills in a specific context. Overall it was clear that the graduates' job demands and their work environments gave rise to very different practices, These practices, together with their personalities, shaped their perceptions of the skills they were using and developing. In other words, skills are heavily context-dependent.

Problems of change in higher education

Personal change in academics

Any innovation has to contend with the established views of practitioners. It is not surprising that academics remain suspicious of the idea of core skills as a central aspect of their work with students. Becher (1989) described the influence of disciplinary study on the lives of academics who took degrees in élite institutions and became leaders in their field. Becher's interviews revealed their perception 'as seekers after knowledge rather than as communicators of it [displaying] satisfaction, enjoyment and even exhilaration in relation to their discipline, as well as having a clear tendency to view the world... from their own disciplinary perspective'. Duke (1992) has attempted some mediation by suggesting that, although notions of preparing citizens for the learning society incline in the direction of instrumentalism, there is 'no necessary discord' with traditional values. Similarly, conceptions of core and transferable skills as being embedded within the disciplinary curriculum, or as enhancing processes of learning, do not have to conflict with traditional study (although they may require, for example, different forms of assessment). However, developments which threaten to undermine the value of 'one's existing intellectual shareholding', which has taken time and trouble to acquire, are unlikely to be welcomed by academics. Middlehurst (1993) claims that in the present onrush of change:

> the boundaries of the known and the valued are no longer clear or certain: in a physical sense where and how teachers and learners operate...; in a cognitive sense, what is taught, researched and learned, for what and for whose purposes; in an emotional sense, who I am as a teacher, learner, researcher or manager, what my role and contribution are, what power I will have or lose, who will judge me and how, what I must protect or surrender. The previous certainties of a life entrenched within a discipline are no longer secure.

If it is possible to empathize with this perspective, then it is also possible to imagine the kind of turmoil that a country such as Lithuania is experiencing, where all the previous certainties – at every level – have been undermined. Yet the particular circumstances have also promoted a desire to embrace change, to learn and to keep learning. There is a sense of enthusiasm and excitement.

From the Baltic State of Estonia, with its new-found political freedom, Indre (1997) reports a very different set of priorities in terms of core skills. She describes how the present transition in Estonia involves rapid changes wherein much has to be re-evaluated: traditions have to be abandoned and new ones adopted; new fields of activity emerge. The country is flooded with Western ideals, its mass culture and its global understanding of effective development. In higher education, access to knowledge from all sources, and open access to textbooks has to be a priority – to catch up with the rest of the world. However what is more important still is that Estonians have to adopt a new system of thinking and values. At the same time, there is a need to 'preserve our critical mind or we may lose our sense of reality and our identity as a nation'. There is a need to acquire a new set of values, new approaches, and to relearn what was previously 'known'. At the same time, economic difficulties cause many people to feel scared and helpless. Complicated relations between people, stress, loneliness, unemployment, homelessness – accompanied by the feeling of emptiness and of being unwanted – are described as: 'some of the psycho-sociological problems which might be called the pathology of our Modern Life. Clearly, our society needs a "doctor". More than that, we need a doctor among us every day. We need a helper, an advisor, a counsellor. These are the most important skills for our society'. This is, of course, the view of one person, but it serves to put a different perspective on the nature and extent of change with which academics, among others, are having to cope, on a daily basis, in certain parts of the world.

Pressures of change, and the accompanying erosion of personal control, are stressful (Fisher, 1994), especially since many academics indicate that they would prefer to spend their time in research activity. Fisher goes so far as to say that stress may undermine the whole ethos of a university. Duke (1992) claims that, if strains and dissonance are not recognized, efforts to revert to the familiar are strengthened. This is important in the light of a teaching union survey in the UK (NATFHE, 1992) which described low staff morale in universities, both old and new. Core skills, whatever their nature and purpose, are unlikely to inspire enthusiasm in this context.

From the USA, Henkel (1987) suggests that academic values *are* being transformed as an inevitable process as academics are exposed to more external norms and influences: they are not, for the most part, helpless pawns in others' games but read the changes and adapt in order to sustain their positions. However, Kogan (1987) concluded that managerial centralizing and instrumental rhetoric, although affecting structure, disposition and content of courses, does not change underlying rules or intellectual ambitions. It seems a question of 'playing the game', but not believing in the reality.

Management and leadership

Green (1994) suggests that: 'The search for economy, efficiency and value for money assumes a degree of management totally foreign to the traditional democratic and collegiate culture of the universities'. Core skills represent yet another issue to deal with. Whether initiated by external or internal pressures, Middlehurst (1993) reports differential consequences and enthusiasm for institutional change. When those at senior level experience a 'buzz of excitement' as they rise to the challenges of major innovations, others may be less enthusiastic. Erosion of personal autonomy or value systems can be threatening, and higher education has traditionally encouraged and valued autonomy. Middlehurst notes that major change in the academic world demands vision and risk-taking, but is concerned that the crucial feature of 'taking people with you' is too often absent. This requires building commitment, enthusiasm and trust in the new directions and strategies. Deep-rooted cultures need leaders to 'work with the grain', to reshape the university 'in the light of the demands of the future while remaining true to what is of enduring value from the past,' using 'support and challenge... in combination'. Whatever the truth of this analysis, or of the need for 'insinuation into the shadowy cultural heartland of the institution wherein change is supported, prevented or subverted' (Duke, 1992), it is clear that ideas of 'core skills' and a 'learning society' have not, in general, been managed in a way that reduces threat. This can go some way to explaining why the powerful rhetoric that assails higher education has still not, in the main, achieved significant changes in internal university priorities and practices.

This should come as no surprise. Stephenson and Weil (1992) argue convincingly that, in general, deep-level change requires not only a reconceptualization of higher education, but also a high level of commitment on the part of the staff and flexibility on the part of the institution. They recommend supportive professional development as crucial together with a clear commitment to incremental steps. However the kinds of professional development that would be required are unlikely to be a priority for academics at present, and commitment to fundamental reconceptualization is unlikely – unless market forces make it clear that survival is dependent on it.

Issues and tensions such as those outlined above are not easily resolved. Any innovation requires determination and persistence, but it also requires money. Although innovators themselves tend to be motivated by a perceived rightness of new methods, there is also evidence that as soon as any additional funding is removed, enthusiasm disperses (DES, 1992). Biggs et al (1994) examined the change process in a wide range of institutions in the Enterprise Programme and showed that innovation failed when it lacked support from top management. The commitment of management needs to be visible in financial planning. Without this, there is a danger that universities may adopt the superficial features of new approaches without really making significant moves. It is quite possible to prepare mission statements citing the importance of skills, of quality in teaching and learning, and of preparing students for the future, for the community, for lifelong learning and for employment. Internal systems can be developed to respond to the recommendations of funding councils that support modularization, clear learning outcomes and skill development. However none of this will matter without the supported commitment of university teachers who have the means of implementing change at the level of everyday practice.

The discourse of a learning society in higher education

The phrase 'a learning society' is one which invites support. It would seem churlish to deny that it is better than its opposite. However it remains unclear what constitutes a learning society. Hughes and Tight (1995) exercise some scepticism when they assert that it has become 'an ideological concept serving ideological purposes' which provides a 'convenient and palatable rationale and packaging for the current and future policies of different power groups within society'. Although Strain and Field (1997) suggest that the aims are broader and 'more transformative than the narrowly instrumental and economistic ones' implied by Hughes and Tight, Coffield (1997b) argues that 'right wing governments have appropriated the terms "a Learning Society" and "lifelong learning" in order to promote a particular view of the future, namely, one where individuals within a market economy are given greater responsibility for their education, training and employment'.

There is no harm in different groups espousing different aims for society. What is difficult is to decide what should be conveyed by either 'lifelong learning' or 'a learning society'. Hämäläinen (1996), for instance, claims quite plausibly that: 'The idea of men and women as maximally efficient instruments of production can only represent a passing phase of social transition'. He goes on to argue that lifelong learning is, at least, in part, about the future that we want for ourselves and our children, asking what is there that is 'so good, so beautiful and so worth while in our lives' that it is worthy of examination and promotion? Surely it is not what we have actually achieved? However from this it is not clear what actual provision would have to be made for 'lifelong learning'.

Barnett (1997) offers a more social, less personal, view. Reminding us that universities are 'in the presence of multiple crises', he addresses the theme of the 'new forms of knowledge', including what he now terms 'state-sponsored operationalism' (of which core skills are a part). He argues: 'institutions living up to the title of university have to engage [with the new definitions of knowledge] or resign themselves to becoming mere recipients and reproducers of others' knowledge. Such a truncation of the role would deprive the university of its historic role as an independent player'. Securing professional identity in the domain of knowledge and understanding in the modern age needs active engagement and intervention by universities, 'recalling their heritage as sites of openendedness and critical reason but also by situating themselves anew in the wider world'.

What Barnett seems to be suggesting is that universities must adopt a political stance in order to preserve their independence of thought, but since the political stance involves adopting the imposed agenda and subjecting this to scrutiny, there may be an inconsistency here. However, the main question is whether this offers a vision of what might be meant by a 'learning society'. It seems to be edging that way by asserting that the public institutions we support must themselves be visibly analytic, visibly responsive. A version of the learning society that refers to the quality of its institutions could be more attractive than one that implies active participation in learning by its individual members at all times. It is attractive, in part, because it places the debate about universities in the same frame as, say, that about public broadcasting. A long tradition of public service in broadcasting is being eroded by a demand to be responsive to the market (identified in terms of viewing figures). It is proving an irresistible demand in a society in which the market is paramount. And it may be in this context that an important aspect of a learning society is seen to be supporting conservatism in the face of pressures always to push back barriers. If the two problems (and others) can be seen as part and parcel of a wider concern, then perhaps the wider concern will begin to be addressed. The crucial question may be seen to be that of how an institution can be publicly funded, accountable and independent. In this way, it might be possible to re-examine the meaning of a learning society and the nature of student provision that this entails.

In 1994, the Director General of UNESCO (United Nations Educational, Scientific, and Cultural Organization) challenged universities to 'offer leadership in the whole educational service in addressing change'. It is all too easy to accept this as implying that universities must adopt change. However, whatever was intended, it also invites being interpreted as a call to dispassionately examine proposed changes, with acceptance and rejection being equally likely. Robertson (1995) observes that, although they will *resist* change, universities seem not to propose and facilitate ideas that would *promote* change. The most pressing cause for concern now is probably that, although discussion about educational reform is being conducted by the civil service, industry and commerce and educational specialists, there are no organized counter-forces. In the context of higher education, academics resist change, at least in the UK; they pay little attention to the issues, often being unaware of the debates. They have not, in the words of Robertson, 'shown themselves capable of leading the social and cultural transformations we need for future success'.

In 1980, Carter (reflecting a turbulent period as Vice-Chancellor of the University of Lancaster) was adamant that 'discussion cannot be left to the academics, who are interested parties with established positions within structures and professional groups'. This, again, may not be so obvious as it seems. It may be that it is not 'established positions' that are problematic, but what the positions are about. In any discipline it is necessary for a strong adherence to established positions to act as a means of conducting sceptical examination of innovation. It should be no less so with teaching, but the positions must be principled, contested, examined, refutable. In short, there needs to be a science of teaching for all academics that is treated as seriously as the other disciplines. Duke (1992) is suggesting something of this sort with two scenarios. On the one hand, academics can offer covert resistance and quiet sabotage, trading on the privileged position of an academic. On the other hand, they can develop a paradigm so that coherence and a rationale can be seen and understood, encouraging 'the kind of conversation, the discursive or dialectical process enjoyed in universities'. Winter (1996) supports the view that 'we retain the fundamental duty to act as "critics" [because] [t]he "new" higher education both summons us and enables us to reinterpret, to reinvigorate and, indeed, to extend that role'. Critics do not work with no knowledge and no understanding; and they do not work without an established paradigm. A learning society may be best conceived as one in which public institutions can engage in debate without fear of being closed for not agreeing. However the cost of this may be a demand for the nature of their disagreement to be visible.

Professionalism and the discourse of learning

It may often be difficult for university teachers who want to concentrate on quality of teaching. They may not be supported and may be criticized for attending to teaching rather than to research and publications. Beyond this, the long-term neglect of learning theory and models of teaching and learning mean there is no solid base of methods, language and discourse on which to draw. Phrases such as 'student-centred learning' or 'autonomy' are used, but this hardly establishes an ethos in which student learning can be given detailed attention. Lacking discourse of this kind, higher education may not qualify as a significant contributor to a learning society. There is a need for academics to be enabled to create a community in which they learn about the ways of thinking of students, and about reactions to provision, so that the development of teaching becomes part of their daily work. It needs a research community for teaching.

There are recently many more instances of teachers writing about their own practice but there is little evidence of these corresponding closely with any situation defined by established models of good practice. However examples can be used to persuade. In the discussion of a law department (Chapter 19), there was evidence of a considerable 'pay-off' from putting time and effort into team development. Students trained to operate in self-managed teams became more responsible for their own long-term learning (which is what employers require) and achieved expected standards in terms of disciplinary knowledge. Although the initiative was demanding of staff time, it had a long-term advantage in reduced contact time. This fact alone provides a reason for others to look to this as a model, which may encourage, in turn, a starting point for developing a language of teaching. Nonetheless, long-term change must be grounded in a more developed approach to the conceptualization of student provision and an enhanced understanding of how students learn.

Provision for learning

In higher education there is a great deal of evidence of the centrality of student learning. The vocabulary – of a learning society, lifelong learning, learning organization, student-centred learning, independent learning, the learner-centred curriculum, learning groups, learning outcomes – all serves to establish the new emphasis. In the UK, it is no longer politically correct to say: 'teaching and learning'; it must be: 'learning and teaching', as if the change in word order would, magically, promote changes in practice. Unfortunately, such change as the latter goes unnoticed and its significance unheeded by the majority of those it is meant to persuade. The problem can be seen vividly in the use of the term 'learning outcomes'. University teachers are being required to rewrite their module or course descriptions to highlight learning outcomes instead of only the content of what is taught. This is intended to create a real focus on learning but it does not necessarily change the practice of teaching or the mode of assessment. The impact on students may be negligible.

Further, despite the terminology of 'learning', little attention is paid to 'what it means to learn', or 'to be a learner'. If the concept of a *learning* society is to be valid, it is crucial that more attention is given to the psychological processes of learning, to the impact of environments and contexts used to promote the act of learning, and to the kinds of teaching which enable and motivate students to learn. Higher education should be able to demonstrate itself to be a society of learners, of people who want to learn and who respond to the challenge of learning, both at the level of student and the teacher.

Structuring the learning context

As student numbers increase and staff:student ratios decline, there will be pressure to find ways of delivering a similar curriculum to that traditionally covered, of balancing this with a skills-oriented curriculum, of maintaining rigour and standards, of ensuring the motivation of students and, in many universities, of ensuring the continued output of high-quality research. An administrative response to this in the UK has been to insist that all courses be designed as a series of modules. This has generated considerable concern about how continuity and progression in learning can be preserved. Resistance to 'modularization' is often represented as the expected resistance to change by academics, but there are major difficulties that are not being given sufficient attention. If learners do not make connections between their learning experiences (and learning theory suggests that this is not straightforward) and if they are not required to practise, apply and reapply skills, in preplanned ways, then it may be that the value of many experiences is lost. In economic terms, this could be seen as wasted learning. Eraut's (1996) notion of the 'cost' of transfer in the workplace might be equally important in higher education. Some universities are now reporting a range of difficulties associated with modular choice and are beginning to provide counselling systems to enable students to make coherent decisions. This response implies that modularization is seen as entirely appropriate, with the problem residing in the students. Again, the assumed wisdom of a new approach is unassailable.

The new emphasis on acquisition of skills is not always convincing to students. The perception often remains of a degree being essentially about disciplinary knowledge, not processes, and that high level knowledge is what employers require. It is also clear that students tend to prefer ways of learning with which they feel most comfortable or successful, and by which they are not challenged (or threatened). Entwistle (1992) has usefully described 'instrumental' learners who work to satisfy a qualification rather than look for quality and depth of understanding, supporting Fullan's (1991) recognition that 'learning a new skill and entertaining new conceptions create doubts and feelings of awkwardness or incompetence, especially when we first try something'. Simons (1997) similarly suggests that 'Learning can (and should) be very painful. Sometimes the *result* of learning is joyful, but the process is energy-taking and very emotional'. One of the problems of introducing new processes of learning is that it tends to be difficult for both those who provide them and for those who should gain from them. There is 'the need to create safe environments to encourage people to take the risk of learning' (Coffield, 1997c).

The future

A focus on teaching is becoming more apparent in government documentation, both in the UK and elsewhere. The issue of professionalization of teachers in higher education is increasingly being seen as important. However reforms in higher education teaching are being imposed on academics who are not equipped to give the same fundamental attention to societal and pedagogic questions that they give to their own discipline. There may be pressures to remove undergraduate courses from their link with research and scholarship so that the bulk of students are taught courses unerringly focused on employment skills. This is an issue that needs the most detailed analysis. The community with the most potential for offering this analysis is the university teachers themselves. Currently this would be difficult because they lack a sense of community in relation to this aspect of their work. When academics do turn their attention to pedagogy, they undoubtedly bring the same analytical rigour to its uncertainties that they practise in their own disciplines. Concentrating on this conversion could provide a major contribution to the debate about what 'a learning society' might come to mean.

Action is needed to involve academics in a debate, central to their work, in which they are currently marginalized. Increased student numbers and a more diverse student group raise questions about teaching methodology that are currently being answered in *ad hoc*, unprincipled ways focused by rhetoric. A professional body for teaching in higher education, drawn from a wide range of disciplines, might turn its attention to the range of issues provoked by contemporary policies. It could examine pedagogic science and enable the development of models of teaching for higher education. It could support the development of 'evidence-based policy and practice', called for by the UK Minister of State (Clarke, 1999) and a move towards research on teaching being as highly valued as research within disciplines.

Clarke aspires for research to 'identify the most effective approaches [to teaching] that will contribute to raising standards at all levels', claiming that 'Research should provide the evidence base to inform and contribute to the decision-making process'. This is an encouraging move given that educational research has recently been heavily criticized by government-sponsored groups. For example, Ofsted (Office for Standards in Education) suggested in July 1998 that two-thirds of journal articles on education were of poor quality. A report later in the year from the Department for Education and Employment concluded that research relating to schools is largely irrelevant and inaccessible, rarely informing policy or practice (Hillage *et al*, 1998). However, the problem – it seems – is that such research 'has been conducted almost entirely independently of the policy and political framework' (Clarke, 1999). But there is a failure to appreciate that research confined to the current policy and political framework most often consolidates its limitations rather than offering principled development.

Time has to be made for informed debate and developing a coherent vision of the roles that universities could play. It is a debate that must be conducted within higher education, not only from outside. There is no appropriate forum for this, but it has been suggested above that there is a need for a professional body, across disciplines, focused on pedagogical science. It could be asserted that this is currently being put into place with the creation of the ILT (Institute for Learning and Teaching) in the UK, with its purpose to set standards of professional practice; to enhance the status of teaching in higher education; and to maintain and improve the quality of learning and teaching (Committee of Vice Chancellors and Principals, 1999). However, it could also be asserted that the creation of this institute illustrates the nature of the problem rather than offering a solution. A predictable pattern is emerging. It is yet another creation of the atheoretical, managerial period in which it is set because it does not provoke the quality of academic debate necessary for developing a robust pedagogical science.

It is atheoretical because it persists with the widespread assumption that all wisdom resides solely in practice that, once described, provides a usable standard. There is a specific claim that the ILT 'will draw on the expertise, experience and professional values of the university and college staff involved in teaching and learning'. The Institute will adopt standards and qualities which 'those who are active in teaching and learning understand as appropriate and relevant'. This comforting recourse to current expertise misses the point. It is not simply a question of finding cases of good practice. It is necessary to be clear about what they are specifically cases of. The whole exercise is one that demands the quality of an explanatory framework that the established disciplines have so painstakingly developed. The same painstaking development is needed for the science of teaching. The willingness to confront uncertain problems (rather than strip every problem of its uncertainty) is what characterizes both the established disciplines and the consensual, political version of democracy that legitimizes the existence of the UK government.

Managerial solutions elevate the need for action above contemplation. Obviously, every act of government has to adopt a managerial approach for some part of its work. It has to be circumscribed by recognition of its limitations. This is the aspect that seems, crucially, to be absent from contemporary developments. What this means is that essentially uncertain problems are being framed to rule out the uncertainty. What constitutes effective teaching? This is a prime example of an important, uncertain problem. It is not being treated as problematic. Legislators have not understood its complexity. They persist with the same tired solution? Find some 'good teaching', describe it, call the outcome 'standards' and enforce it. The solution becomes an exercise in writing statements that are not required to reflect the complexity of the question. It is a managerial solution.

In order to understand why a managerial approach has become endemic it is necessary to look beyond the immediate manifestations. To do this, it is important to look at current practice in government, that is, to look at the nature of political life. Any legitimate government has the authority to pursue policies consistent with its legitimacy. This is not true only of democratic governments but of all governments. What is peculiar to democratic governments is only that they achieve their legitimacy via a democratic process. It is the nature and limits of its legitimacy that determines a government's freedom of action.

Democratic government in the UK has developed over the centuries into a relatively stable process that has a particular sensitivity to minority views. It is a process of government that seeks to make decisions about complex, contested questions without simple recourse to majority opinion. It is this tradition that has been unusually sceptical about holding any referendum; and it is a process that has held the line, for instance, against reintroduction of the death penalty without overt demonstration by its supporters. It is characterized by decision-making that, susceptible to the criticism of being less than transparent, exhibits, arguably, considerable wisdom. It is not dominated by a management model but exhibits instead a consensual, almost generous, agreement (even in the face of mistakes). It has an almost old-fashioned allegiance to a set of guiding principles. It is seemingly driven by a view of life that is closer to that of the academic disciplines than it is to schools of management. It does not focus only on solutions acceptable to its constituency (it does not, for instance, reintroduce capital punishment when it is demanded, but continues to treat it as a complex, uncertain problem).

This is the tradition of government that has developed. Governments elected in this context have a legitimacy that is not simply 'democratic' but defines a particular version of democracy, and they have a particular responsibility to respect this fragile legitimacy. There is an implicit trust that is not incorporated into any list of responsibilities or rights. It has denied the elevation of managerial approaches above fragile, uncertain, consensual, active contemplation.

This implicit trust is under threat by the manner in which a series of reforms are being driven. The trust that lies at the heart of UK government is being abandoned in a flight to managerial transparency. Once a problem is defined ('lack of skills among the workforce', or whatever) then that problem is solved by the installation of 'a system'. The contemplative mode is one that seeks to see what light has been shed on the nature of the initial problem by the supposed solution. And it is most often the case that the original characterization is seen to be faulty. This is the nature of the established disciplines and the nature of the framework which legitimizes the government. It is different from seeking only to satisfy majority opinion. It is in this sense that current reforms are intrinsically undemocratic. They rule out the possibility of contemplation. They seek to reduce the problem rather than to understand it. They fail to seek the wisdom in traditional lore.

The proposed ILT is likely to become yet another example of a managerial approach antithetical to the fragile trust placed in government. A parallel development, 'benchmarking', is one of the latest moves in the process of outlining curriculum content and standards. It is likely to gain some support because it does refer to the established disciplines to be more explicit about the outcomes of higher education. It remains, however, resolutely managerial in its approach. It does not address the fundamental issues of teaching and learning. It is this that could be regained by a professional body of the kind suggested above. It would provide at least a chance that teaching could be understood and characterized in a manner that captures its essential feature of induction into a well-developed explanatory framework. This is radically different from contemporary approaches.

The distinctive feature of established disciplines is having an explanatory framework accepted by its practitioners so there are agreed criteria for testing the validity of new assertions, findings or methods. It is this feature that requires urgent work in university teaching and would be an imperative for the cross-discipline professional body advocated above. It would be a pedagogical framework that is sufficiently robust for it to be applied to all the disciplines. At the moment there is no such framework and the attendant problems are becoming increasingly critical as the university system comes under pressure from managerial thinking. In current circumstances any assertion about teaching and course design is as valid as another. For example, it has become popular to describe lectures as 'transmission knowledge', with the implication that this is in some way unsavoury. It is contrasted with 'independent learning' which is taken to be unproblematically valid. There is an absence of any established view of the nature of learning that enables practitioners to examine these assertions in terms that can be debated in detail. Little attention is given to what might make a lecture centrally important to a course of study, or in what circumstances transmission knowledge (whatever that means, and it is certainly problematic) is essential.

This unprincipled approach to course planning has led to some bizarre scenarios (although none look strange to their advocates). In one instance, 100 first-year students were required to seek computer access to a Web-based lecture which could more profitably have been given in a lecture theatre. The justification for this was located in the need, firstly, for the development of IT-based skills; secondly, a flexible timetable so that students manage their own learning; thirdly, more time for the lecturer to engage in research. Each of these criteria reflects a managerial influence on the nature of teaching.

The influence of managerial priorities on teaching in higher education (and the consequent absence of shared theoretical frameworks) is widespread and typified by Nightingale and O'Neil (1994). They contribute to mistaken ideas of teaching when they uncritically accept that 'the facilitation of learning is contrasted with conceptions of teaching as the transmission of knowledge and of teaching as the efficient orchestration of teaching skills'. Seemingly unaware of the dangers of making a false distinction (since none of them constitutes teaching without the others) they proceed to a series of further claims that mimic the managerial view. This kind of uncritical and uninformed approach reinforces that teaching in higher education requires a theoretical framework of the type that characterizes the established disciplines. This has the same purpose in teaching as in the disciplines: to provide a relatively stable test of the validity of innovation.

The direction of argument so far has been from recognition of the established success of the disciplines towards the need to cater for identified deficiencies in the conceptualization of teaching. Interestingly, the same conclusion can be reached by arguing in the opposite direction. Let us start from current interest in the notion of a learning society, lifelong learning and learning organizations. Each of these remain somewhat ill-defined. Leitch *et al* (1995) discuss the idea of a learning organization and, pointing out that there is little consensus about what organizational learning is, suggest 'the critical issue is how individual learning or self-development... can be transferred to the organisation'. They assert that an explicit distinction has to be made between individual and organizational learning, otherwise there is a danger of over-simplifying the latter'. This is important because it is a rare recognition of the need to conceive the 'learning' of an organization as something different from the sum of the individual learning of its members.

A similar warning needs to be applied to the notion of 'lifelong learning', that it is not a continuing process of adding more knowledge or abandoning previous knowledge in preference to new employment requirements. Each of these present a major conceptual problem. It can be solved by conceiving the required wider view of learning as one that provides codification for the relevant knowledge. This means that the extent to which an organization can be characterized as *'learning'* is the extent to which knowledge is codified. The challenge is to codify relevant knowledge in ways that make it possible for inividuals to contribute to and access it in economical ways. This is precisely the purpose of a theoretical framework in the established disciplines: it provides a codification that, in the way it operates, offers a test of the validity of a new contribution and points to the rationale for inclusion of established contributions. It can be seen that this direction of argument brings the same conclusion that induction into a discipline has all the advantages that contemporary managers aspire to as preparation for work in a learning society. A problem has been created in spite of its solution being available.

Preparation for work must include not only some experience of working in a discipline but also the disposition to work in that way. This is, of course, what has always been meant by induction into a discipline: it is a cognitive apprenticeship. Training must conform to the essence of disciplinary work. This central purpose of higher education has been distorted by the imposition of the competing demand to provide 'student satisfaction' for a wider range of students (for retention of students and continued payment of fees). When teachers respond, for instance, by reducing the demands of the task, they are most often failing adequately to represent the nature of disciplinary study. A wider range of students are usually taken as sufficient incentive to design courses that are 'more practical' and 'less theoretical'. Far more important is the need for understanding 'underlying meaning and constructing a mental representation' (Simons, 1997), and it is this, most importantly' 'that forms a basis for future applications'.

In the absence of a principled pedagogic framework, teachers in higher education have assumed that less talented students need matters simplified. However such students are in more need of being taught the theoretical ideas because it is these that provide the crucial connections in a discipline. They need the ideas to be clarified. The tendency for simplification makes it even more difficult for less talented students to identify and respond to the essence of disciplinary study. They are, therefore, less well prepared for any work in what aspires to be a 'learning organization'. Interestingly, the tendency to reduce the demands of the task is not necessarily popular with the students for whom it is done. James and McInnis (1995) have shown this in a national study of first-year higher education students in Australia. Despite 'increasing numbers of students who are academically less well prepared', they found a strong desire and expectation for intellectual challenge. It may be that they require special support, but the support should be for clarification of the essential features of the discipline, not by removal from the curriculum of the central features of that discipline.

It has been argued here that the most appropriate focus for characterizing a learning society, and for framing research on teaching and learning within that society, is through the notion of scholarship. There are other advocates of this. An ongoing project in four Australian universities, funded by the Committee for University Teaching and Staff Development, focuses on the development of scholarship in teaching (www, 1999). The two main intentions are to 'develop and support university teachers in their scholarly practice' and to 'communicate the scholarship of teaching widely throughout the Australian higher education community'. The 'practice of scholarship' is perceived as developing 'within a community, a community of scholars. Communication is central to the idea of community and it is the medium for scrutiny, debate and learning to take place'. For them, communicating the scholarship of teaching is premised on three starting points:

1. talking through practice issues with colleagues;
2. sharing knowledge gained through reading research into student learning;
3. collaborating to enable the development and refinement of ideas, the illumination of practice through theory.

Underpinning the project is the 'assumption that teaching will be properly valued in higher education when it is publicly seen to be a scholarly pursuit'. This is a step in the right direction, but there is a danger that 'communication' will not necessarily include the development of the robust theoretical perspective argued for here. There must be a determination to emphasize the 'science' in pedagogical science.

Coffield has directed a major programme of British research into different versions of a learning society over the past five years. He has expressed his concern (Coffield, 1999) that the 'official list of skills culled from the ubiquitous rhetoric' will not serve us well for success in the next century. What, then, is the significance of the official list (information technology, communication and teamwork etc) to which he refers? They are, of course, worthwhile attributes to develop, in the same way that it was worth while learning to use a quill several centuries ago, but they are inadequate as the central planks of a programme in higher education. However it is against rhetoric such as this that we need the secure defence of pedagogical science. When it is asserted that, say, teamwork should be central to a curriculum, we need practitioners who are able to evaluate the extent to which it is a valid concept, knowing what are the criteria for validity in their own science, employing a robust evaluative language. What they would not do, as scientists, is to resist considering the merits of a new vocabulary or concept. What they would do is to examine it from a principled position.

Those who seek to establish skills as the centre of higher education, so that graduates become more employable in an increasingly complex world, have one direction to move in. They should advocate the induction of all students into principled disciplinary knowledge and provide university teachers with the resources to create the new discipline of pedagogy. There is much to be learnt and a great challenge to be met before higher education can be recognized as a 'learning society' that is as knowledgeable about pedagogy as it is about the established disciplines.

References

Abrami, PC *et al* (1993) *Using Cooperative Learning*, Brown and Benchmark, Dubuque, Iowa

ACLEC (The Lord Chancellor's Advisory Committee on Legal Education and Conduct) (1996) *First Report on Legal Education and Training*, Lord Chancellor's Department, London

AGR (Association of Graduate Recruiters) (1995) *Skills for Graduates in the 21st Century*, AGR, Cambridge

AGR (Association of Graduate Recruiters) (1996) *Graduate Salaries and Vacancies*, Summer Update Survey, AGR, Cambridge

Allen, M (1991) *Improving the personal skills of graduates*, Final Report, University of Sheffield, Sheffield

Angelil-Carter, S (1995) *Uncovering plagiarism in academic writing: developing authorial voice within multivoiced text*, MEd thesis, Rhodes University, Rhodes

Angelo, TA (1993) A teacher's dozen – 14 general research-based principles for improving higher learning in our classrooms, *American Association for Higher Education Bulletin*, April

Angelo, TA, and Cross, KP (1993) *Classroom Assessment Techniques: A handbook for college teachers*, 2nd edn, Jossey-Bass, San Francisco, CA

Assiter, A, ed (1995) *Transferable Skills in Higher Education*, Kogan Page, London

Astin, A (1993) *What Matters in College: Four critical years revisited*, Jossey-Bass, San Francisco, CA

Australian Government discussion paper, *Learning for life – questions and answers*, http://www.deetya.gov.au/divisions/hed/hereview/reports/learning.htm

Barnett, R (1990) *The Idea of Higher Education*, Open University Press, Buckingham

Barnett, R (1994) *The Limits of Competence: Knowledge, higher education and society*, Open University Press/SRHE, Buckingham

Barnett, R (1997) A knowledge strategy for universities, in *The End of Knowledge in Higher Education*, eds R Barnett and A Griffin, pp 166–79, Cassell, London

BBC2 (1996) *Firsts among equals?* Broadcast (5 November)

Becher, T (1989) *Tribes and Territories*, Open University Press, Buckingham

Bell, J and Johnstone, J (1998) *General transferable skills in the law curriculum*, Report of a Discipline Network Project, Law Department, University of Leeds, Leeds

Bennett, N, Dunne, E and Carré, C (1999) Patterns of core and generic skill provision in higher education, *Higher Education*, **15** (1), pp 1–23

Bernstein, B (1971) On the classification and framing of educational knowledge, in *Knowledge and Control*, ed MFD Young, pp 47–69, Macmillan, London

Beven, F and Duggan, L (1996) A conceptualisation of generic skills and context-dependent knowledge and a methodology for examining practice, in *Learning in the Workplace: Tourism and hospitality*, ed J Stevenson, Centre for Skill Research and Development, Griffith University, Brisbane

Biggs, C, Brighton, R, Minnit, P, Pow, R and Wicksteed, W (1994) Thematic evaluation of EHEI, *Research Series*, **30**, Employment Department, Sheffield

Boekaerts, M (1993) Being concerned with well-being and with learning, *Educational Psychologist*, **28** (2), pp 149–67

Bossert, ST (1988) Cooperative activities in the classroom, *Review of Educational Research*, **15**, pp 225–50

Boud, D, ed (1981) *Developing Student Autonomy in Learning*, Kogan Page, London

Boud, D (1986) *Implementing Student Self-Assessment*, HERDSA Green Guides, no 5, Higher Education Research and Development Society of Australasia, Kensington, New South Wales

Boud, D (1989) The role of self-assessment in student grading, *Assessment and Evaluation in Higher Education*, **14** (1), pp 20–29

Boud, D (1995) *Enhancing Learning through Self-Assessment*, Kogan Page, London

Boud, D, Keogh R and Walker, D (1985) Promoting reflection in learning: a model, in *Reflection in Learning: A model*, eds D Boud, R Keogh and D Walker, pp. 18–40, Kogan Page, New York

Boughey, C (1994) *Towards a Model of 'Writing to Learn': Reflections on two years' work at UWC*, UWC, Bellville

Boyer, E (1987) *College: The undergraduate experience in America*, Jossey-Bass, San Francisco, CA

Brown, A (1997) The development of key skills across contexts and over time, *Capability*, **3** (2), pp 16–20

Brown, JS, Collins, A and Duguid, P (1989) 'Situation cognition and the culture of learning', *Education Researcher*, **18**, pp 32–42

Bruffee, K (1978) The Brooklyn plan: attaining intellectual growth through peer-group tutoring, *Liberal Education*, **64**, pp 447–68

Bruffee, KA (1983) Writing and reading as social or collaborative acts, in JN Hays (ed) *The Writer's Mind: Writing as a mode of thinking*, pp 159–169, NCTE, Urbana IL

Business/Higher Education Round Table (1991) *Aiming higher: the concerns and attitudes of leading business executives and university heads to education priorities in Australia in the 1990s* (Commissioned Report no 1), Melbourne

Business/Higher Education Round Table (1992) *Educating for excellence part 2: achieving excellence in university professional education* (Commissioned Report no 2), Melbourne

Business/Higher Education Round Table (1993) *Graduating to the workplace: business students' views about their education* (Commissioned Report no 3), Melbourne

Business/Higher Education Round Table (1995) *Identifying future leaders: a study of career progression and development* (Commissioned Report no 4), Melbourne

Candy, PC (1991) *Self-direction for Lifelong Learning*, Jossey-Bass, San Francisco

Candy, PC, Crebert, G, and O'Leary, J (1994) *Developing lifelong learners through undergraduate education* (Commissioned Report no 28), National Board of Employment, Education and Training, Canberra

Chalmers, D, and Fuller, R (1995) *Teaching for Learning at University*, Edith Cowan University, Perth

Chambers, EA (1992) Workload and the quality of student learning, *Studies in Higher Education*, **17** (2), pp 141–53

City and Guilds (1993) *Core Skills For GNVQs*, City and Guilds, London

Clarke, C (1999) Resurrecting research to raise standards, *Economic and Social Research Council, Updates*, **2**, http://www.esrc.ac.uk/news2.html

Cleary, LM (1991) *From the Other Side of the Desk: Students speak out about writing*, Heinemann, Portsmouth

Coffield, F (1997a) Attempts to reclaim the concept of 'the learning society', in Perspectives on defining 'the learning society', *Journal of Educational Policy*, **12** (6), pp 1–18

Coffield, F (1997b) A tale of three little pigs: building the learning society with straw, in *A National Strategy for Lifelong Learning*, ed F Coffield, pp 77–93, School of Education, University of Newcastle upon Tyne

Coffield, F (1997c), Nine learning fallacies and their replacement by a national strategy for lifelong learning, in *A National Strategy for Lifelong Learning*, ed F Coffield, pp 1–35, School of Education, University of Newcastle upon Tyne

Coffield, F (1999) *Breaking the consensus: lifelong learning as social control*, inaugural lecture, University of Newcastle, Newcastle

Collis, B (1996) *Tele-learning in a Digital World*, International Thomson Computer Press, London

Cooper, JL *et al* (1990) *Cooperative Learning and College Instruction: Effective use of student learning teams*, California State University, Dominguez Hills Foundation on behalf of the California State University Institute for Teaching and Learning, Carson, California

Cuseo, JB (1996) *Cooperative Learning: A pedagogy for addressing contemporary challenges and critical issues in higher education*, Oryx Press, Ohio

CVCP (Committee of Vice Chancellors and Principals), CBI (Confederation of British Industry) and CIHE (Council for Industry and Higher Education) (1996) *Declaration of Intent*, CVCP, London

CVCP (Committee of Vice Chancellors and Principals), DfEE (Department for Education and Employment) and HEQE (Higher Education and Employability) (1998) *Skills Development in Higher Education*, CVCP, London

CVCP (Committee of Vice Chancellors and Principals) (1999) *Institute for Learning and Teaching Consultation: The national framework for higher education teaching, 1/99/14*, CVCP, London

Danish Ministry of Education (1997) *National kompetenceudvikling*, Danish Ministry of Education, Copenhagen
http://www.uvm.dk/eng/publications.engonline.htmDanish Ministry of Education (1998a) *Kvalitet i uddannelsessystemet* Danish Ministry of Education, Copenhagen

Danish Ministry of Education, (1998b) *Det 21. århundredes uddannelsesinstutioner*, Danish Ministry of Education, Copenhagen

de la Harpe, B, Radloff, A and Parker, L (1997) *Time spent working and studying in the first year: what do students tell us?*, paper presented at the Teaching Learning Forum, Murdoch University, Perth

Dearing Report (1997) *Higher Education in the Learning Society*, HMSO, London

Denicolo, P, Entwistle, N and Hounsell, D (1992) What is active learning? in *Effective Learning and Teaching in Higher Education*, Module 1, CVCP Universities' Staff Development and Training Unit [now UCoSDA], Sheffield

Department of Employment (1995) *Strategy paper on core skills*, paper presented to the Committee of Vice Chancellors and Principals, DoE, London

DES (Department of Education and Science) (1987) *Higher Education: Meeting The Challenge*, HMSO, London

DES (Department of Education and Science) (1991) *Higher Education: A New Framework*, HMSO, London

DES (Department of Education and Science) (1992) *A Survey of the Enterprise in Higher Education Initiative*, DES, London

Director General of UNESCO (1994) Opening address, cited in R Waterhouse, *Lifelong Learning – a European perspective*, paper presented at the Conference of the Trans-European Exchange and Transfer Consortium, Hogeschool Gent, Gent

Dohmen, G (1996) *Lifelong Learning: Guidelines for a Modern Education Policy*, Bundesministerium fuer Bildung, Wissenschaft, Forschung und Technologie, Bonn

Drummond, I, Nixon, I and Wiltshier, J (1997) *Transferable skills in higher education: the problems of implementing good practice*, draft project paper, Universities of Hull and Newcastle, Newcastle upon Tyne

Duke, C (1992) *The Learning University: Towards a new paradigm*, SRHE/Open University Press, Buckingham

Dunne, E (1995) *Personal transferable skills*, Internal Report, University of Exeter, Exeter

Dunne, E, Bennett, N and Carré, C (1997) Higher education: core skills in a learning society, in Perspectives on defining 'the learning society', *Journal of Educational Policy*, **12** (6), pp 511–25

Dunne, E, Carré, C and Davies, N (1997) *The graduate experience of work: core skills*, paper presented at the 5th Conference of the European Association for Research into Learning and Instruction (EARLI), Athens

Dunne, E and Fraser, M (1998) The acquisition and development of core skills: practices and perceptions, in *Improving Student Learning*, proceedings of the

Fifth International Symposium on Improving Student Learning, ed C Rust, pp 171–81, Oxford Centre for Staff and Learning Development, Oxford

Dunne, R (1992) *Curriculum coordination and management*, Module 11: Inset at a distance, University of Exeter, Exeter

Edwards, R (1994) From a distance? Globalisation, space-time compression and distance education, *Open Learning,* **9** (3), pp 9–17

Edwards, R (1997) *Changing Places? Flexibility, lifelong learning and a learning society,* Routledge, London and New York

Elliot, J (1991) A model of professionalism and its implications for teacher education, *British Education Research Journal,* **16,** pp 94–103

Engeström, Y (1995) *Training for Change,* ILO, London

Entwistle, N (1987) *Understanding Classroom Learning,* Hodder and Stoughton Educational, London

Entwistle, N (1988) *Styles of Learning and Teaching: An integrated outline of educational psychology,* David Fulton, London

Entwistle, N (1992) *Student learning and instructional principles in higher education,* in Committee of Scottish University Principals, *Teaching and Learning in an Expanding Higher Education System, Appendix A,* pp 52–62, SFC, Edinburgh

Entwistle, N and Ramsden, P (1983) *Understanding Student Learning,* Croom Helm, London

Eraut, M (1994) *Developing Professional Knowledge and Competence,* Falmer, London

Eraut, M (1996) *The new discourse of vocational education and training: a framework for clarifying assumptions, challenging the rhetoric and planning useful, theoretically informed research,* paper presented at the European Conference on Educational Research (ECER), Seville

European Commission (1995) *Teaching and Learning: towards the learning society,* European Commission, Brussels

Evans, K, Brown, A and Oates, T (1987) Developing work-based learning: an evaluation of the YTS Core Skills Project, Employment Department, Sheffield

Evans, TD (1989) Taking place: the social construction of place, time and space, and the (re)reading of distances in distance education, *Distance Education,* **10** (2), pp 170–83

Evans, TD (1994) *Understanding Learners in Open and Distance Education,* Kogan Page, London

Evans, TD (1995) Globalisation, post-Fordism and open and distance education, *Distance Education,* **16** (2), pp 241–55

Evans, TD (1997) (En)countering globalisation: issues for open and distance education, in *Shifting Borders: Globalisation, localisation and open and distance education,* eds LO Rowan, VL Bartlett, and TD Evans, pp 11–22, Deakin University Press, Geelong

Evans, TD and Nation, DE (1989) Dialogue in practice, research and theory in distance education, *Open Learning,* **4** (2), pp 37–43

Evans, TD and Nation, DE (1993a) Educational technologies: reforming open and distance education, in *Reforming Open and Distance Education*, eds TD Evans and DE Nation, pp 196–214, Kogan Page, London

Evans, TD and Nation, DE (1993b) Theorising open and distance education, in *Key Issues in Open Learning*, ed AW Tait, pp 45–62, Longman, London

Evans, TD and Nation, DE (1996) Educational futures: globalisation, educational technology and lifelong learning, in *Opening Education: Policies and practices from open and distance education*, eds TD Evans and DE Nation, pp 1–6, Routledge, London

Evans, TD and Rowan, LO (1997a) Place matters: exploring issues of globalisation and localisation through sites of open and distance education, in *Research in Distance Education*, 4, eds TD Evans, D Thompson and V Jakupec, Deakin University Press, Geelong

Evans, TD and Rowan, LO (1997b) *Globalisation, localisation and distance education: issues for research*, paper presented at the Australian Association for Research in Education Globalisation and Education Symposium, Brisbane

Evans, TD and Rowan, LO (1997c) *Globalisation, localisation and distance education: issues of policy and practice*, paper presented at the Open and Distance Learning Association of Australia Conference, Launceston

Field, J (1996) Universities and the learning society, *International Journal of University Adult Education*, 35 (1), pp 1–12

Finegold, D and Soskice, D (1988) The failure of training in Britain: analysis and prescription, *Oxford Review of Economic Policy*, 4, pp 21–53

Finn Report (Australian Education Council Review Committee) (1991) *Young people's participation in post-compulsory education and training*, Australian Capital Territory: Australian Government Publishing Service, Canberra

Fisher, S (1994) *The Mental Assembly Line*, SRHE/Open University Press, Buckingham

Fullan, M (1991) *The New Meaning of Educational Change*, Cassell, London

Fulton, Gordon and Williams (1982) cited in Dunne, R (1992) *Curriculum coordination and management*, Module 11: Inset at a distance, University of Exeter, Exeter

Further Education Unit (1979) *A Basis for Choice*, FEU, London

George, R (1997) Language and learning in open and distance education, in *Shifting Borders: Globalisation, localisation and open and distance education*, eds LO Rowan, VL Bartlett and TD Evans, pp 39–51, Deakin University Press, Geelong

Gibbs, G (1991) *Teaching Students to Learn*, Open University Press, Buckingham

Gibbs, G (1992) Control and independence, in *Teaching Large Classes in Higher Education*, eds G Gibbs and A Jenkins, pp 37–59, Kogan Page, London

Gibbs, G (1995) *Assessing Student Centred Courses*, Oxford Brookes University, Oxford

Gibbs, G and Jenkins, A, eds (1992) *Teaching Large Classes in Higher Education: How to maintain quality with reduced resources*, Kogan Page, London

Gibbs, G and Lucas, L (1995) *Using research to improve student learning in large classes*, paper presented at the Third International Symposium on Improving Student Learning, Using research to improve student learning, University of Exeter, Exeter

Giddens, A (1991) *The Consequences of Modernity*, Cambridge, Polity Press

Green, D (1994) What is quality in higher education? Concepts, policy and practice, in *What is Quality in Higher Education*, ed D Green, Open University Press/SRHE, Buckingham

Gubbay, J (1994) A Critique of Conventional Justification for Transferable Skills, in *Transferable Skills in Higher Education*, ed D Bridges, University of East Anglia/ERTEC, Norwich

Guile, D and Young M (1996) *Connecting work, learning and higher level qualifications: a new role for theory and practice in Masters degrees*, unpublished paper, Post-16 Centre, Institute of Education, University of London, London

Guy, RK (1997) Contesting borders: knowledge, power and pedagogy in distance education in Papua New Guinea, in *Shifting Borders: Globalisation, localisation and open and distance education*, eds LO Rowan, VL Bartlett and TD Evans, pp 53–64, Deakin University Press, Geelong

Hager, P, Gonczi, A and Athanasou, J (1994) General issues about assessment of competence, *Assessment and Evaluation in Higher Education*, **19** (1), pp 3–16

Halal, WE and Liebowitz, J (1994) Telelearning: the multimedia revolution in education, *The Futurist*, November–December, pp 21–26

Hämäläinen, K (1996) We make the future, editorial, *LLinE (Lifelong Learning in Europe)*, **2**, p 2

Hartley, J (1994) *Designing Instructional Text*, 3rd edn, Kogan Page, London

Harvey, L, Moon, S and Geall, V (1997) *Graduates' Work: Organisational change and students' attributes*, Centre for Research into Quality, University of Central England, Birmingham

Hattie, J, Biggs, J and Purdie, N (1996) Effects of learning skills interventions on student learning: a meta-analysis, *Review of Educational Research,* **66** (2), pp 99–136

Hausman, DR (1982) Causal explanatory symmetry, *Philosophy of Science Association*, **1** (9)

Healy, T (1996) Lifelong learning for all: international experience and comparisons, in *A National Strategy for Lifelong Learning*, ed F Coffield, pp 53–64, School of Education, University of Newcastle upon Tyne

Hemmings, B and Battersby, D (1989) Textbook selection: evaluative criteria, *Higher Education Research and Development,* **8** (1), pp 69–78

Henkel, M (1987) *The discipline: still the dominant force in higher education?*, International Conference, Swedish National Board of Universities and Colleges Research on Higher Education Programme, Dalaro

HEQC (Higher Education Quality Council) (1996) *Understanding Academic Standards in Modular Frameworks*, HEQC, London

HEQC (Higher Education Quality Council) (1997) *Assessment in Higher Education and the Role of Graduateness*, HEQC, London

Hertz-Lazarowitz, R (1995) Using group investigation to enhance Arab–Jewish relationships, *Cooperative Learning and College Teaching*, **5**, pp 2–4

Higher Education Council (1992) *The quality of higher education: discussion papers* (National Board of Employment, Education and Training Publication), Canberra, Australian Capital Territory: Australian Government Publishing Service

Hillage, J et al (1998) *Excellence in research on schools*, DfEE Research Report no 74

Hounsell, D (1994) Educational development, in D Watson and J Bockock (eds) Managing the Curriculum in the Year 2000, SRHE and Open University Press, Milton Keynes

Hounsell, D (1997) *Changing assessment practices in Scottish higher education*, paper presented at the Invitational Symposium on Assessment, Seventh Biennial Conference of the European Association for Research on Learning and Instruction, Athens

Hounsell, D (1998) Learning, assignments and assessment, in *Improving Students as Learners*, proceedings of the Fifth International Symposium on Improving Student Learning, ed C Rust, Oxford Centre for Staff and Learning Development, Oxford

Hounsell, D, Day, K and Grant, R (1998) *Reviewing Your Teaching*, University of Edinburgh, TLA Centre/CVCP Universities' and College' Staff Development Agency, Edinburgh and Sheffield

Hounsell, D, Marton, F and Entwistle, N eds (1984) *The Experience of Learning*, Scotish Academic Press, Edinburgh

Hounsell, D, McCulloch, M and Scott, M (1996) *The ASSHE Inventory: Changing assessment practices in Scottish higher education*, Edinburgh and Napier Universities and the Universities' and Colleges' Staff Development Agency (UCoSDA), Edinburgh and Sheffield

Hughes, C and Tight, M (1995) The myth of the learning society, *British Journal of Educational Studies*, **43** (3), pp 290–304

Husén, T (1974) *The Learning Society*, Methuen, London

Hyland, T (1994) *Competence, Education and NVQs: Dissenting perspectives*, Cassell, London

Illeris, K (1998) Adult learning and responsibility, in *Adult Education in a Transforming Society*, Roskilde University Press, pp 107–25

Indre, K (1997) Challenges in adult education in Estonia: helping, counselling and encouragement, in Lifelong learning, Conference Proceedings, University of Kaunas, Kaunas

Industry in Education (1995) *Towards Employability: Addressing the gap between young people's qualities and employers' recruitment needs*, Industry in Education, London

James, R and McInnis, C (1995) *Responding to student diversity: strategies for enrichment and retention in the first year*, paper presented at the Society for Research in Higher Education Conference, University of Central England, Birmingham

Janssen, PJ (1996) Studaxology: the expertise students need to be effective in higher education, *Higher Education*, **31**, pp 117–141

Jaques, D (1991) *Learning in Groups*, 2nd edn, Kogan Page, London

Jarvis, P (1990) *An International Dictionary of Adult and Continuing Education*, Routledge, London and New York

Jessup, G (1991) *Outcomes: NVQs and the Emerging Model of Education and Training*, Falmer, London

Jessup, G (1997) *Establishing a learning society*, paper presented at a Conference on 'The Learning Society', Bristol

Johnson, DW and Johnson, RT (1989) *Cooperation and Competition: Theory and practice*, Interaction Books, Edina, Minnesota

Kagan, S (1994) *Cooperative Learning: resources for teachers*, San Juan Capistrano, California

Kaldeway, J and Korthagen, F (1995) Training in studying in higher education: objectives and effects, *Higher Education*, **30**, pp 81–89

Keep, E (1997) *There is no such thing as society: some problems with an individual approach to creating a learning society*, paper presented at a Conference on 'The Learning Society', Bristol

Khaladjan, N (1996) Landmarks in the formation of the new school, in earning and learning, *International Higher Education*, **3**, pp 35–37

Kirkpatrick, A and Mulligan, D (1996) *Cultures of learning in Australian universities: reading expectations and practice in the Social and Applied Sciences*, paper presented at the Applied Linguistics Association of Australia, 21st Annual Conference, Worlds of Discourse, Sydney, New South Wales

Klenowski, V (1995) Student self-evaluation processes in student-centred teaching and learning context of Australia and England, *Assessment in Education*, **2** (2), pp 145–63

Kogan, M (1987) *The responsiveness of higher education to external influences*, International Conference, Swedish National Board of Universities and Colleges Research on Higher Education Programme, Dalaro

Kuhn, T (1970) *The Structure of Scientific Revolutions*, University of Chicago Press, Chicago

Kurfiss, JG (1988*) Critical thinking: theory, research, practice, and possibilities*, ASHE-ERIC Higher Education Report no 2, Association for the Study of Higher Education, Washington, DC

Kwan, KP and Leung, R (1996) Tutor versus peer group assessment of student performance in a simulation training exercise, *Assessment and Evaluation in Higher Education*, **21** (3), pp 205–14

Lamble, K (1998) *Perceptions of undergraduate science education as a preparation for employment*, Final Report, Industrial Links Programme, University of Plymouth, Plymouth

Lave, J (1991) Situated learning in communities of practice, in *Perspectives on Socially Shared Cognition*, eds L Resnick, J Levine and S Behrend, American Psychological Association, Washington, DC

Lave, J and Wenger, E (1991) *Situated Learning: Legitimate peripheral participation*, Cambridge University Press, Cambridge

Leitch, C, Harrison, R and Burgoyne, J (1995) *Understanding the Learning Company: A constructivist approach*, Centre for Executive Development, Ulster Business School, Jordanstown

Lengrand, P (1989) Lifelong education: growth of the concept, in *The International Handbook of Lifelong Learning*, ed C Titmus, pp 5–9, Pergamon Press, Oxford

Levin, H and Kelley, C (1997) Can education do it alone?, in *Education: Culture, economy and society*, in AH Halsey et al (eds), Oxford University Press, Oxford

Levin, P (1997) *Making Social Policy: The mechanisms of government and politics and how to investigate them*, Open University Press, Buckingham

Longworth, N and Davies, WK (1996) *Lifelong Learning*, Kogan Page, London

MacDonald, J and Mason, R (1997) Information handling skills and resource based learning, *OTD Project no 10*, Open University, Milton Keynes

MacDonald-Ross, M and Scott, B (1995) *Results of the survey of OU students' reading skills, text and readers programme*, Technical Report no 3, Institute of Educational Technology, Open University, Milton Keynes

MacLennan, HM (1997) Using action research to develop a resource-based Professional Studies programme for BA Hons Fine Art students, in *Using Research to Improve Student Learning through Course Design*, Proceedings of the Fourth International Symposium on Improving Student Learning, ed C Rust, Oxford Centre for Staff and Learning Development, Oxford

MacLennan, HM (1998) An investigation of students' changing perceptions of professional studies provision for Fine Art, in *Improving Students as Learners*, Proceedings of the Fifth International Symposium on Improving Student Learning, ed C Rust, Oxford Centre for Staff and Learning Development, Oxford

Main, A (1988) Reflection and the development of learning skills, in *Reflection: Turning experience into learning*, eds D Boud, R Keogh and D Walker, Kogan Page, New York

Marshall, R and Tucker, M (1992) *Thinking for a Living: Education and the wealth of nations*, Basic Books, New York

Mason, R (1998) *Globalising Education*, Routledge, London

Matthews, RS et al (1995) Building bridges between cooperative and collaborative learning, *Change*, **2**, pp 88–89

Mayer Report (1992) *Employment related key competencies: a proposal for consultation*, Mayer Committee, Melbourne

McInnis, C, James, R and McNaught, C (1995) *First year on campus: diversity of initial experiences of Australian undergraduates*, Centre for the Study of Higher Education, University of Melbourne, Melbourne

McKeachie et al (1986) *Teaching and learning in the college classroom: a review of the research literature* (Technical Report no 86-B-001.0), National Center for Research to Improve Postsecondary Teaching and Learning, University of Michigan, Michigan

McPeck, J (1981) *Critical Thinking and Education*, St Martin's Press, New York

Meagher, N (1998) *Employability: the skills and attitudes employers look for in young school leavers*, paper presented at the European Conference on Educational Research (ECER), Ljubljana

Mertens, D (1974) Schüsselqualifikatione: Thesen zur Schuburg einer modernen Gesellschaft [Key qualifications: themes for education and training in a modern society], Mitteilungen aus der Arbeitsmarkt- und Berufsforschung [Reports from studies of the labour market and vocational research], **7**, pp 314–25

Meyers, C and Jones, TB (1993) *Promoting Active Learning: Strategies for the college classroom*, Jossey-Bass, San Francisco, CA

Middlehurst, R (1993) *Leading Academics*, SRHE/Open University Press, Buckingham

Morgan A and Beaty, E (1997) The world of the learner, in *The Experience of Learning,* eds F Marton, D Hounsell and N Entwistle, pp 217–37, Scottish Academic Press, Edinburgh

Morgan, A R (1983) Theoretical aspects of project-based learning in higher education, *British Journal of Educational Technology*, **14** (1) pp 66–78

Morgan, AR (1993) *Improving your Students' Learning: Reflections on the experience of study*, Kogan Page, London

Morgan, A R (1997) Still seeking the silent revolution? Research, theory and practice in open and distance education, in *Research in Distance Education*, **4**, eds TD Evans, V Jakupec and DC Thompson, Deakin University Press, Geelong

NATFHE (National Association of Teachers in Further and Higher Education) (1992) *Managing the university curriculum in the year 2000*, conference papers, NATFHE, London

National Board of Employment, Education and Training (1992) *Skills sought by employers of graduates* (Commissioned Report no 20), Australian Capital Territory: Australian Government Publishing Service, Canberra

National Skills Task Force (1999) *Towards a national skills agenda*, First Report of the National Skills Task Force, Department for Education and Employment, Suffolk

Neer (1987) The development of an instrument to measure classroom apprehension, *Communication Education*, **36**, pp 154–66

Nightingale, P and O'Neil, M (1994) *Achieving Quality Learning in Higher Education*, Kogan Page, London

Nordic Council of Ministers (1995) *The Golden Riches in the Grass – Life long Learning for All*, NORD, Oslo

Nordic Council of Ministers (1996) Nordic 'folkeoplysning' and Adult Education, Nordic Council of Ministers, Copenhagen

Northedge, A (1990) *The Good Study Guide,* Open University, Milton Keynes

Nystrand, M (1986) Learning to write by talking about writing: A summary of intensive peer review in expository writing instruction at the University of Wisconsin, Madison, in M Nystrand (ed) *The structure of written communication*, pp 179–211, Academic Press, Orlando, FL

O'Neil, HF, ed (1997) *Workforce Readiness: Competencies and assessment*, Erlbaum, Mahwah, New Jersey

OECD (1998) *Education Policy Analyses*, OECD, Paris

Okamoto, K (1994) *The Lifelong Learning Movement in Japan: Strategy, practices and challenges*, Ministry of Education, Science and Culture, Tokyo

Onstenk, J (1997) Kernproblemen, ICT en de innovatie van het beroepsonderwijs [Core problems, information and communication technologies and innovation in vocational education and training], SCO Kohnstamn Institut, Amsterdam

Onstenk, J *et al* (1990) Leerprocessen in stages [Learning processes during practical training], SCO Kohnstamn Institut, Amsterdam

Orsmond, P, Merry, S and Reiling, K (1996) The importance of marking criteria in the use of peer assessment, *Assessment and Evaluation in Higher Education*, **21** (3), pp 239–50

Otala, L (1993) *Trends in lifelong learning in Europe*, paper presented at a Conference on the Trans-European Exchange and Transfer Consortium, Accreditation of In-company Training, Dublin

Parlett, M (1977) The learning milieu, *Studies in Higher Education*, **2** (2), pp 173–81

Parlett, M and Hamilton, D (1977) Evaluation as illumination, in *Beyond the Numbers Game*, eds D Hamilton *et al*, pp 6–22, Macmillan, Basingstoke

Perry, WG (1970) *Forms of Intellectual and Ethical Development in the College Years: A scheme*, Holt, Rinehart & Winston, New York

Pintrich, PR and Schrauben, B (1992) Students' motivational beliefs and their cognitive engagement in classroom academic tasks, in *Student Perceptions in the Classroom*, eds DH Schunk and JL Meece, pp 149–183, Lawrence Erlbaum Associates, Hillsdale, New Jersey

Project Panel on the General Professional Education of the Physician and College Preparation for Medicine (1984) *Physicians for the twenty-first century*, part two, *Journal of Medical Education,* **59**, p 11

QCA (Qualifications and Curriculum Authority) (established November 1997) London

QHE (Quality in Higher Education) (1993) *Update (6)*, the newsletter of the quality in higher education project, University of Central England, Birmingham

QHE (Quality in Higher Education) (1994) *Update (7)*, the newsletter of the quality in higher education project, University of Central England, Birmingham

Radloff, A (1996) *Integrating life long learning skills into the curriculum*, unpublished raw data

Radloff, A and Styles, I (1997) *The development of self-regulation in adult university students*, paper presented at the Fifth European Association for Research into Learning and Instruction (EARLI), Athens

Raggatt, P, Edwards, R and Small, N, eds (1996) *The Learning Society: Challenges and trends*, Routledge in association with the Open University, London and New York

Ramsden, P (1992) *Learning to Teach in Higher Education*, London, Routledge

Ramsden, P (1993) What is good teaching in higher education? in *The Audit and Assessment of Teaching Quality*, ed PT Knight, pp 43–52, Standing Conference on Educational Development

Robbins, Lord (1963) *Higher education* (Report of the Committee under the Chairmanship of Lord Robbins), HMSO, London

Robertson, D (1995) The reform of higher education for social equity, individual choice and mobility, in *Higher Education in a Learning Society*, ed F Coffield, pp 45–66, University of Durham, Durham

Robinson, P and Cooper J (1995) *An Annotated Bibliography of Cooperative Learning in Higher Education: Part III – the 1990s*, New Forums Press, Stillwater, Oklahoma

Rogers, C (1969) *Freedom to Learn*, Merrill, Columbus, Ohio

Rowan, LO and Bartlett, VL (1997) Feminist theorising on open and distance education, in *Shifting Borders: Globalisation, localisation and open and distance education*, eds LO Rowan, VL Bartlett and TD Evans, pp 117–34, Deakin University Press, Geelong

Rowan, LO, Bartlett, VL and Evans, TD, eds (1997) *Shifting Borders: Globalisation, localisation and open and distance education*, Deakin University Press, Geelong

Rowntree, D (1987) *Assessing Students: How shall we know them?*, rev edn, Kogan Page, London

Rowntree, D (1990) *Teaching Through Self-instruction: How to develop open learning material*, Kogan Page, London

Royal Society for Arts (1997) *NVQ Key Skills*, RSA, London

Saljo, R (1982) Learning and understanding, in *Goteborg Studies in Educational Sciences*, **41**, Acta Universitatis, Gothenburg

SCANS (Secretary's Commission on Achieving Necessary Skills) (1991) *What Work Requires of Schools*, US Department of Labor, Washington, DC

Schön, D (1983) *The Reflective Practitioner*, Basic Books, New York

Schön, D (1987) *Educating the Reflective Practitioner*, Jossey-Bass, San Francisco, CA

Scottish Higher Education Funding Council (1996a) *Higher Education Institutions: Students and Staff 1994–95*, Statistical Bulletin no 3/96 (October), Table 6, SHEFC, Edinburgh

Scottish Higher Education Funding Council (1996b) *Facts and Figures 96*, SHEFC, Edinburgh

Shuell, TJ (1990) Phases of meaningful learning, *Review of Educational Research*, **6** (4), pp 531–47

Simons, PR-J (1997) From Romanticism to practice in learning, *Lifelong Learning in Europe* **II** (1), pp 8–15

Simons, R-J (1990) *Transferability*, Quick Print, Nijmegen

Slee, P (1989) A consensus framework for higher education, in *Higher Education in the 1990s: New dimensions*, eds C Ball, and H Eggins, SRHE/OUP, Milton Keynes

Snow, CP (1959) *The Two Cultures and the Scientific Revolution*, Cambridge

Soden, R (1993) *Teaching thinking skills in vocational education*, Department of Employment, Sheffield

Squires, G (1990) *First Degree: The undergraduate curriculum*, SRHE/OUP, Milton Keynes

Stalker, K (1996) *The antinomies of choice in community care*, paper presented at a Seminar on 'The Learning Society', Bristol

Stasz, C *et al* (1996) *Workplace skills in practice: case studies of technical work*, RAND, Santa Monica, National Center for Research in Vocational Education, University of California at Berkeley

Steen, LA (1992) 20 questions that deans should ask their mathematics department (Or, that a sharp department will ask itself) *AAHE Bulletin*, **44**(9) pp 3–6

Stephenson, J and Weil, S, eds (1992) *Quality in Learning*, Kogan Page, London

Stock, A (1996) Lifelong learning: thirty years of educational change, in *The Learning Society: Challenges and trends*, eds P Raggatt, R Edwards and N Small, pp 10–25, Routledge in association with the Open University, London and New York

Strain, M and Field, J (1997) On 'the myth of the learning society', *British Journal of Educational Studies*, **45** (2), pp141–55

Svinicki, MD (1990) So much content, so little time, *Teaching Excellence*, **2** (8), pp

Tate, H and Entwhistle, N (1996) 'Identifying students at risk through ineffective study strategies', *Higher Education*, **31**, pp 97–116

Thaman, K (1997) Considerations of culture in distance education in the Pacific Islands, in *Shifting Borders: Globalisation, localisation and open and distance education*, eds LO Rowan, VL Bartlett and TD Evans, pp 23–34, Deakin University Press, Geelong

Thomas, JW (1988) Proficiency at academic studying, *Contemporary Educational Psychology*, **13**, pp 265–75

Times Higher Education Supplement (1997) *What Dearing says/summary*, 25 July

Tribe, J (1996) Core skills: a critical examination, *Educational Review*, **48** (1), pp13–27

Trivellato, P (1997) Japan as a learning society: an overall view by a European sociologist, in *A National Strategy for Lifelong Learning*, ed F Coffield, pp 185–206, University of Newcastle, Newcastle

Tuijnman, (1996) The expansion of adult education and training in Europe: trends and issues, in *The Learning Society: Challenges and trends*, eds P Raggatt, R Edwards and N Small, pp 26–44, Routledge in association with the Open University, London and New York

UNESCO (1996) *Learning: the treasure within*, Report to UNESCO of the International Commission for the Twenty-first Century, UNESCO, Paris

University of Exeter (1995) *Into the twenty-first century: a strategy for the next decade*, Internal Report, University of Exeter, Exeter

Unwin, S (1997) *Analysing Architecture*, Routledge, London

van der Vleuten, C *et al* (1996) Flexibility in learning: a case report on problem-based learning, *International Higher Education*, **2**, pp 17–24

van der Zee, H (1996) The learning society, in *The Learning Society: Challenges and trends*, eds P Raggatt, R Edwards and N Small, pp 163–183, Routledge in association with the Open University, London and New York

Van Zolingen, S (1995) Gevraagd: sleutelkwalificaties: een studie van sleutelkwalificaties voor het middelbaar beroepsonderwijs [Wanted: key qualifications: a study of key qualifications for upper secondary vocational education and training], UDN, Nijmegen

Van Zolingen *et al* (1997) *Towards broad initial vocational education and training : a method for the formulation of key qualifications and core problems*, paper presented at the CEDEFOP Conference on Core Skills, Amsterdam

Vanna, K (1997) *The political and educational conditions of adult education in Estonia*, paper presented at the Lifelong Learning Conference, Vytautas Magnus University, Kaunas

Wah, R (1997) Distance education in the South Pacific – issues and contradictions, in *Shifting Borders: Globalisation, localisation and open and distance education*, eds LO Rowan, VL Bartlett and TD Evans, pp 69–82, Deakin University Press, Geelong

Walker, L (ed) (1994) *Institutional Change – Towards an Ability-Based Curriculum in Higher Education*, Oxford Brooks University, Oxford

Wang, MC and Palincsar, AS (1989) Teaching students to assume an active role in their learning, in *Knowledge Bases for the Beginning Teacher*, ed MC Reynolds, pp 71–84, Pergamon Press, Oxford

Wegerif, R (1995) Collaborative learning: creating an on-line community, *CITE Report* 212, Institute of Educational Technology, Open University, Milton Keynes

Winter, R (1996) New liberty, new discipline: academic work in the new higher education, in *Working in Higher Education*, ed R Cuthbert, SRHE/Open University Press, Buckingham

Winter, R and Maisch, M (1996) *Professional Competence and Higher Education: The ASSETT programme*, Falmer, London

Wolf, A (1991) Assessing core skills: wisdom or wild goose chase, *Cambridge Journal of Education*, **21** (2), pp 189–201

Wright, D L (1987) Getting the most out of your textbook, *Teaching at the University of Nebraska, Lincoln*, **8** (3), pp 1–3

www.creative contingencies.com (1999) *Developing scholarship in teaching* – home page, RMIT University

Young, M and Guile, D (1997) *New possibilities for the professionalisation of UK VET professionals*, Post-16 Centre, Institute of Education, University of London, London

Young, M, Hayton, A and Leney, T (1997) *Report on the ASDAN Youth Award Scheme, London*, Post-16 Centre, Institute for Education, University of London, London

Zemsky, R (1997) Turning Point, *Policy Perspectives*, **7** (2), pp 1–10

Zemsky, R and Oedel, P (1994) *Higher education and the changing nature of the American workforce – responses, challenges and opportunities*, National Centre on the Educational Quality of the Workforce, University of Pennsylvania, Philadelphia

Zimmerman, BJ and Martinez-Pons, M (1992) Perceptions of efficacy and strategy use in the self-regulation of learning, in *Student Perceptions in the Classroom,* eds DH Schunk and JL Meece, pp 185–207, Lawrence Erlbaum Associates, Hillsdale, New Jersey

Zimmerman, BJ and Paulsen, AS (1995) Self-monitoring during collegiate studying: an invaluable tool for academic self-regulation, *New Directions for Teaching and Learning*, **63**, pp 13–27

Index

Visit Kogan Page on-line

Comprehensive information on
Kogan Page titles

Features include

- complete catalogue listings,
  including book reviews and
  descriptions

- special monthly promotions

- information on NEW titles and
  BESTSELLING titles

- a secure shopping basket facility
  for on-line ordering

PLUS everything you need to know
about KOGAN PAGE

http://www.kogan-page.co.uk